SIMPLE GREEN SUPPERS

A Fresh Strategy for ONE-DISH Vegetarian Meals

SUSIE MIDDLETON

Photographs by RANDI BAIRD

ROOST BOOKS

Boulder

2017

Roost Books
An imprint of Shambhala Publications, Inc.
4720 Walnut Street
Boulder, Colorado 80301
roostbooks.com

9 8 7 6 5 4 3 2 1

First Edition
Printed in the United States of America

⊗This edition is printed on acid-free paper that
meets the American National Standards Institute
Z39.48 Standard.
♻ Shambhala Publications makes every effort to
print on recycled paper. For more information please
visit www.shambhala.com.

Distributed in the United States by
Penguin Random House LLC and in
Canada by Random House of Canada Ltd

Designed by Toni Tajima

Library of Congress Cataloging-in-Publication Data

Names: Middleton, Susie, author. |
Baird, Randi, photographer (expression)
Title: simple green suppers: a fresh strategy for
one-dish vegetarian meals / Susie Middleton;
photographs by Randi Baird.
Description: First edition. | Boulder: Roost Books,
2017. | Includes index.
Identifiers: LCCN 2016018114 |
ISBN 9781611803365 (pbk.: acid-free paper)
Subjects: LCSH: Vegetarian cooking. | Cooking
(Vegetables) | One-dish meals. | LCGFT: Cookbooks.
Classification: LCCTX837 .M565 2017 |
DDC 641.5/636—dc23 LC record availbable at
https://lccn.loc.gov/2016018114

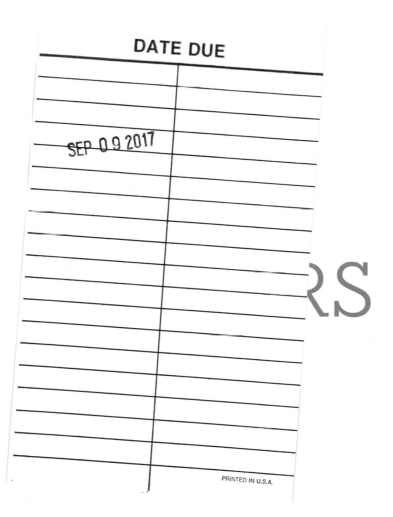

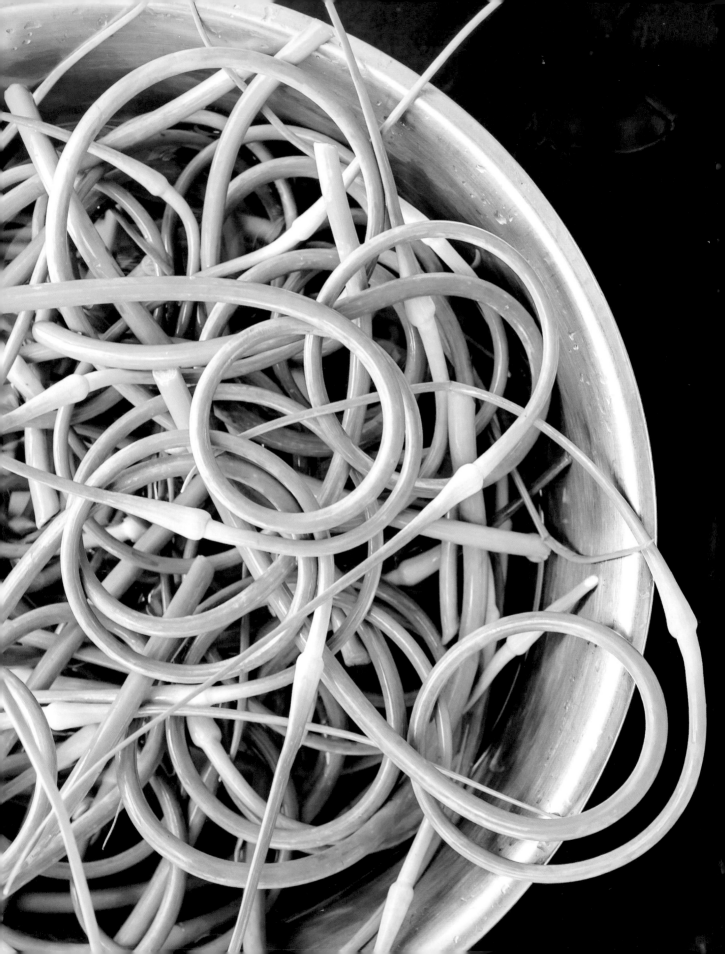

For Eliza, always

CONTENTS

INTRODUCTION
The One-Dish Veggie Supper Strategy

Life is funny. You're busy doing one thing, focusing on the road ahead, and meanwhile something else entirely unplanned is taking shape around you.

I was pretty sure that my chief job as Miss-Spread-the-Vegetable-Gospel was to share everything I knew about cooking vegetables with you and everyone else who wanted to eat more vegetables. And by everyone else, I mean not just vegetarians. I didn't want to leave anyone stranded out there with a fennel bulb and no chef's knife, if you know what I mean.

So I wrote three vegetable cookbooks filled with useful vegetable-cooking techniques and flavorful recipes. Meanwhile, I started growing and selling my own vegetables (dozens of different varieties), and my overall crazed enthusiasm for vegetables did not exactly wane. I went into my kitchen with fistfuls of baby kale, armloads of pattypan squash, and baskets of Sun Gold cherry tomatoes and French fingerling potatoes. I dared those vegetables to be boring, to give up trying to be so versatile, to disappoint me. And it simply didn't happen. Not only were they star performers, but they also played so darn well with all the other kids in my pantry and larder.

Gradually, I began to eat less meat, and then . . . even less. (There were a few other reasons for this, and I'll spare you the details, but let's just say that after my Winter of Pork, which followed the Summer of Raising Three Pigs, I was, I guess, meat exhausted.) One day I realized that the fence between my (metaphorical) vegetarian neighbors and me was awfully low. So I just stepped over it.

And that day, I tumbled into one of the most engaging creative challenges in my cooking career: making a veggie supper every night. (And when I say "every night" I mean that. I live on the island of Martha's Vineyard year-round, and options for dining out are slim during the off-season and expensive in the summer. Most Islanders cook at home regularly.)

I didn't mention to anyone—family or friends—that I had every intention of taking up this path as a permanent occupation. I didn't want to put anyone off, and maybe I doubted whether my resolution would be steadfast. (Who ever really knows about the future, right? And also, you never want to be the bore who insists on knowing what's best for everyone!) But right from the start, I had a curious sense of contentment about eating and cooking vegetarian.

For one thing, it immediately made my life simpler, as I didn't have those agonizing moments in the grocery store, staring once again at the over-priced, under-inspiring meat selection. And now there were natural parameters for what I could cook. Yet instead of feeling limited by this challenge, I felt stimulated: How would I turn all those beautiful veggies (whether they came from my garden or the grocery) into a filling, satisfying supper tonight—and every night? I began to look forward to my time in the kitchen each evening with a new sense of pleasure and excitement. Here was a fun puzzle to solve.

A puzzle that called for a strategy, I soon realized.

The One-Dish Veggie Supper Strategy

I'll tell you straight out that this book is the result of my honing, day after day, week after week, my own veggie supper strategy. What I will deliver to you here, in the next few hundred pages, is a simple explanation of my strategy, plus a whole lot of (delicious!) ways to practically execute it. I'll also point out lots of veggie cooking tips and tricks along the way. And, thanks to my collaboration with photographer Randi Baird, you'll also get a sense of the real enjoyment that lies ahead when you create delicious, substantial, *and* beautiful meals out of fresh vegetables and a well-stocked larder. ("Larder" is an old-fashioned concept referring to a pantry with cold storage, but it's also a handy modern term for all of our ingredient-storage spots, including the pantry, fridge, and freezer.)

Before I get into the strategy, I should probably tell you that you *will* be cooking. This is not meal assembly (though we'll definitely talk about building blocks)—this is about the sensual pleasure and physical satisfaction you get from cooking, from feeding yourself and others well. By now we all know that there is no magic bullet, no perfect diet. But cooking for ourselves and striving for balance and variety in what we eat are some of the best things we can do for our long-term well-being. So we've got to get into the habit of doing it—and of enjoying it, too—so we also have to be realistic about how much time we can devote to cooking every day (or night).

All of the recipes in this book can be made in under an hour—most in under 45 minutes and many *theoretically* in 30 (that is, when you don't have a child, a dog, a glass of wine, the news, the phone, or anything else to distract you). Although I can't promise you "superfast," the great news is that if you embrace some make-ahead suggestions (see page xiv), you can easily cut your evening supper-prep time to 20 minutes. For instance, if you've got cooked chickpeas (page 236), cooked brown rice (page 235), avocados, toasted walnuts, arugula, and our Farmhouse Vinaigrette (page 100) in the fridge, you can make a warm or cool salad in under 10 minutes. Even by making only one thing ahead—say Spicy Peanut Sauce (page 25)—you could be eating something like Chinese Egg Noodles and Broccoli with Spicy Peanut Sauce (page 24) in less than 20 minutes.

Now about that strategy.

1. THE STARTING POINT: ADOPT A NEW FORMULA CALLED "VEGGIES + 1."

I'm going to ask you to think of veggie suppers as equal to (one or more) fresh veggies *plus* one major player from your pantry or larder:

veggies + noodles	veggies + toast
veggies + grains	veggies + tortillas
veggies + beans (and other legumes)	veggies + eggs
veggies + leaves	veggies + broth

Let's say you've got a nice head of cauliflower in your fridge. How can you turn that into dinner? Well, you start by picking a pantry item to pair it with. You could pair it with chickpeas (Indian Curry with Chickpeas, Cauliflower, Spinach, Tomatoes, and Coconut Milk, page 76). You could pair it with eggs (Puffy Oven Pancake with Spiced Cauliflower Sauté, page 190). Or you could pair it with broth (Miso-Ginger Broth with Cauliflower and Baby Kale, page 223). Or, let's say you got a nice fresh bunch of carrots at the farmers' market. You could match them up with couscous (Couscous with Colorful Carrots and Citrus Tarragon Butter Sauce, page 21) or combine them with greens (Roasted Carrot, Bell Pepper, and Red Onion Salad with Endive, Radicchio, and Carrot Top–Pecan Pesto Dressing, page 112). Got brussels sprouts? How about making Yukon Gold Potato and Brussels Sprouts Hash with Parmesan-Fried Eggs (page 188) or Mini Savory Bread Puddings with Brussels Sprouts, Cheddar, Dijon, and Shallots (page 202)?

Your nice fresh veggies (though a few frozen ones now and then are fine and convenient, too) are the stars of the show, and your larder is providing the essential supporting actors. The eight "supporting actors" I've chosen for this book—noodles, grains, beans and other legumes, leafy green vegetables, toasted bread, tortillas, eggs, and broth for soups—are the ingredients that I think have enough star power to hold their own with the veggies, and that's why they're the ones I turn to, night after night, to make supper.

2. NEXT, REFRESH AND RESTOCK YOUR LARDER.

In addition to depending on your larder for the important whole foods like beans, grains, and eggs, you'll also want to lean on it to round out the flavor equation. If we're going to eat veggies-plus-something every night, we'll need some other fun stuff—let's call them "accessory ingredients"—to help keep things interesting. That doesn't mean having twelve different kinds of mustard and twenty-nine bottles of vinegar on hand. It does mean having a supply of your favorite raw nuts in the freezer and maybe a container or two of already toasted nuts in your pantry. It might mean putting avocados, a couple of fresh herbs, and maybe a fresh cheese like feta on the shopping list every week. It means some carefully chosen condiments: A can of coconut milk on the shelf can open up a world of recipe opportunities. Maybe you don't need six kinds of hot sauce, but a bottle of sriracha or a jar of Asian chili-garlic paste could be the workhorse you're looking for.

Refreshing your larder also means taking advantage of the more than thirty homemade dressings, sauces, and condiment recipes in this book—from Lime-Chipotle Sauce (page 164) to Quick-Roasted Cherry Tomatoes (page 133). These can all be made ahead and stored in the fridge for several days or for weeks in the freezer. (See the complete list of bonus recipes on page 241.) If you were to do nothing but make one of these at the beginning of every week, you would be already well on your way to a week of tasty veggie suppers.

Take a hard look at your pantry with an eye toward updating its contents. But don't get overwhelmed—I'm going to help you through this. First, weed out things that have been hanging around forever, unused. (Remember, many whole grains and nuts can go rancid, so take a sniff if you're not sure and also check for any pests while you're at it.) Next, part with packages of highly processed food. Whenever possible, we'll be cooking with whole foods plus the most minimally processed ingredients we can find to make our veggie suppers. That way, we get a lot of creative control (you're welcome, control freaks!) over how things taste, and, oh, a few other little benefits, like more fiber, more nutrients, and fewer additives and preservatives.

Even if you can't get rid of much, take an hour or two to reshelve and reorganize things. At the very least, put like ingredients with like: all your pasta and noodles together, your canned beans in one place, and your grains in another.

Then read through the introduction to each of the following eight chapters. (OK, you can scan them if you're busy.) In each one, you'll find a list of suggested "plus" items—the varieties of noodles, beans, grains, bread, greens, and so on that I find most useful and versatile.

You'll also find a second list in every chapter: some favorite "accessory" pantry ingredients that I use frequently—things like tamari, maple syrup, tapenade, limes, and fresh ginger. Most likely you'll already have many of these things on hand, but maybe there's something like miso paste or dried porcini mushrooms that you've needed a good excuse to try.

Make a list that includes a few new purchases to make in every category, and then take a trip to your favorite large grocery or natural foods store that will have the best selection. I don't want you to think you have to go crazy on one shopping trip, but in order to expand your veggie supper repertoire, you'll have to stretch your pantry wings and try some new things. And I think you'll be surprised at how much more likely you are to try something new if you've already got that interesting ingredient—the farro, the rice noodles, the ciabatta—on hand. Plus, by having a nice variety around, you're free to make substitutions or begin improvising after you've tried some of the recipes.

Go ahead and do this shopping now, before you even start cooking from the book. After all, one of our goals (getting back to the question of time, especially when cooking on weeknights) is to eliminate some of those inconvenient shopping stops you'd rather not make on the way home from work. By having your larder in good shape, you only have to procure your fresh veggies. And honestly, many vegetables keep longer in the fridge than meat does, so if you play your cards right, you can really cut down on grocery trips once you get in the groove of cooking veggie suppers. If you're lucky enough to have your own vegetable garden or access to a nearby farmers' market, you're in even better shape, because very fresh local vegetables will last several days longer than well-traveled grocery store veg (especially greens).

Come home with your new goodies and finish your pantry refresh. I've included storage suggestions in each chapter, too. I'm a total organization geek, so I love doing things like putting all my grains and beans into glass mason jars. Yes, it looks pretty (can't help myself!), but there are other advantages. Filling your own storage containers from bulk bins can be less expensive, and if you buy at a natural foods store where there is a good turnover rate, bulk ingredients may be fresher. Also, heavy-duty well-sealed containers are your best defense against pantry bugs. Get a sharpie out and label jar tops with the item name and the purchase date. (It's a good idea to write the date on any kind of packaging, really. I do this with my spices, too—when I remember.)

Some of my storage tips may seem like no-brainers: for example, put things close to where you will use them; don't hide ingredients in the back of the cupboard; keep Scotch tape near your pasta boxes. I apologize in advance for stating the obvious, but because I always need basic reminders and tips, I'm thinking you might, too. Although I like organizing things, I'm also no minimalist; I constantly have space issues and too much stuff, and I have to tidy my pantry often.

3. EMBRACE MAKE-AHEADS.

So far, we've got a formula for supper, and we've refreshed our pantry. The next most important component of our strategy is committing to making some things ahead. As I said before, you are certainly not *required* to make anything ahead for these veggie-supper recipes (this is not a college course, only supper!). But I desperately want you to share that gleeful feeling I get when I open the fridge at suppertime and see that I've already got a batch of cooked rice or wheat berries on hand. Maybe I've got a little bowl of Quick-Roasted Root Vegetables (page 83) in there, too, and a batch of Rosemary Roasted Walnuts (page 107) or a jar of Farmhouse Vinaigrette (page 100).

An even better feeling is when you open the fridge for *the second night in a row* and find you've still got more of that rice, those nuts, and that vinaigrette; you don't have to make an extra-big batch of these things up front—even one recipe will carry you through a few nights.

Here are the make-aheads that give you the biggest bang for your buck, so to speak.

Cooked grains. You can cook many rice varieties, plus wheat berries, farro, quinoa, and barley, using the easy "pasta" method described on page 235. Drain and cool the grains thoroughly, pack them into fridge containers, and refrigerate for five to six days, or freeze for a month.

Cooked chickpeas. Because chickpeas are the most versatile of all the beans and other legumes (they can be sautéed, roasted, stir-fried, braised, or pureed), I find that the extra effort it takes to cook them fresh (as opposed to using canned ones, which I recommend with most other beans for convenience) is worth it. Freshly cooked chickpeas will last longer in your fridge as well, and you are never far from supper when they're around.

Toasted nuts. For adding texture and deep flavor (not to mention protein and antioxidants), there's no substitute for toasted pecans, almonds, walnuts, and other nuts. To me, toasting nuts is almost like roasting coffee beans: I think the flavor transformation (in this case from something starchy to something dark and rich) is astounding. Any veggie supper will be more satisfying with the addition of toasted nuts, and it sure is nice when you've already got them done. Store them in the freezer if you like.

Workhorse sauces and dressings. Rich, thick sauces such as Creamy Blender Caesar Dressing (page 103), Quick Lemony Tahini Sauce (page 19), and Spicy Peanut Sauce (page 25) also contain protein from eggs or nuts, so a batch of one of these can add real substance to a supper. They hold up well for several days in the fridge, too. But even something as simple as our Farmhouse Vinaigrette (page 100) can be a workhorse—meaning you can use it in any number of different preparations.

Roasted vegetables. I'm not necessarily encouraging you to cook all your vegetables ahead of time. In fact, the techniques I use the most for cooking veggies for quick suppers are stir-frying and sautéing, and I like the texture of veggies when freshly cooked. But I do find that some roasted vegetables can hold up decently in the fridge for a few days. Quick-Roasted Cherry Tomatoes (page 133) are so flavorful (and keep so well), they're almost like a condiment. And Quick-Roasted Root Vegetables (page 83) cut into small dice can be just the thing to have on hand for filling a quesadilla or for tossing with some beans or greens in a salad.

Washed and properly stored greens and herbs. This make-ahead doesn't involve any cooking, but it is still a big time saver during the week. If you can take a few extra minutes to trim, wash, and dry your greens when you get them home, you'll save time later in the week. Also, by removing those awful twist-ties and placing your greens in paper-towel-lined zip-top bags, you can extend their life for up to several days.

4. FORGET THE "THREE THINGS ON A PLATE" NOTION AND FOCUS ON "ONE-DISH" RECIPES THAT HAVE IT ALL.

The last important part of our veggie supper strategy is to focus our energies on producing just one delicious dish. We may eat this dish out of a bowl (fun and comforting!) or arrange it on a pretty platter (impressive!) to serve ourselves and our family; however we present it, that one dish will be our entire supper. By concentrating on cooking this one dish, we get to drop all the angst about what to serve with it. The recipes have made those decisions for us by combining complementary ingredients and contrasting textures within one dish. By their very nature, the combinations offer maximum flavor impact, so your meals will always be interesting, never dull.

Another remarkable thing about one-dish suppers is that they have a generous ability to take on additional ingredients—or let some go. (Swapping is OK, too.) A spicy soup of noodles and greens can handle an egg or a handful of beans if you want to add them, and at the same time it will still be tasty if you leave off the garnish of peanuts and scallions. With every dish, we'll build some flavor from the bottom up so that we can be flexible at the finish.

You'll understand what I mean when you start improvising your own one-dish suppers—something I'm convinced you'll do, once you cook your way through some of the recipes in this book. By following the recipes, you'll begin to see how different components work together to make up that one satisfying dish.

OK, now a few minor housekeeping issues before we start cooking. (Not really housekeeping, but you know what I mean. We're having a meeting here, after all!) First, I'm sorry to say that a "one-dish" supper does not mean that you will use only one pot or one bowl or one spoon to prepare it. (I am not a genie in this department, but if you figure out how to do it and still make an interesting meal every night, do let me know!)

Second, there is a reason this is a "supper" book, not a "dinner" book: these meals are not heavy. I'm not a big fan of eating a huge meal in the evening anymore. Yes, I'm hungry after work and I want to feel satisfied. But I don't want to feel overstuffed or logy. I enjoy eating a few smaller meals throughout the day, partly because I love food so much that I'd rather eat a variety of things in small amounts than a large amount of one thing. I generally don't want to commit *all* my calories to one evening meal (as delicious as it can be!). That said, portions are flexible, and obviously some recipes are denser than others, so I hope you'll find plenty to satisfy you, even when you're in the mood for a feast.

Last, I'm not a huge fan of meat substitutes, so you will not find a lot of soy-based proteins in these recipes. I find that beans, grains, eggs, greens, nuts, and the vegetables and fruits themselves, along with some dairy and of course the necessary fats found in plant oils, keep me full and satisfied. These ingredients, plus the support crew in my larder, let me cook and eat a different kind of delicious veggie supper every night of the week.

How to Design Your Own Veggie Supper

At the heart of this book lies an approach to creating veggie suppers every night that, I hope, will become second nature to you when you follow the strategy tips on pages xi–xvii and then begin cooking recipes from this book. If you get inspired, I think you'll feel, like I did after creating these recipes, that the possible combinations for veggie suppers are practically endless. So if you're ready to try improvising, here are some tips for mapping out your own recipes.

Begin by pairing two elements: a vegetable and one of our substantial pantry players. For instance, think mushrooms + eggs; carrots + couscous; cauliflower + chickpeas; Tuscan kale + white beans; or corn + tortillas.

Next, consider how you'd like to cook the vegetables. Sauté those mushrooms? You're one step away from a frittata. Roast those carrots? Then perhaps you're thinking of a warm couscous salad. Stir-fried cauliflower and chickpeas can easily segue into a saucy curry right in the pan. Fresh corn could pile up on a crisp tortilla, salad-style, or join other veggies and some cheese between two soft tortillas for a quesadilla.

Then layer in contrasting flavors and textures. Take advantage of fresh herbs, aromatic veggies, citrus, yogurt, tamari, and all our little sauces and condiments to make simple flavor boosts (one or two of these is plenty). And add contrasting texture (and sometimes temperature) with things like nuts, seeds, pea shoots and raw baby greens, herb sprigs, tortilla strips, shredded cabbage, fresh salsa, and more. For example, add shallots, fresh thyme, and sharp cheese to that frittata. Add a few arugula leaves to the carrot and couscous salad, then drizzle it with Spicy Lime-Chili Oil (page 83). Maybe add Quick-Roasted Cherry Tomatoes (page 133) and toasted pine nuts to the Tuscan kale and white beans.

Last, keep a light hand when you assemble your one-dish veggie supper. Toss the ingredients together loosely or layer them in a bowl. Don't overwhelm the dish with any one ingredient; keep a nice balance. And, take some notes—you'll want to jot down your favorite combinations so you can make them again!

SIMPLE
GREEN
SUPPERS

VEGGIES + NOODLES

NOODLE. Just say the word and it's hard not to smile. Silly, slippery, comely, comforting—we love our noodles. And for once, a childhood favorite is actually our grown-up ally. From whole-grain pasta to gluten-free macaroni, Chinese egg noodles to Japanese buckwheat soba, the delicious noodle options—all quick-to-cook and veggie-friendly—are multiplying. We still love our Italian durum wheat pasta, for sure, but for veggie suppers, it's nice to know there are so many different directions to go in—and that we don't have to avoid pasta for fear of carb overload. The truth is, even though a dish of spaghetti with really good (and quick) homemade tomato sauce is a comforting treat (recipe on page 11), most of the time we can enjoy our noodles in more equal proportion to other ingredients. (And yes, I like to use the word "noodles" loosely, because technically, not all pasta is noodles, though most noodles *are* pasta. Oh, never mind!)

My favorite destinations for noodles are stir-fries, pan sautés, braises and brothy dishes, and salads, both warm and cool. These are the kinds of dishes where vegetables and aromatics, as well as sauces and vinaigrettes, can contribute great flavors that starchy noodles love to absorb. In fact, there are certain vegetables that have a natural affinity with noodles. Aromatics (like onions, peppers, and mushrooms) that release a lot of moisture when they cook tend to coat

1

pasta with their juices. Greens, either wilted or braised, instantly create a pan "liquor" (especially flavorful when garlic, ginger, or chilis have been added in) that begs for noodles to lap it up. Other meaty vegetables, like eggplant and broccoli, are so commanding when sautéed or grilled that they practically beg for a pillow of pasta to lean on. Bold seasoning (and a little fat to carry its flavor) is important with pasta, which is why infused oils and sauces that contain both creamy and spicy elements work so well with noodles.

Tips and Strategies for Noodles

EVERYTHING IN ITS PLACE.

Before stocking the pantry with a nice assortment of noodles (see lists that follow), let's consider equipment, storage, and cooking tips that will help guarantee the best results. First, do yourself a favor and find a convenient place for your favorite pasta pot and your colander. I know that seems obvious, but sometimes I find myself struggling (again and again) to unearth a piece of cooking equipment that I use a lot (say, my salad spinner), only to realize one day when putting the dishes away that the waffle maker is taking up a perfectly convenient spot where the salad spinner should go! You know what I mean, I'm sure.

I have a six-quart nonstick pasta pot that I love, and it lives in a cabinet near my sink, right next to a few colanders nested together. (I find that having more than one colander is also convenient. A simple mesh one might be already in use draining canned beans while a sturdier metal one is in the sink cradling hot pasta.) The nonstick pasta pot is also handy for cooking grains using the method I detail on page 235. In either case, if you put the drained pasta or grain back into the warm pot, either for holding or for mixing with sauce, you won't have to worry about any sticking if you use a nonstick pot. Whether you go with nonstick or not, something in the six- to eight-quart range is plenty big enough for the recipes in this book, so if you've only got a giant pasta pot that's cumbersome to move around, consider adding a smaller one to your batterie de cuisine.

As much as I love noodles, they can be cumbersome to store. But because we're updating our supplies, this is a good opportunity to at least try to store them efficiently. My suggestion is to find a dedicated shelf (or two). In the ideal world, these would be shallow shelves, at or just above eye level. (Up high is fine, too, for boxes of pasta, as long as the shelf is shallow and you can reach them.) To save space, tip the boxes on their sides and stack them with the relevant label facing out.

I love shallow pantry shelves because things can't disappear into the black hole that is the back of the cabinet. My kitchen is very small, rustic, and decidedly unfancy. But I do have an open, floor-to-ceiling shelving unit with shallow wooden shelves that hold all my dry pantry ingredients. I can see what I've got at a quick glance, and it's a lovely feeling, I tell you!

An easy-to-access drawer deep enough to hold noodle boxes would work, too. Just be sure that you can see everything, or you'll never use some of it. There's a reason Julia Child had all her pots and pans on the wall, all her utensils in crocks, and all her vinegars and oils on the countertop. If you're going to cook, being able to reach for your favorite things quickly makes it more pleasurable and encourages spontaneity.

For Asian noodles and others that come in cellophane packages, find a shoe box or a shoe box–shaped plastic storage container that will hold all the bags. Once a bag is open, fold or roll the bag back on itself lengthwise and secure it with a rubber band, especially one of those thick rubber bands that come with your asparagus and broccoli, or use a small binder clip or clothespin to secure it. (Keep extra ones in the box.) Otherwise, you'll have tiny broken noodles all over the place. I keep Scotch tape near my pasta boxes, too, so I can quickly seal up a half-used box of spaghetti before it spills all over the floor.

TIME IT AND TASTE IT.

When it's time to cook your noodles, sure, go ahead and read the suggested cooking time on the box or package. But be aware that those suggested cooking times (especially in the case of Asian noodles) are often too long and will deliver mushy pasta. When possible, I've given you cooking times in the recipes, but you will still want to check by tasting a noodle at the short end of the cooking time. Be sure you're cooking your noodles in plenty of well-salted water (1 or 2 teaspoons of salt) for the best flavor.

COOK NOODLES FIRST, AND SEPARATELY.

Most of the recipes you'll find in this chapter call for boiling the noodles separate from other ingredients, and then draining them well and seasoning them before using in the recipe. Seasoning noodles separately (with a little salt, tamari, or flavored oil) before they get added to the rest of the dish gives you a stronger flavor base. It's a little trick chefs use to layer flavors and prevent blandness.

To season the pasta, it must, of course, be relatively dry first. Usually, a spell in the colander is enough, but sometimes, when the noodles are headed for a salad or another kind of dish where too much residual water might dilute a dressing or seasoning, I take an extra step. I transfer the noodles from the colander onto a clean, dry dish towel for a few minutes. (And, by the way, I usually don't rinse wheat pasta after cooking; it removes the starchy coating that helps sauces cling to it. Rinsing rice noodles and some other Asian noodles destined for salads can be a good idea, though, to deter clumping.) If I want to keep the noodles warm for a short while, I often put them back in the warm (empty) pasta pot, where as a bonus some extra moisture will steam off.

The hidden convenience factor is that in most of these recipes, you don't have to time your pasta to be done the exact moment that the rest of the dish is finished. This means that the minute you decide you're going to cook one of the recipes in this chapter, you can put a pot of water on, put a colander in the sink, and go ahead and cook your noodles.

Keep in mind that cooking noodles separately is an especially good idea when it comes to noodle soup or any other broth-heavy dish. It's tempting to cook noodles right in a soup, but often they will absorb far too much of the liquid and possibly overcook as well. It's much nicer to add a tangle of cooked noodles to your carefully flavored broth at the time of serving so that both elements retain their integrity.

SUBSTITUTIONS? YES.

There is one other subversive reason I have for suggesting you treat the noodles as a separate ingredient. It means I'm basically giving you permission to substitute one noodle for another. (Don't tell the purists, who might kill me.) Maybe it's not the best idea, but look, if you can't find fresh Chinese egg noodles, fresh Italian linguine will work. If you're making a traditional Italian pasta but you're going gluten-free, the gluten-free spaghetti on the market now is a fine substitute, and so on. You probably don't want to use thick udon noodles in place of rice vermicelli, but I trust you. You'll do the right thing.

For the Pantry

This brings us back to the whole notion of stocking up. Filling out the noodle pantry is really about as simple as it sounds. We are not going to visit Chinatown for a noodle adventure. (I mean, we could, and it would be fun, but we don't need to for our everyday veggie suppers.) However, I am going to push you out of your comfort zone a little bit.

The reason (as I mentioned in the introduction to the book) is that I think you're more likely to expand your noodle-veggie supper repertoire if you've got some of the interesting stuff on hand. You already know the miracle of finding a box of spaghetti in the pantry when there is virtually nothing else to eat. Wouldn't it be fun, on a busy Tuesday night, to discover that a cheery Israeli couscous or Thai rice noodles were also options for supper?

In that spirit, I'm offering a list of suggestions for your noodle pantry. Most of my favorite noodles are now available in major supermarkets—hurrah! You might have to make a short list of those you couldn't find and pick them up at a natural foods market, but that should do it. And certainly, you don't have to keep every one of these noodles on hand at all times. These are my favorites, but the important thing is for you to come up with a nice mix of old friends and interesting newcomers. Then invite a few of the accessory ingredients from the following list into your pantry and fridge for completing your noodle-supper prep. Last, follow a few tips (see page 2) for getting that noodle pantry a bit more organized.

The Noodles

GLUTEN-FREE (DRIED)

Thai rice noodles, pad thai–style—Thin, flat rice noodles, most commonly available in two widths; similar to linguine and fettuccine

Vermicelli rice noodles—Very fine, thin rice noodles, not to be confused with cellophane noodles, which are made from beans

Japanese soba noodles—Thin, flat brown noodles made from buckwheat; if necessary, check packaging to ensure all-buckwheat (gluten-free) content, because some brands contain wheat (Eden Brands is 100 percent buckwheat)

Gluten-free spaghetti or linguine—Made from corn, quinoa, and/or rice flour; I like Barilla's corn- and rice-based pasta and Ancient Harvest quinoa and corn-based pasta

Gluten-free medium shapes, such as elbows or rotini

WHEAT-BASED (DRIED)

Italian-style durum wheat spaghetti and linguine

Italian-style durum wheat medium shapes, such as gemelli or cellentani

Italian-style durum wheat small shapes, such as orzo or ditalini

Whole-grain spaghetti or linguine

Couscous

Pearl (Israeli) couscous—Small balls of toasted semolina flour, called *ptitim* in Israel

Japanese somen noodles—Very fine, thin white wheat noodles; packages contain small bundles bound with ribbons

Japanese udon noodles—Thick, flat, dried wheat noodles, also available fresh

Chinese-style or Japanese-style curly noodles—Quick-cooking, thin wheat noodles in a wavy shape; a good alternative to ramen noodles, as they are not fried; look for Kame brand

EGG-BASED (FRESH)

Italian-style fresh linguine or fettuccine—Will keep, unopened, in the fridge for a week

Chinese egg noodles—Lo mein–style flat, yellow noodles; available fresh in the produce section; will keep, unopened, in the fridge for five or six days

Accessory Ingredients

Aromatics: Garlic, shallots, and onions

Asian chili-garlic paste

Canned full-fat coconut milk

Capers

Extra-virgin olive oil

Feta cheese

Fresh ginger

Fresh goat cheese

Fresh herbs

Grapeseed oil

Lemons and limes

Low-sodium tamari

Mirin (rice wine)

Miso paste (see page 209)

Oil-packed sun-dried tomatoes

Olive tapenade

Parmesan cheese

Pitted Kalamata olives

Red pepper flakes

Toasted nuts (see page 237)

Toasted sesame oil

Tomato paste

SPRING FARMERS' MARKET STIR-FRY

OF BABY JAPANESE TURNIPS, RADISHES, AND SOBA

SERVES 2

Kosher salt

2 ounces dried soba (buckwheat) noodles

10 to 12 small or 6 to 8 larger Japanese turnips (aka Hakurei or "salad" turnips) with greens

8 to 10 small radishes with greens

2 teaspoons grapeseed or vegetable oil

¼ cup thinly sliced scallions, plus 1 to 2 tablespoons for garnish

2 teaspoons chopped fresh ginger

2 teaspoons chopped fresh garlic

½ teaspoon red pepper flakes, or ½ small fresh serrano pepper, sliced

1 tablespoon white (shiro) miso, plus more to taste

¼ cup coarsely chopped fresh cilantro (leaves and tender stems), plus a few whole sprigs for garnish

Low-sodium tamari

Japanese turnips are a revelation; crisp and almost sweet, these little spring beauties are nothing like fall globe turnips, and the greens are light and delicious. You can eat Japanese turnips raw or lightly steamed, but they also shine in a stir-fry like this one, paired up with their garden buddy, radishes (which are also surprisingly delicious cooked—and yes, their greens are edible). This noodle dish is also a great template: replace the turnips and radishes with any other spring veg-and-green combo.

1 Bring a medium saucepan of lightly salted water to a boil. Add the soba noodles and cook until tender, about 3 minutes. (Beware of the package instructions, which will tell you to cook them for much longer.) Drain, rinse briefly with cold water, and allow to drain well.

2 Separate the turnip greens from the roots, and cut the turnip roots into ½-inch dice or wedges. You should have about 1 cup (a little more or less won't matter). Separate the greens from the radish roots, then trim the radishes and quarter them, if they are small, or cut into ½-inch dice. You should have about ½ cup. Trim the lower stems off the turnip greens and discard. Roughly chop the combined turnip greens and radish greens and measure out 2 cups loosely packed.

3 In a small saucepan, heat 1 cup of water to a very gentle simmer.

4 Meanwhile, in a large (12-inch) nonstick stir-fry pan, heat the oil over medium heat. Add the diced turnips and radishes and ¼ teaspoon of salt. Cook, stirring, until all the veggies are slightly browned, about 5 to 6 minutes. Add ¼ cup of the scallions and the ginger, garlic, and red pepper flakes. Cook, stirring, until fragrant and softened, about 1 minute. Add the 2 cups of chopped greens and cook, stirring, until wilted, about 30 seconds. Remove the pan from the heat.

5 Whisk the miso into the hot water, then add the mixture to the stir-fry pan. Add the cooked soba noodles, the chopped cilantro, and a splash of tamari. (If necessary, return the pan to low heat for a minute or two to heat everything through.) Transfer to two bowls and garnish with the remaining 1 to 2 tablespoons of scallions and the cilantro sprigs.

BABY BOK CHOY AND RICE NOODLES

IN FRAGRANT COCONUT SAUCE

SERVES 3 OR 4

6 ounces thin rice noodles (linguine width)

¾ cup canned full-fat coconut milk (preferably organic), well stirred

2 tablespoons low-sodium tamari

2 tablespoons freshly squeezed lime juice, plus 4 lime wedges for serving

2 tablespoons packed brown sugar

2 teaspoons Asian chili-garlic paste

1 tablespoon plus 1 teaspoon vegetable or peanut oil

6 ounces cremini mushrooms, cut into thick slices (about 2½ to 3 cups)

Kosher salt

8 to 10 ounces baby bok choy leaves and stalks, sliced crosswise into ½-inch-thick ribbons (about 4 to 5 cups)

2 teaspoons chopped fresh ginger

2 teaspoons chopped fresh garlic

continued opposite

This brightly flavored Thai-inspired noodle dish is a lovely destination for one of my favorite veggies: baby bok choy. I harvest the last of my spring baby bok choy just as the shell-pea harvest is beginning, and both vegetables pair naturally with coconut. (Any greens would be good in this soup, though.) An easy ginger- and garlic-spiced sauce and quick-cooking rice noodles help this come together quickly. I usually use a combination of cilantro and mint in this dish, but it's also a great place to try out Thai basil, which has a bright, cinnamon aroma and is a wonderful addition to any Asian noodle dish, if you can get your hands on some. Have fun with garnishes here too and try toasted coconut flakes, fresh bean sprouts, or whole herb sprigs. Be sure to pass around wedges of lime for squeezing.

1 In a large saucepan, bring 2 quarts of water to a boil. Take the pan off the heat, add the rice noodles, and let sit until well softened, about 10 minutes. Drain.

2 In a glass measuring cup, whisk together the coconut milk, 1 cup of water, and the tamari, lime juice, brown sugar, and chili-garlic paste and set aside.

3 In a large (12-inch) nonstick stir-fry pan, heat 1 tablespoon of the oil over medium-high heat. Add the mushrooms and ¼ teaspoon of salt and cook, stirring, until the mushrooms are browned and shrunken, 5 to 7 minutes. Add the remaining 1 teaspoon of oil, the bok choy, and a big pinch of salt. Cook, stirring, until the bok choy is wilted and a bit shrunken, 3 to 4 minutes. Reduce the heat to medium, add the ginger and garlic, and cook, stirring, until fragrant, about 30 seconds. Add the peas and the coconut milk mixture, and stir well. Cook until heated through, 1 to 2 minutes. Remove from the heat and add the chopped herbs.

⅔ cup frozen peas, thawed, or fresh peas, blanched or microwaved for 30 seconds

2 tablespoons chopped fresh cilantro or a combination of chopped fresh mint, cilantro, and/or Thai basil, plus a few sprigs for garnish

2 to 3 tablespoons toasted unsweetened coconut flakes (optional)

1 cup fresh bean sprouts (optional)

4 Distribute the rice noodles among three or four wide, shallow serving bowls. Ladle the veggies and sauce over each and garnish with the toasted coconut or bean sprouts (if using) and the herb sprigs and lime wedges. Serve with a fork and spoon.

STIR-FRIED GREENS, MUSHROOMS, AND UDON NOODLES

WITH SPICY PONZU SAUCE

SERVES 3

Kosher salt

6 ounces dried udon noodles

2 teaspoons toasted sesame oil

2 tablespoons low-sodium tamari

1 tablespoon freshly squeezed lemon juice

1 tablespoon mirin (rice wine)

2 teaspoons packed dark brown sugar

2 teaspoons Asian chili-garlic paste

3 tablespoons grapeseed or vegetable oil

2 cups sliced or quartered mixed mushrooms (any kind)

½ cup sliced shallots

2 cups thinly sliced green cabbage (any kind)

2 cups thinly sliced kale, bok choy, collards, or mustard greens

2 to 3 teaspoons chopped fresh ginger

2 to 3 teaspoons chopped fresh garlic

You might be familiar with udon noodles from noodle shops, where they're often served in savory broths. But their thick, meaty texture also makes them great candidates for stir-fries that have lots of veggies and bold sauces. Here, I was inspired by the soy-citrus flavors of Japanese ponzu sauce to create an assertive combination of ginger, garlic, tamari, lemon, and plenty of chili-garlic paste. The sauce thickens and coats the noodles, mushrooms, and greens in a most delightful way. I like to use both cabbage and another green in this recipe, so I've given you some options for this. Kale, bok choy, collards, or even spicy mustard greens would work well. Choose your favorite mushrooms, too. Dried udon noodles are in many grocery stores, but you could also use whole wheat or durum wheat linguine in this recipe.

1 Bring a small (5- or 6-quart) stockpot of salted water to a boil. Add the udon noodles and cook until just tender, about 6 minutes. (They will be tender in a little less time than most package directions indicate. You want them to be al dente.) Drain, rinse briefly, and let sit in the colander to dry a bit. Transfer to a bowl and toss with a big pinch of salt and 1 teaspoon of the sesame oil.

2 In a small bowl, whisk together the tamari, lemon juice, mirin, brown sugar, chili-garlic paste, 1 tablespoon of water, and the remaining 1 teaspoon of sesame oil. Set aside.

3 In a large (12-inch) nonstick stir-fry pan, heat 2 tablespoons of the grapeseed oil over medium heat. Add the mushrooms, shallots, and ½ teaspoon of salt and increase the heat to medium-high. Cook, stirring, until the veggies are shrunken and browned, 5 to 7 minutes. Add the remaining tablespoon of grapeseed oil, the cabbage, the kale, and ¼ teaspoon of salt. Cook, stirring, until the cabbage begins to brown and the greens are very wilted, 3 to 4 minutes. Add the ginger and garlic and cook, stirring well, until fragrant, about 30 seconds. Lower the heat to medium-low and stir in the noodles and the tamari mixture. Cook, stirring, just until the noodles are heated through and well incorporated and the sauce is clingy, about 1 minute. Transfer onto a serving platter or into shallow bowls and serve.

SPAGHETTI

WITH QUICK-ROASTED PLUM TOMATO SAUCE, BASIL, AND PINE NUTS

SERVES 2

Kosher salt

8 ounces angel hair or thin spaghetti (durum, gluten-free, or whatever variety you like)

1 recipe Quick-Roasted Plum Tomato Sauce (recipe follows)

1 tablespoon unsalted butter

¼ cup coarsely grated Parmesan cheese

2 to 3 tablespoons finely sliced fresh basil leaves or tiny whole basil leaves

1 to 2 tablespoons toasted pine nuts

Inspired by Marcella Hazan's famous tomato sauce, which has a good bit of butter in it (not olive oil!), I combined my delicious Quick-Roasted Plum Tomato Sauce (page 12) with a little butter to make a simple and satisfying sauce for spaghetti. I sauce my spaghetti lightly, as the Italians do, and I toss everything together in the pasta-cooking pot. With fresh basil, toasted pine nuts, and Parmesan cheese, you have a delicious supper—and a classic repertoire recipe you'll come back to again and again.

1 Bring a small stockpot of well-salted water to a boil. Add the pasta and cook until al dente, according to the package instructions. (If cooking gluten-free pasta, be sure to taste early—it can overcook quickly.) Drain well in a colander and then return the pasta to the hot pan. Toss the pasta around a bit with tongs to dry it out a bit further.

2 Combine the tomato sauce and butter in a small saucepan over low heat. Heat, stirring, until the butter is melted and the sauce is hot. Scrape the sauce into the pan with the pasta and toss gently until the pasta is nicely coated with the sauce. Portion the pasta into two serving bowls and top with the cheese, basil, and pine nuts. Serve right away.

Quick-Roasted Plum Tomato Sauce

MAKES 1¼ CUPS

1½ pounds plum tomatoes (about 6 to 7 large tomatoes)

3 tablespoons extra-virgin olive oil

2 large garlic cloves, peeled and cut in half

½ teaspoon kosher salt

Pinch of red pepper flakes (optional)

3 to 4 sprigs of fresh thyme (optional)

Balsamic vinegar

I've never been able to settle on a store-bought tomato sauce that I really love; I find most of them too acidic. But I'm crazy about the flavor of roasted tomatoes, so it wasn't hard to find a way to make delicious sauce at home by quick-roasting plum tomatoes and tossing them into the food processor. In less than 45 minutes, this easy technique turns ordinary grocery-store plum tomatoes into a versatile sauce every vegetarian would be happy to have in her repertoire. I use it on pasta (Spaghetti with Quick-Roasted Plum Tomato Sauce, Basil, and Pine Nuts, page 11) and in egg dishes (Baked Egg Pizziola, page 195), but you'll find other uses, too. This recipe makes just a little over a cup—enough for pasta for two. You can easily double the yield: just be sure to use two baking pans and rotate them halfway through cooking; also add a few minutes of cooking time to allow the moisture in the extra tomatoes to steam off.

1 Preheat the oven to 450°F. Cut the tomatoes in half and scoop out most of the seeds. (Don't worry if you don't get all the seeds. You can also cut out the stem end if you want, but try to retain the inner ribs.) Cut each half into quarters (or into sixths if they are very large) and toss them into a 9 x 13-inch glass or ceramic baking dish. (I like Pyrex.) Add the olive oil, garlic, salt, and red pepper flakes and thyme (if using) and toss well. Roast, stirring from time to time with a silicone spatula, until the tomatoes have collapsed, softened, and browned a bit, about 30 minutes.

2 Let the tomatoes cool for 10 minutes or so. Then, while the baking dish is still hot, add 2 to 3 tablespoons of hot water and use a wooden spoon to scrape off any caramelized bits on the sides and corners of the dish. (This will add flavor to your sauce.) Remove the thyme sprigs and scrape the tomato mixture into a food processor. Process until smooth. Add a few drops (up to ¼ teaspoon) of balsamic vinegar to taste.

3 Use the sauce right away, or transfer to an airtight container and store in the refrigerator for up to 4 days or in the freezer for up to 2 months.

GRILL-BASKET GREEN BEANS

WITH WHOLE-GRAIN PASTA AND BASIL "PESTO" OIL

SERVES 2

Kosher salt

5 ounces whole-grain or gluten-free linguine or spaghetti

Freshly ground black pepper

8 to 10 ounces thin green beans, trimmed and cut in half

1 medium red onion, cut into ½-inch wedges

1 tablespoon extra-virgin olive oil

Handful of torn radicchio or sliced red cabbage leaves

1 recipe Basil "Pesto" Oil (recipe follows)

¼ cup grated Parmesan cheese (optional)

Basil "Pesto" Oil

MAKES ⅓ CUP

1 medium garlic clove, peeled

2 tablespoons toasted sliced almonds or toasted pine nuts

½ cup fresh basil leaves

¼ cup extra-virgin olive oil

1 teaspoon fresh lemon zest

Freshly ground black pepper

Large pinch of kosher salt

How I love to mix warm veggies fresh from my grill basket with a tangle of noodles and a spoonful or two of a flavorful oil. It's a casual and easy match-up that you can take in any direction you like. Here I'm focusing on green beans, whole-grain noodles, and a quick basil oil that's a bit like a loose pesto.

1 Put an enameled grill basket on a gas grill, cover, and preheat to medium heat.

2 Bring a large saucepan of well-salted water to a boil. Cook the pasta according to the package directions and drain well. Return the pasta to the warm pot and toss with ¼ teaspoon of salt and several grinds of black pepper. Cover and set aside.

3 In a medium bowl, toss together the green beans, red onion, olive oil, and ½ teaspoon of salt. Transfer to the hot grill basket, cover the grill, and cook, stirring occasionally with tongs, until the beans and onions are shrunken, browned, and tender, 10 to 12 minutes. Add the radicchio and cook, tossing continuously, just until wilted, 1 to 2 minutes. Remove the veggies from the grill and immediately add to the pot with the pasta.

4 Add three-quarters of the basil oil and toss until well coated. Taste and season generously with more salt and pepper, and/or a bit more of the basil oil, as desired. Transfer to two shallow bowls and serve with Parmesan cheese, if desired.

This little flavored oil comes together quickly in a small or regular food processor, and it is best made fresh for the brightest color and flavor. It has nuts, garlic, and lemon but no cheese, so it's a good vegan dressing, too.

In a small or regular-size food processor, combine the garlic, nuts, and basil. Process until everything is finely chopped, stopping to scrape down the sides as necessary. Add the olive oil, lemon zest, several grinds of black pepper, and the salt. Process again until well combined. The mixture will be loose.

CORN, ZUCCHINI, AND PEARL COUSCOUS

WITH CORIANDER AND SUMMER HERBS

SERVES 3

2 tablespoons unsalted butter

1 cup finely diced yellow onion

Kosher salt

1 cup uncooked pearl couscous

1½ teaspoons ground coriander

1 tablespoon olive oil

2 cups finely diced zucchini or summer squash (about 10 ounces)

2 cups fresh corn kernels (from about 4 ears)

2 teaspoons minced fresh garlic

2 teaspoons freshly squeezed lemon or lime juice, plus more to taste

Freshly ground black pepper

2 tablespoons chopped fresh mint, cilantro, basil, or any combination of these

A fresh corn and zucchini sauté gets a boost from easy-to-cook pearl couscous—that lovely little pasta also known as Israeli couscous. (Look for Bob's Red Mill brand.) Delicious hot, warm, or at room temperature, this versatile summer supper speckled with fresh herbs and brightened with citrus juice can also take on a bit of salty cheese (finely grated Parmesan or finely crumbled feta) if you like, or you could also serve it scattered over lettuce. (It makes a great taco filling, too.) For a vegan version, simply substitute olive oil for the butter.

1 In a medium saucepan with a lid, melt 1 tablespoon of the butter over medium-low heat. Add ¼ cup of the onion and a pinch of salt. Cook, stirring frequently, until the onions have softened and are beginning to brown, 4 to 6 minutes.

2 Add the couscous and ½ teaspoon of salt. Raise the heat to medium and cook, stirring frequently, until much of the couscous has taken on some browning, 3 to 5 minutes. Add ½ teaspoon of the ground coriander and stir. Add 1¼ cups of water to the pan, bring to a boil, then reduce the heat to low, cover, and simmer until the water has been absorbed and the couscous is tender, 9 to 12 minutes. Remove the pan from the heat. Fluff the couscous with a fork, then cover to keep it warm in the pan.

3 In a large (12-inch) nonstick skillet, heat the remaining 1 tablespoon of butter and the olive oil over medium heat. When the butter has melted, add the remaining ¾ cup of onion and ½ teaspoon of salt. Cook, stirring occasionally, until the onions are softened and just starting to brown, 5 to 7 minutes.

4 Raise the heat to medium-high and add the zucchini and ¼ teaspoon of salt. Cook, stirring, until the squash is somewhat shrunken and browned on some sides, about 5 to 7 minutes. Add the corn kernels and another ¼ teaspoon of salt. Cook, stirring frequently, until the corn is glistening, bright, and slightly shrunken, 3 to 5 minutes. Add the garlic and the remaining 1 teaspoon of coriander and cook, stirring and scraping the bottom of

the pan, until fragrant and well mixed, about 1 minute. Remove the skillet from the heat and let sit for a couple of minutes. Sprinkle 2 teaspoons of the lemon juice over the sauté and stir and scrape any browned bits off the bottom of the pan.

5 Add the cooked couscous to the skillet, stir, and season with black pepper to taste. Stir in most of the fresh herbs and taste for seasoning. Add more salt, pepper, or citrus juice to taste. Serve garnished with the remaining herbs.

TUSCAN PASTA

WITH NO-COOK TOMATO, OLIVE, BASIL, AND CAPER SAUCE

SERVES 4

¼ cup mild extra-virgin olive oil

2 tablespoons orange juice

1 tablespoon finely chopped capers

2 teaspoons fresh lemon juice

1 teaspoon freshly grated lemon zest

2 teaspoons chopped fresh garlic

2 teaspoons honey

¼ teaspoon red pepper flakes

Kosher salt

Freshly ground black pepper

2 cups diced ripe beefsteak tomatoes, cored but not seeded or skinned, juices included (about 2 medium-large tomatoes)

½ cup pitted Kalamata olives, cut lengthwise into quarters

4 ounces feta cheese, crumbled

⅓ cup torn and packed fresh basil leaves

8 ounces gemelli or other twisty or curly pasta shape

You're going to love this technique—tossing warm pasta with a cool no-cook tomato sauce—for its simplicity and its great flavor. Part of my summer repertoire for many years, this type of "cool" pasta (not a pasta salad) gets its personality from juicy tomatoes combined with bright ingredients like olives, capers, basil, garlic (of course), citrus juice, and red pepper flakes. There's even a little feta cheese for its salty, creamy note. Fresh from the pot, the warm pasta (I like a twisty shape like gemelli) soaks up all that flavor. Eat this warm or at room temperature. And, although I did say that this isn't a pasta salad (cold pasta tends to get gummy), I won't tell anyone if you eat some of the leftovers cold the next day. It's delicious—or so I've heard. Whatever you do, be sure to use ripe summer tomatoes for the best flavor.

1. In a large, wide mixing bowl, whisk together the olive oil, orange juice, capers, lemon juice, lemon zest, garlic, honey, red pepper flakes, ½ teaspoon of kosher salt, and several grinds of black pepper. Add the tomatoes, olives, feta, and half of the basil and toss well. Let sit for 15 to 20 minutes while you cook the pasta.

2. Bring a small (5- or 6-quart) stockpot of well-salted water to a boil. Add the pasta and cook until al dente, about 12 minutes. Drain well in a colander but do not rinse. Transfer the warm pasta to the mixing bowl with the tomato mixture. Season the pasta directly with a big pinch of salt, then add most of the remaining basil and toss gently but thoroughly. If needed, season with more salt and pepper to taste.

3. Transfer to a large, shallow serving bowl or three individual bowls or plates. Garnish with any remaining basil and eat warm.

STIR-FRIED EGGPLANT AND ROMAINE HEARTS

WITH SOBA NOODLES AND QUICK LEMONY TAHINI SAUCE

SERVES 2

2 ounces soba (buckwheat) noodles

Kosher salt

1 tablespoon plus 2½ teaspoons grapeseed or vegetable oil

2 romaine lettuce hearts

8 to 10 ounces slim Japanese eggplant or globe (regular) eggplant, unpeeled, cut into ½-inch pieces

1 teaspoon chopped fresh ginger

1 teaspoon minced fresh garlic

4 to 5 tablespoons Quick Lemony Tahini Sauce (recipe follows)

3 tablespoons thinly sliced fresh mint or basil, or a combination

1 to 2 teaspoons toasted sesame seeds, for garnish

2 lemon wedges, for serving

This rustic warm salad is a delicious destination for slim, sexy, fast-cooking Japanese eggplants, though it will certainly work with any kind of eggplant. My favorite element might be the stir-fried romaine hearts, which take on such a great flavor when browned. But I also love that this gives me an excuse to mix up a batch of Quick Lemony Tahini Sauce (page 19), which I can then use on grilled or roasted veggies another night. I like to cook the soba noodles, eggplant, and romaine separately and compose the elements on the plate for the best presentation (keeping in mind that what the sauce lacks in beautiful color it provides in great flavor!), but once served, the salad is best enjoyed if everything is chopped together.

1 Bring a large saucepan of water to a boil and cook the soba noodles until tender, about 3 minutes. (Beware of the package instructions, which may tell you to cook them for much longer.) Drain, rinse briefly with cold water, and let the noodles sit in the colander to dry a bit. Transfer to a medium bowl and toss with ¼ teaspoon of salt and ½ teaspoon of the oil. Set aside.

2 Remove the longest and bulkiest outer leaves from the romaine hearts and trim just a sliver off the stem end of each heart. Cut the hearts lengthwise into quarters (keeping the stem end intact). You should have 8 long wedges of romaine weighing about 8 ounces total. Don't worry if some of the wedges are falling apart.

3 In a large (12-inch) nonstick stir-fry pan, heat 2 teaspoons of the oil over medium-high heat. Add the romaine wedges and a big pinch of salt and cook, gently tossing occasionally with tongs, until nicely wilted (they will still have a little heft) and browned in many spots, about 5 to 6 minutes. Lift from the pan and transfer to a plate.

4 Add the remaining 1 tablespoon of oil to the hot pan. When the oil is hot, add the eggplant and ¼ teaspoon of salt. Cook, stirring frequently, until the eggplant is shrunken and well browned, about 6 to 7 minutes. Add the ginger and garlic and cook, stirring constantly, until softened and fragrant, about 1 minute. Remove the pan from the heat and let the eggplant

mixture sit for a few minutes. It will continue to steam and cook. Have ready two dinner plates (oval ones are nice) or one round or oval platter for sharing.

5 Transfer the eggplant into a medium bowl. Add about 2 tablespoons of tahini sauce and about 1 tablespoon of the herbs and toss. Add 1 to 2 tablespoons of the tahini sauce and about 2 teaspoons of the herbs to the bowl of cooked noodles and toss. Arrange a nest of noodles on each plate, then arrange the romaine hearts alongside the noodles. Spoon the eggplant mixture next to them, dividing it evenly between plates. Drizzle it all with a bit more tahini sauce. Garnish with the remaining herbs, and the sesame seeds and lemon wedges.

Quick Lemony Tahini Sauce

MAKES ⅔ CUP

¼ cup well-mixed tahini (see Note)

¼ cup fresh lemon juice, plus more if needed

2 tablespoons low-sodium tamari

2 tablespoons pure maple syrup

1 teaspoon minced fresh garlic

¼ teaspoon kosher salt

2 tablespoons very hot water

This powerhouse sauce will keep for a week in the refrigerator, so go ahead and make a batch in early summer when cucumbers and the first tomatoes, zucchinis, and eggplants are coming in. It is delicious on all these veggies (and broccoli and cauliflower as well), especially if the veggies are grilled or roasted. Try it with naan bread, too. If the sauce has been refrigerated, bring it to room temperature before using, or warm it very gently in a saucepan over low heat.

Put the tahini, lemon juice, tamari, maple syrup, garlic, and salt into a blender and blend until well combined. Scrape down the sides, add the hot water, and blend again. If you like, add more lemon, salt, or tamari to taste.

Note: If you are opening up a new can of tahini and the solids are very hard to mix with the liquids, scrape everything out into a food processor or blender and mix until well combined and smooth.

COUSCOUS WITH COLORFUL CARROTS

AND CITRUS TARRAGON BUTTER SAUCE

SERVES 2 OR 3

4 tablespoons unsalted butter

¼ cup orange juice

1½ teaspoons Dijon mustard

1 teaspoon freshly grated lemon zest

1 teaspoon lemon juice

1 teaspoon white balsamic vinegar

1 teaspoon kosher salt, plus a pinch

1 cup uncooked couscous

1 tablespoon extra-virgin olive oil

12 ounces colorful carrots (orange, yellow, and red, if possible), peeled and cut into sticks between 2 and 3 inches long and ⅜ to ½ inch wide (yielding about 9 ounces or 3 cups)

2 large shallots, cut into ½-inch-wide wedges

½ cup frozen peas, thawed, or fresh peas, blanched or microwaved for 30 seconds

2 teaspoons finely chopped fresh tarragon

¼ cup coarsely chopped toasted hazelnuts (optional)

Comforting and colorful, a saucy slow-sauté of carrots, shallots, and peas nestles into a bed of quick-cooking couscous for a satisfying supper with the flavor of a much longer-cooked dish. My "slow-sauté" technique is a great one for dense veggies, provided they are all cut into about the same size. In a crowded covered pan, the veggies both brown and steam at the same time, so they not only cook through but gain flavor, too. Stealing a sauce trick from the French, I add a little acid (orange, lemon, or Dijon) to the finished sauté and then toss in some very cold butter so that it melts into a creamy consistency. The vegetables and their glazy sauce find a perfect home on a bed of couscous, but you could serve them over noodles too.

1 Cut 1½ tablespoons of the butter into 6 pieces and keep chilled in the refrigerator.

2 In a small bowl, whisk together the orange juice, mustard, lemon zest, lemon juice, and vinegar; set aside.

3 In a small saucepan, combine 1 cup of water, 1 tablespoon of the butter, and ½ teaspoon of salt and bring to a boil. Stir in the couscous, then cover the pan and remove from the heat. Let sit 5 minutes, then fluff with a fork. Cover to keep warm.

4 In a small (4- or 5-quart) Dutch oven or other deep, wide pot, heat the remaining 1½ tablespoons of butter and the olive oil over medium-low heat. When the butter has melted, add the carrots and ½ teaspoon of salt. Cover loosely and

cook, uncovering frequently to gently stir, for 5 minutes. Add the shallots and a pinch of salt and stir, then cover loosely and continue cooking and stirring frequently until the carrots are tender and very nicely browned, about 8 to 10 minutes. Add the peas and the orange juice mixture and immediately stir well, quickly scraping up any browned bits. Remove the pan from the heat, add the cold butter, and stir until just melted and creamy. Stir in the tarragon.

5 Portion the couscous between two or three bowls or spoon onto one platter. (You may not use all the couscous if only serving two.) Spoon the carrot sauté over the couscous and garnish with hazelnuts (if using). Serve right away.

YOU-SAY-MIZUNA, I-SAY-TATSOI NOODLE SALAD

WITH GRILLED MAPLE-TAMARI SHIITAKES AND GARLIC-CHILI OIL

SERVES 2

2 tablespoons grapeseed or vegetable oil

1½ teaspoons minced fresh garlic

¼ teaspoon red pepper flakes

½ teaspoon freshly grated lime zest, plus 2 large lime wedges

Kosher salt

2 ounces thin somen noodles

1 cup mizuna or other baby Asian greens

1 cup tatsoi leaves or other baby Asian greens, or thinly slivered hearty greens

1 recipe Grilled Maple-Tamari Shiitakes (page 141)

There are zillions of Asian greens, it seems. Two of my favorites are mizuna and tatsoi. The fine-toothed mildly mustardy mizuna and the dark green spoon-shaped tatsoi are both delicious and versatile, so when I have them growing in my garden, I add them not only to green salads but also to stir-fries, light soups, and noodle dishes, too. Here I pair them with thin somen noodles (substitute buckwheat soba for a gluten-free alternative) and my umami-delicious Grilled Maple-Tamari Shiitakes (page 141). A quick little garlic-chili oil brings everything together in this pretty dish. These days you might find bunches of mizuna or heads of tatsoi at the farmers' market and occasionally at natural foods markets. But don't worry if you can't find them; any other Asian greens, such as baby mustard or bok choy, broccoli leaves, or even thinly slivered collards, will work, too.

1 In a small skillet, combine the oil, garlic, and red pepper flakes. Place over medium heat and bring to a simmer, stirring occasionally, until the garlic is sizzling. Continue cooking just long enough to infuse the oil but not long enough to brown the garlic, about 1 minute. Remove the skillet from the heat and stir in the lime zest and a pinch of salt. Set aside.

2 In a large saucepan of well-salted boiling water, cook the pasta according to the package instructions, about 3 minutes. Drain well and let sit in the colander until somewhat dry, tossing occasionally, about 10 minutes. Transfer to a bowl.

3 Season the pasta with a big pinch of salt, and toss with 2 or 3 teaspoons of the garlic-chili oil (along with the garlic bits).

4 In a separate medium bowl, toss the mizuna and tatsoi with 1 to 2 teaspoons of the garlic-chili oil.

5 Arrange two-thirds of the greens on two serving plates or in two shallow serving bowls. Top with most of the mushrooms (reserve a few) and then the noodles. Top with the remaining greens and mushrooms and sprinkle a little salt over all. Garnish with lime wedges for squeezing generously over the salad before eating. Serve when still a bit warm or at room temperature.

CHINESE EGG NOODLES AND BROCCOLI

WITH SPICY PEANUT SAUCE

SERVES 3 OR 4

Kosher salt

8 ounces fresh Chinese egg noodles, torn into shorter pieces

1 tablespoon plus 1 teaspoon peanut or vegetable oil

5 cups small broccoli florets, cut through the center to create one flat side (about 10 ounces)

2 large shallots, cut into thick slices (about ¾ cup)

5 radishes, topped and cut lengthwise into wedges (about ½ cup)

¾ cup plus about 2 tablespoons Spicy Peanut Sauce (recipe follows), at room temperature

Chopped fresh cilantro or parsley, for garnish (optional)

Chopped scallions, for garnish (optional)

The earthy, slightly bitter edge of stir-fried broccoli meets a perfect match in a nutty, sweet, and spicy peanut sauce. Pick up a package of fresh Chinese egg noodles (sometimes labeled "lo mein") in the produce section of your grocery store when you're doing your regular shopping, because they'll keep for 5 or 6 days in the fridge. They're quick and comforting, so if you've also made your peanut sauce ahead, this satisfying supper will come together quickly. Even if you haven't made the sauce ahead, it's quick to make, and then you'll be happy to have extra to use another night. Radishes make an unexpectedly delicious, and pretty, addition to the stir-fry.

1 Bring a small (5- or 6-quart) pot of salted water to a boil. Add the egg noodles and cook until tender, about 3 minutes. Drain, rinse briefly, and let sit in the colander to dry a bit. Transfer to a medium bowl and toss with a big pinch of salt and 1 teaspoon of the oil.

2 In a large (12-inch) nonstick stir-fry pan, heat the remaining 1 tablespoon of oil over medium heat. When the oil is hot, add the broccoli, shallots, radishes, and 1 teaspoon of salt. Cover and cook, uncovering occasionally to stir, until the shallots are limp and browned and the broccoli is bright green and browning in places, about 6 to 7 minutes. (If your stir-fry pan does not have a lid, improvise with a baking sheet.)

3 Carefully add ¼ cup of water to the skillet, stir, and quickly cover the pan. Cook until the liquid is gone, about 1 minute. (The steam will finish cooking the broccoli.) Uncover, turn the heat to medium-low, and add the egg noodles, tossing to combine. Cook, stirring, until the noodles are hot, 1 to 2 minutes. Add ¾ cup of the peanut sauce and toss to combine. Transfer to a serving platter or shallow bowls. Drizzle with the remaining 2 tablespoons of peanut sauce, if you like, and garnish with chopped fresh cilantro and scallions (if using).

Spicy Peanut Sauce

MAKES 1½ CUPS

1 large or 2 medium garlic
cloves, peeled

4 thin slices of fresh ginger
(no need to peel)

⅔ cup smooth natural peanut
butter, well stirred

⅓ cup canned full-fat coconut
milk (preferably organic),
well stirred

2 tablespoons packed
dark brown sugar

2 tablespoons
low-sodium tamari

2 tablespoons fresh lemon juice

2½ teaspoons Asian
chili-garlic paste

¼ cup hot water

This smooth, pourable peanut sauce is versatile, easy to make, and keeps for 5 days in the fridge, so it's a great tool in our make-ahead arsenal. It's delicious on Chinese egg noodles, in chopped salads, or on grilled or roasted veggies. Rewarm gently in a saucepan over very low heat to loosen it up after refrigeration.

Put the garlic and ginger in the bowl of a food processor and pulse until finely chopped. Add the peanut butter, coconut milk, brown sugar, tamari, lemon juice, and chili-garlic paste. Process until smooth, stopping to scrape down the sides of the bowl as necessary. Add the ¼ cup of hot water and process again (scraping down the sides as necessary) until loosened and smooth. Store in an airtight glass container in the fridge for up to 5 days.

CURRIED SINGAPORE NOODLES

WITH STIR-FRIED VEGGIES

SERVES 2

2 tablespoons
low-sodium tamari

1 tablespoon mirin (rice wine)

1 tablespoon packed
dark brown sugar

4 ounces vermicelli rice noodles

2 tablespoons grapeseed or
vegetable oil

2 cups very thinly sliced
green cabbage

1 cup thinly sliced snow peas

¾ cup very thinly sliced
red bell pepper

¾ cup thinly sliced red onion

½ teaspoon kosher salt

2 teaspoons minced fresh ginger

2 teaspoons minced fresh garlic

2 teaspoons Asian
chili-garlic paste

2 teaspoons Madras
curry powder

Ordering Singapore noodles at a Chinese restaurant is always fun, but most come with shrimp or pork. The good news is that this dish of curried rice noodles and slivered stir-fried veggies is totally easy and delicious to make without meat. The initial curry-ginger-garlic seasoning gets smoothed out at the end when the noodles absorb a simple tamari sauce. For the veggies, I like a combination of cabbage, red bell pepper, snow peas, and red onions, as each of these is easy to slice in thin strips that pair well with the thin rice noodles. You could certainly add slivered carrots or zucchini. Also, as with fried rice, you can stir-fry an egg or two before or after you cook the noodles for garnish or to toss in.

1 In a small bowl, stir together the tamari, mirin, brown sugar, and 1 tablespoon of water and set aside.

2 Bring a large saucepan of water to a boil. Add the rice noodles, remove from the heat, and let sit for 3 minutes. Drain well. Rip the noodles into 5 or 6 manageable clumps. (They will be much easier to toss in the stir-fry pan.)

3 In a large (12-inch) nonstick stir-fry pan, heat the oil over medium-high heat. Add the cabbage, snow peas, bell pepper, red onion, and salt and cook, tossing and stirring, until the veggies are lightly browned but not completely limp, 3 to 4 minutes. Add the ginger, garlic, chili-garlic paste, and curry powder to the vegetables and cook, stirring, until fragrant, about 30 seconds. Lower the heat to medium. Add the cooked rice noodles and cook, stirring, until well incorporated (most of the noodles should have some color). Stir in the tamari mixture and cook for a few seconds, then remove from the heat. Taste the noodles and season with a bit more salt if necessary. Transfer to a serving platter or two plates and eat hot or warm.

BROCCOLI RAAB AND CREAMY GOAT CHEESE BAKED PASTA GRATIN

SERVES 2 TO 3

Unsalted butter, for greasing pan

Kosher salt

4 ounces small- to medium-size pasta, such as gemelli or small elbows (a generous 1 cup)

4 cups roughly chopped tender tops and leaves of broccoli raab (thin stems are fine, too)

1 cup fresh bread crumbs (I like to use English muffins)

¼ cup plus 3 tablespoons coarsely grated Parmesan cheese

1 tablespoon extra-virgin olive oil

1½ cups heavy cream

2 large garlic cloves, smashed and peeled

Freshly ground black pepper

½ teaspoon freshly grated lemon zest

2 to 3 ounces fresh goat cheese, crumbled while still cold

This is a yummy old-school Susie-style gratin: cream, cheese, bread crumbs—hurrah! (I've made a lot of these over the years.) And I'm not apologizing for its richness. Sometimes you simply need this level of filling deliciousness in your day, especially on a cold winter's evening. I've always loved pairing bitter greens with goat cheese, particularly in a creamy gratin, and this time I've added pasta to make it even heartier. I guess you could call it a macaroni gratin, but that might be selling it short. I like to use a medium-size oval gratin dish (about 1½ quarts), but any shape will work as long as it is shallow enough to allow the cream to reduce.

1 Preheat the oven to 400°F. Grease the bottom and sides of a 5- or 6-cup shallow gratin dish with butter. Bring a small (5- or 6-quart) stockpot of salted water to a boil and add the pasta. Cook the pasta until just 2 or 3 minutes shy of the suggested cooking time on the package. Add the broccoli raab to the boiling water and cook for 2 or 3 more minutes. Drain the pasta and raab in a fine-mesh colander. Let sit for a few minutes, tossing occasionally to release water.

2 In a small bowl, combine the bread crumbs, 3 tablespoons of the Parmesan, the olive oil, and a pinch of salt and stir well. Set aside.

3 In a medium saucepan over medium-high heat, bring the cream and the smashed garlic just to a boil (watch it carefully so that it doesn't suddenly bubble up and overflow). Remove the pan from the heat and let sit for 10 minutes to allow the garlic to infuse the cream. Remove the garlic cloves (or not!) and season the cream with ½ teaspoon of salt, a few grinds of black pepper, and the lemon zest. Stir well.

4 Put the pasta and broccoli raab into a medium mixing bowl. Add the goat cheese and the remaining ¼ cup of Parmesan. Pour the infused cream over the pasta mixture and stir well. Transfer to the prepared gratin dish and spread evenly. Top with the bread crumb mixture. Bake the gratin until the crumbs are golden brown and the liquids have reduced to below the crumb level (there will be a light brown ring around the edge of the dish), about 35 minutes. Let sit for 5 to 10 minutes before serving.

VEGGIES + GRAINS

WHEN I was learning to cook on my own in my first (New York City) apartment, I fell in love with grains. I made millet stew and bulgur pancakes, quinoa pilafs and barley risotto. I bought Bert Greene's *The Grains Cookbook* and later Sheryl and Mel London's *The Versatile Grain and the Elegant Bean*. I made polenta and paella, congee and tabbouleh. My interest eventually waned (as things do, you know, over the years), but then it rebounded when I began to think more about putting vegetables at the center of the plate. Grains are such a natural partner to veggies. I developed new recipes for *Vegetarian Times* magazine, using everything from amaranth and buckwheat to cornmeal and oats. And then, when I wrote my second cookbook, *The Fresh and Green Table*, I brought wheat berries, brown rice, and quinoa into the picture. More recently, I learned about the resurgence of farro, including delicious ways to cook it, from an excellent book by journalist Maria Speck, titled *Simply Ancient Grains*. And by the time I read Amy Chaplin's *At Home in the Whole Food Kitchen*, I had started to really appreciate the holistic value of cooking with and eating more grains.

But I was still all over the map. Frankly, I hadn't settled into a comfortable way of cooking with grains on a regular basis. I was hung up on "grains recipes"—elaborate preparations that had me cooking grains in a different way every time I used them. Where was the common denominator? Because I'm a recipe developer, I tend to come at cooking from a technique-based point of view, and I wanted the take-away.

It was when I started cooking veggie suppers every night that I had a breakthrough. I happened upon a method for cooking grains that was different from the "pilaf" method I was familiar with (where you cook grains in a measured amount of water) and also, I soon realized, much more versatile. I call this the "pasta" method (see page 235). Now I had clarity: to cook grains for supper, I simply had to choose one of these two methods and go for it.

Tips and Strategies for Grains

First, choose your cooking method. The "pasta" method involves cooking grains in plenty of boiling water until done, and then draining them as you would pasta (see "How to Cook Grains Using the Pasta Method," page 235). Grains cooked this way are generally firmer and plumper, and without any added flavors, a batch of these grains is very versatile. Also, unlike grains cooked with the pilaf method, they don't tend to stick together, making them easy to fold into other dishes. They are also a great make-ahead ingredient—one that can be stored in the fridge or even in the freezer to use in small amounts as you please.

Being able to use small amounts of grains in salads, stir-fries, and sautés means that you don't have to give a giant bear hug to grains every time you use them. You can enjoy them in balance with vegetables, nuts, fruits, greens, and dressings; in fact, you can use them to make any dish more satisfying. Heck, you could eat them *almost every night of the week*.

The pilaf method still has its place, especially when it comes to cooking white rice. I'm fond of incorporating flavors into a dish "from

the bottom up": by sautéing rice with aromatics like onions and garlic—maybe a few spices, too—and adding just enough liquid to cook it properly, you get a flavor-infused dish that still welcomes veggie additions into its arms (such as Green Rice, page 50). But the pilaf method is unpredictable when cooking whole grains: it's hard to estimate the correct amount of water, so you're often left with extra liquid or undercooked grains.

Using the pasta method for cooking grains has helped me to hone my "short" list of favorite grains. I always had trouble cooking brown rice consistently (and in less than 45 or 50 minutes), but now I can cook it perfectly in 30 minutes (and I frequently do). Instead of cooking farro or wheat berries once in a blue moon, I now cook them nearly as often as rice. I find I can use either the pasta or the pilaf method for quinoa, which I especially enjoy in the summer because it feels lighter. With barley and rices, I now have a manageable list of favorites.

For our veggie supper strategy, I think three or four whole grains and a few rices are enough to cook with regularly, especially to begin with, and certainly simpler than stocking fifteen different varieties. Of course you'll have to try cooking with several different grains to see what you like, but won't it be a feat when you wind up with your very own short list of grains you can enthusiastically rely on for veggie suppers? Let's see if we can get you there.

SHOP SMART: READ THE FINE PRINT.

You have to play a bit of the sleuth when shopping for whole grains. The grocery store or the natural foods market is full of clues, but you may need a magnifying glass to find them. The problem is that grains—whether you buy them from bulk bins or in plastic packaging or cardboard boxes—often don't have obvious labeling or labeling that is consistent from one brand to the next. Be vigilant about reading the fine print on a package or a bulk bin label to make sure you're getting something that can be cooked in a reasonable amount of time but is not stripped of all its nutrients to achieve this.

Consider farro: One brand may simply be labeled "farro," but another brand will be properly labeled to specify "whole," "pearled" (or *perlato*), or "semi-pearled." Semi-pearled or pearled farro cooks much more quickly than whole farro, which can take hours, especially if not soaked overnight first. Fortunately, semi-pearled farro is the type most widely available. (There is one other form of farro on the market: par-cooked farro. Trader Joe's calls it "10-Minute Farro." It is not bad, all things considered.)

Sometimes farro is labeled as spelt, which isn't necessarily a mistake. Farro is, in fact, a general name for a set of three ancient cereal grains that are related to and predate modern wheat: einkorn (known as *farro piccolo*), emmer (*farro medio*), and spelt (*farro grande*). Farro of the emmer variety is the one most commonly imported into the United States from Italy (as a whole grain), but all three varieties are grown in the United States now, too.

Wheat berries can be tricky, too, but both "hard" wheat berries (from summer or winter wheat) and "soft" wheat berries will work in our recipes, especially when soaked overnight. Soft will be quicker cooking.

Barley is usually sold "pearled" (which we will use for quicker cooking), but it is sometimes available "hulled," retaining more of its fiber. There is also a par-cooked barley on the market; I am not crazy about it.

Quinoa is actually the seed of an ancient edible Peruvian plant, but we use it like a grain. It is available in three colors, white being the most common. To my taste, the red (which is pretty, too) has the mildest flavor, but all quinoa needs to be rinsed (even if the package says it has been already) to remove its tannic coating. Conveniently, all quinoas cook in the same amount of time—which is only about 12 minutes using the pasta method.

Rices are usually more clearly labeled, but it's still smart to pay attention. For instance, you could see any brown rice and grab it. It might wind up being long-grain brown rice. There's nothing wrong with that, but the short-grain variety (which I love) will have a firmer texture that holds up better in salads and soups. Never buy instant or par-cooked rice.

KEEP IT CONVENIENT.

As I mentioned earlier, I do like to buy grains from bulk bins if the store has a good turnover rate. It's fun to look at all the choices—plus you can buy only the amount you want. But also look for packaged brands like Bob's Red Mill and Anson Mills, which offer an increasingly interesting variety of both whole grains and whole-grain flours. Most important, try to find products that you like at a store you frequent. Yes, we are planning to stock up here, but we have only so much room. And I find I use something more often if I can replenish it on a regular shopping trip. (My view of this may be a little warped, though, as I have to get on a ferry boat and then drive many miles to get to a specialty grocer!)

When you get your grains home, store them in a well-sealed container in a cool, dry place. I like glass mason jars or cookie jars with tight-fitting lids so that I can see what I've got. Whatever containers you choose, label and date them. (Farro and wheat berries look very much alike.) You have probably heard the advice that you should store your grains in the refrigerator or freezer, but it really isn't necessary (and whose fridge has room for it?). It's a great place for whole-grain flours that can go rancid, but as long as you're keeping them in a well-sealed container in a cool place, whole grains will have a shelf life of many months.

LOVE YOUR COLANDER.

We don't need a lot of special equipment for cooking grains. I do like my nonstick pasta pot (see page 2) for cooking both noodles and grains (pasta-style). And you'll need a good medium-size (2½-quart) nonstick saucepan for rice. But there is one other thing you might want: a fine-mesh colander or strainer, or both.

Colanders with big holes are fine for draining pasta, but little grains will run right through those holes. So I have a coarse-mesh colander for draining pasta as well as a handheld fine-mesh strainer that I can use to drain or rinse grains.

CONSIDER SOAKING.

There is no doubt that soaking chewy grains like wheat berries or whole farro overnight will speed up the cooking process the next day, but many health experts suggest that there's another good reason to soak most any whole grain. Whole grains contain a naturally protective substance called phytic acid, which inhibits nutrient availability and may make grains less digestible; soaking can decrease the phytic acid. I don't give most quick-cooking grains an overnight soak, but I want you to know that you have that option. It might take on more importance if you start to consume large amounts of grains on a regular basis.

For the Pantry

To stock our grains pantry, I've divided my recommendations into two lists: grains that I stock pretty regularly, and those I cook with occasionally. As I said at the start of this chapter, our goal isn't to make cooking with fifteen different grains a regular habit, so please don't be put off by the length of these lists. However, by all means, do feel empowered to try as many as you like on your way to getting friendly with a few.

I can't overemphasize the usefulness of grains for veggie suppers; I dearly wish I had room to give you more recipes using them. Instead I've tried to give you one or two recipes using each of my favorite grains, and then I encourage you to try more varieties on your own, knowing that cooking them is not nearly as complicated as you or I might have guessed. Feel free to make grain substitutions in these recipes, too. I've also included grains in other recipes throughout the book, including some great ones in the "Veggies + Broth" chapter (page 205) that use grain-cooking liquid as a soup base.

I've also included my list of favorite "accessory" ingredients for grains. Grains love fruits and nuts, bright herbs like parsley and mint, and always a nice bright hit of vinegar or citrus. Add a few grain "accessories" to your shopping list, and your grain larder will be good to go.

The Grains

USUALLY ON MY SHELF

Short-grain brown rice

Long-grain brown rice

Texmati (white) rice

Basmati (white) rice

Arborio (medium-grain white) rice

Sushi rice

Farro

Wheat berries

Pearled barley

Quinoa (red and white)

Coarse cornmeal

Rolled oats

SOMETIMES ON MY SHELF

Black rice

Red rice

Wild rice

Buckwheat groats

Bulghur

Millet

Freekeh

Accessory Ingredients

Toasted pecans, walnuts, almonds, and hazelnuts

Dried cherries, cranberries, and dates

Low-sodium tamari

Rice vinegar

White balsamic vinegar

Dijon mustard

Fresh limes

Fresh garlic

Fresh ginger

Shallots

Fresh parsley

Fresh mint

Curry powder

Chili powder

Miso paste

ASPARAGUS AND GRAPEFRUIT SALAD

WITH SUSHI RICE AND GINGER-MISO DRESSING

SERVES 2

1 cup uncooked sushi rice

1 tablespoon rice vinegar

2 teaspoons cane sugar

¾ teaspoon kosher salt

12 medium asparagus spears

1 pink grapefruit

10 to 12 small leaves of Bibb lettuce or other small, pretty lettuce leaves

1 recipe Crystallized Ginger-Miso Dressing (recipe follows)

Coarse sea salt (optional)

4 to 6 sprigs of fresh cilantro, for garnish (optional)

Amazingly, the bright flavor of a potent ginger dressing perfectly bridges the earthy and tart flavors of asparagus and grapefruit. Paired with warm sushi rice and crisp lettuce, this supper salad is both stunning and satisfying. I love the plump kernels of quick-cooking sushi rice, which glisten after the traditional toss with rice vinegar and sugar. The salad can be served completely at room temperature or, as I like it, with slightly warm sushi rice and asparagus and cool (but not cold) grapefruit, lettuce, and vinaigrette. In a pinch, sushi rice can be made ahead and gently reheated.

1 Put the rice in a small bowl and rinse it in several changes of cool water until the water runs clear. Drain well. Put in a medium saucepan with 1 cup of water and bring to a boil over high heat, then cover, reduce the heat to very low, and cook for 15 minutes. Remove the pan from the heat and let sit for 10 minutes.

2 Using a silicone spatula, transfer the rice into a shallow mixing bowl. In another small bowl, stir together the rice vinegar, sugar, and ¼ teaspoon of the salt until the sugar is mostly dissolved. Drizzle the vinegar mixture over the cooked rice and stir gently until the rice is coated and glistening.

3 Arrange the asparagus in a single layer in a large skillet. Season with the remaining ½ teaspoon of salt and cover with enough water that the asparagus begins to float. Bring to a boil over high heat, then reduce the heat to low and simmer until the asparagus are very flexible when lifted with tongs but still bright green, about 3 minutes. Transfer spears to a dish towel.

4 Peel the grapefruit and cut it crosswise into 6 or 8 round slices.

5 On two dinner plates or small platters, arrange equal portions of the lettuce leaves, the grapefruit slices, the asparagus, and the rice in rows next to each other (or any pleasing way you like). Spoon a few tablespoons of dressing over each salad (you may not need all the dressing, but be sure to scoop out plenty of crystallized ginger for each portion), sprinkle with coarse sea salt (if using), and garnish with the cilantro sprigs (if using).

Crystallized Ginger-Miso Dressing

MAKES ABOUT ⅓ CUP

1 tablespoon peanut oil

1 tablespoon rice vinegar

1 tablespoon plus 1 teaspoon
fresh lime juice

1 tablespoon plus 1 teaspoon
minced crystallized ginger

1 tablespoon maple syrup

1 tablespoon minced
fresh cilantro

1½ teaspoons white (shiro) miso

I have to admit this ginger dressing is one of my favorite recipes. It features crystallized ginger with assists from lime, maple, and miso. I love it with asparagus and grapefruit, but it is equally good with broccoli, green beans, or cabbage. You may want to double or triple the recipe.

Whisk together all the ingredients in a small bowl. Store the dressing in a glass jar or other container in the fridge for up to 2 weeks. Bring it to room temperature and stir well before using.

CURRIED BASMATI RICE

WITH PEAS, SHALLOTS, DATES, ALMONDS, AND COCONUT

SERVES 3

2 tablespoons unsalted butter

1 tablespoon grapeseed or vegetable oil

3 large shallots, cut crosswise into thin rings (about 1 cup)

1¼ teaspoons kosher salt

1 tablespoon curry powder

1 cup basmati rice

½ cup canned full-fat coconut milk (preferably organic), well stirred

1 cup frozen peas, thawed, or fresh peas, blanched or microwaved for 30 seconds

⅓ cup finely chopped pitted Medjool dates (about 3 or 4 dates)

⅓ cup coarsely chopped toasted almonds

⅓ to ½ cup toasted unsweetened coconut flakes (large flakes)

This lovely and fragrant rice dish is reminiscent of Persian rice recipes, which feature spices, dried fruit, nuts, and crispy onions or shallots. This one isn't fussy to make, but it does require a couple of items—dates and unsweetened coconut flakes—that you might not have in your pantry. Both dates and coconut keep well (coconut flakes store for months in the freezer), so if you have some left over, no worries. Look for the Bob's Red Mill brand of unsweetened flaked coconut in the grains or baking section of a natural foods store or well-stocked grocery. Fresh peas bring this rice into springtime, but it is just as tasty with frozen peas in fall or winter (or any time!).

1 Heat 1 tablespoon of the butter with the oil in a medium nonstick saucepan over medium heat. Add the shallots and ¼ teaspoon of the salt and cook, stirring, until all the shallots are well browned and crinkly, about 10 minutes. Transfer three quarters of the shallots to a plate and set aside. Add the remaining 1 tablespoon of butter, the curry powder, and the remaining 1 teaspoon of salt and cook for 1 minute, stirring well. Add the rice and stir very well to incorporate the spices.

2 Add the coconut milk and 1¼ cups water to the rice and stir well. Bring to a boil, then reduce the heat to the lowest setting, cover the pan, and cook for 20 minutes. Remove the pan from the heat. Put the peas and dates on top of the rice, then replace the lid and let sit for 10 minutes. Uncover, stir with a fork, and transfer to a medium mixing bowl.

3 Add the chopped almonds and most of the toasted coconut and stir well. Transfer to a serving platter and garnish with the remaining coconut and the reserved shallot rings.

STIR-FRIED BLACK RICE

WITH BABY BOK CHOY, ASPARAGUS, SHIITAKES, AND LEMON-MISO BUTTER

SERVES 2

½ pound baby bok choy

2 tablespoons peanut oil

4 ounces shiitake mushrooms, stemmed and cut into thick slices

4 ounces asparagus, cut into thin slices at a sharp angle

¾ teaspoon kosher salt

2 teaspoons minced fresh garlic

⅓ cup sliced scallions (white and light green parts)

1½ cups cooked black rice (see page 235), at room temperature or warm

1 recipe Lemon-Miso Butter (recipe follows)

1 to 2 teaspoons toasted sesame seeds

2 lemon wedges, for serving

I fell in love with black rice (sometimes called "forbidden rice") many years ago when I was an editor at *Fine Cooking* magazine looking for interesting new ingredients. These days, black rice is getting a lot of attention for its nutritional benefits: it's particularly high in anthocyanins, antioxidants that give the rice its purple color. It has a nutty flavor and a slightly sticky texture, so I love to pair it with stir-fried baby bok choy, which takes on a delicious nutty flavor when browned. This fun twist on fried rice also includes shiitakes, asparagus, and a finish of lemon-miso butter (which makes everything taste delicious). Of course, you can use white or brown rice in place of the black if you like.

1 Cut the bok choys in half lengthwise. Then cut them in half crosswise, separating the leafy greens from the stalks. Cut both the greens and the stalks lengthwise into ½-inch-wide pieces. (The core will hold pieces of the stalk together.) Dunk the stalks and the greens separately into clean tepid water and swish to release dirt. Spin-dry separately.

2 In a large (12-inch) nonstick stir-fry pan, heat 1 tablespoon of the oil over medium-high heat. When the oil is hot, add the shiitakes, asparagus, and ½ teaspoon of the salt and cook, stirring, until the shiitakes and asparagus are browned and shrunken, 3 to 4 minutes. Remove to a plate.

3 Add the remaining 1 tablespoon of oil, the bok choy stalks, and the remaining ¼ teaspoon of salt to the pan. Cook, stirring, until the bok choy stalks are browned in places and have lost their stiffness, 3 to 4 minutes. Add the bok choy leaves, the garlic, and half of the scallions and cook until the leaves are wilted, about 1 minute. Add the asparagus and shiitakes back to the pan along with the rice and cook, stirring, until the rice is heated through, 1 to 2 minutes.

4 Remove the pan from the heat and add three quarters of the miso butter. Stir until the butter melts and coats the rice. Taste, and add the rest of the miso butter if you like.

5 Transfer to a serving platter or bowls and garnish with the remaining scallions, the sesame seeds, and the lemon wedges.

Lemon-Miso Butter

MAKES ¼ CUP

2 tablespoons unsalted
butter, softened

2 tablespoons white (shiro) miso

1 teaspoon freshly grated
lemon zest

Make this handy flavor booster ahead, then cover it and keep it in the fridge for up to a week. Use it in the Stir-Fried Black Rice with Baby Bok Choy, Asparagus, Shiitakes, and Lemon-Miso Butter recipe (page 38), in the Parsnips and Creminis with Wheat Berries (page 56), or on your own stir-fried or sautéed veggies. Don't hesitate to double this recipe if you like. (If you need to soften the butter quickly when making this, cut it into pieces and microwave for a few seconds, but be careful not to melt it.)

Put all the ingredients in a small bowl. Use a small silicone spatula or wooden spoon to mash them together until well combined.

QUICK-ROASTED BEET, ARUGULA, AND WHEAT BERRY SALAD

WITH STRAWBERRY-BALSAMIC DRESSING

SERVES 4

1 pound beets (6 to 8 small to medium), any color, unpeeled

¼ cup plus 1 tablespoon grapeseed or olive oil

1¼ teaspoons kosher salt, plus 2 large pinches

1 tablespoon plus 2 teaspoons white balsamic vinegar or a combination of red balsamic vinegar and white wine vinegar

1 tablespoon maple syrup

1 tablespoon fresh lemon juice

3 tablespoons diced fresh strawberries, plus 8 to 10 strawberries, cored and sliced

1½ cups cooked wheat berries (see page 235)

4 cups arugula (preferably small or baby leaves)

⅓ cup chopped toasted pistachio nuts, or toasted sliced almonds (see page 237)

2 ounces fresh goat cheese, crumbled while still cold

1 tablespoon fresh baby mint leaves or slivered mint (optional)

In my garden, strawberries begin to ripen about the same time the first beets are ready to harvest. One day I realized that the sweet, citrusy acidity of my Ozark Beauty strawberries would be the perfect foil for the earthy nuances of beets, and that both go well with maple syrup and balsamic vinegar. Because wheat berries also love maple and balsamic, I had found the perfect pairing for a beautiful and tasty salad. (Cook your wheat berries ahead of time, or if you need a quicker-cooking grain here, use farro.) The cool flavors of arugula and goat cheese add the perfect contrast, but you could certainly leave out the goat cheese for a vegan version. Ideally, use a large platter or two smaller platters for this salad, which gets a whimsical character from scattering and layering the ingredients rather than mixing them in a deep bowl.

1 Preheat the oven to 450°F. Line two heavy-duty rimmed baking sheets with parchment paper.

2 Using a sharp, thin-bladed knife, trim the ends of the beets and then slice each beet crosswise into rounds between ⅛ and ¼ inch thick. (Don't use a mandoline, which would cut them too thin.) If a beet wobbles around while you are trying to cut it, cut a thin piece off the bottom to stabilize it.

3 If you have both red and yellow beets, put them in separate bowls. Toss the beets with 2 tablespoons of the oil and ¾ teaspoon of the salt. Spread out the beets in a single layer on the baking sheets (preferably keeping red and yellow beets separate) and bake, flipping with a spatula and rotating the pans halfway through cooking, until the beet slices are tender, glistening, and shrunken, a total of 16 to 18 minutes.

4 In a small bowl, whisk together the remaining 3 tablespoons of oil, the vinegar, maple syrup, and lemon juice, and a big pinch of salt. Stir in the diced strawberries.

5 Put the wheat berries into a small bowl and season with ½ teaspoon of the salt. Stir in 2 tablespoons of the strawberry dressing and let sit for 10 to 20 minutes to allow the grain to absorb some of the dressing.

6 Have ready four large dinner plates, two medium platters, or one large platter. (Both ovals

and rounds look nice; just aim for a lot of surface area.) Reserve a few leaves of arugula, then divide the arugula evenly among your serving dishes, scattering it over the dishes. Sprinkle it all with the remaining big pinch of salt and drizzle with 2 tablespoons of the strawberry dressing, divided up among the dishes.

7 Over the arugula, arrange or scatter the roasted beets, strawberry slices, and seasoned wheat berries. Drizzle with the remaining dressing, then sprinkle with the goat cheese, the pistachios, the remaining arugula leaves, and the mint leaves (if using). Serve right away.

COLORFUL QUINOA AND BEAN SALAD

WITH TOMATO-NECTARINE-CURRY DRESSING

SERVES 4

3 tablespoons extra-virgin olive oil

2 tablespoons plus 2 teaspoons white balsamic vinegar

1 tablespoon honey or maple syrup

1 tablespoon minced fresh ginger

2 teaspoons minced fresh garlic

1½ teaspoons Madras curry powder

1 teaspoon kosher salt

2 cups halved or quartered cherry tomatoes (depending on their size)

2 cups peeled and diced or sliced ripe-but-firm nectarines or peaches (about 3 medium fruits)

½ small red onion, cut into thin slices

3 cups cooked red or white quinoa (see page 235)

One 15-ounce can white beans, drained and rinsed

½ cup coarsely chopped fresh herbs (any combination of parsley, mint, and cilantro)

½ cup toasted pepitas (pumpkin seeds)

Vibrant red quinoa with a sexy tomato-nectarine dressing makes this a colorful and flavorful grain salad you won't forget. You'll love it for supper—the addition of beans makes it totally filling. But you might also find yourself bringing it to a summer potluck because this is a "big bowl" salad, as opposed to the kind that is best served on a platter. There is a bit of chopping to do here, but then it will all come together in a snap. The flavor of this salad improves as it sits, so you can make it a little ahead of time. I love the juiciness and flavor of a really good ripe peach; so if you've got one, certainly use it in place of the nectarines. However, nectarines do hold up slightly better in the salad. Make sure your curry powder is recently purchased for the best flavor.

1 In a large mixing bowl, whisk together the oil, vinegar, honey, ginger, garlic, curry powder, and ½ teaspoon of the salt. Add the tomatoes, nectarines, and onion. (If you like, you can put the onion slices in hot water for a few minutes to soften them.) Stir gently and let marinate for a few minutes, stirring occasionally.

Add the quinoa, the beans, most of the herbs, and the remaining ½ teaspoon of salt to the bowl. Stir together gently and let sit a few minutes, or up to 30 minutes.

2 Right before serving, stir in half of the pepitas and transfer to a large serving bowl. Garnish with the remaining herbs and pepitas.

GRILLED SUMMER VEGGIE AND BARLEY SALAD

WITH BASIL AND SUN-DRIED TOMATO DRESSING

SERVES 4

½ pound summer squash, zucchini, Asian eggplant, and/or Fairy Tale eggplant in any combination

½ pound cremini mushrooms, bell peppers, shishito peppers, onions, snap peas, and/or green beans in any combination

¼ cup extra-virgin olive oil, plus more for brushing vegetables

¼ teaspoon of kosher salt, plus 2 large pinches

¼ cup coarsely chopped fresh basil leaves, plus some small whole leaves for garnish (optional)

1 tablespoon plus 2 teaspoons white balsamic vinegar

2 tablespoons finely chopped sun-dried tomatoes

2 tablespoons chopped, pitted Kalamata olives

1 teaspoon minced fresh garlic

2 cups cooked barley (see page 225)

continued opposite

The smoky flavors of grilled veggies combine with the briny, sweet-tart flavors of olives, sun-dried tomatoes, and fresh basil to give this barley salad a lot of personality. I like to grill a combination of squashes, eggplants, peppers, onions, and mushrooms, but you can choose your own favorites. Cooking the smaller veggies is easiest in a grill basket or on a grill topper, but if you don't have one, no problem: cut the veggies into extra-big pieces for grilling, then chop them smaller afterward. Cook the barley a day or two ahead if you like, but because it will take only about 35 minutes, you could still make this tonight. This salad holds well, too.

1 Preheat a gas grill to medium heat. Put a grill basket or grill topper on the grill to preheat, if using either or both (see "How to Grill Veggies," page 239). Trim the ends off the squashes and/or eggplants and cut them diagonally into long slices about ⅜ inch thick. (Cut Fairy Tale eggplants only in half lengthwise.) Cut the remaining vegetables into 1- to 2-inch hunks, leaving the smallest ones whole. (You can quarter small onions, leaving the stem ends intact to hold the layers together, or cut them into thick rings.) Brush the sliced vegetables on all sides with olive oil and sprinkle with a large pinch of salt. Place on a baking sheet to transport to the grill. Put the remaining chopped vegetables in a bowl and toss with 2 tablespoons of the olive oil and a large pinch of salt.

2 Arrange the sliced vegetable pieces on the grill topper, cover, and cook until well marked on the first side, 3 to 5 minutes. Turn them over, cover again, and continue cooking until the bottom side is marked and the veggies are tender, 2 to 3 minutes. Transfer to a tray or plate and cover loosely to keep warm. Place the remaining chopped vegetables in a grill basket or on the grill topper, cover, and cook, occasionally flipping or stirring if in a basket, until browned and tender, about 5 to 8 minutes total. (If your grill is big enough, you can cook all the veggies at the same time.)

3 Put the barley into a medium bowl. In a small bowl, stir together the remaining 2 tablespoons of olive oil and the basil, vinegar, sun-dried tomatoes, olives, garlic, and the

8 to 12 medium-size pretty lettuce leaves, such as Bibb, romaine, or any other loose-leaf variety

2 to 3 tablespoons sliced or chopped toasted almonds

Dark local honey (optional)

remaining ¼ teaspoon of salt. (The dressing will be chunky.) Add 2 tablespoons of the sun-dried tomato dressing to the barley and stir well.

4 Arrange 2 or 3 leaves of lettuce on each of four serving plates or arrange all the lettuce leaves around the edges of one medium-large platter. Arrange some of the sliced grilled veggies over the lettuce and spoon over a little more of the sun-dried tomato dressing. Sprinkle with half of the barley, distributing it evenly among plates. Arrange the remaining grilled veggies over the barley and spoon over a little more dressing. Sprinkle with the remaining barley and drizzle with the remaining dressing, then garnish with the whole basil leaves (if using) and the almonds. Drizzle with a bit of honey if you like. Serve warm or at room temperature.

RED QUINOA AND BABY KALE SALAD

WITH SWEET POTATO FRIES AND BLACKBERRY DRESSING

SERVES 4

1½ pounds sweet potatoes (unpeeled), cut into sticks 2 to 3 inches long and ⅜ to ½ inch wide (about 2 large potatoes)

¼ cup plus 2 tablespoons grapeseed or olive oil

1 teaspoon kosher salt, plus 2 large pinches

1 tablespoon plus 1 teaspoon balsamic vinegar

1 tablespoon maple syrup

1 tablespoon blackberry jam

2 to 3 teaspoons fresh lime juice

½ teaspoon Dijon mustard

4 to 5 cups packed baby kale leaves

1½ cups cooked red quinoa, cooled (see page 235)

⅓ cup chopped toasted pecans

6 ounces fresh blackberries or defrosted frozen blackberries or raspberries (about 1¼ cups)

I had to laugh at myself when I realized that I had put together a nutritional powerhouse, accidentally. I was just aiming for color and flavor, but with high-protein quinoa, super-food kale, antioxidant blackberries, and beta-carotene-rich sweet potatoes, this is all-around good for you. I've gone light on the quinoa here, sprinkling it over the dressed kale and under the taters for a bit of texture that doesn't overwhelm. In the vinaigrette, blackberry jam marries with maple syrup, balsamic vinegar, and lime juice for delicious results, but you could use any berry jam. Cook the quinoa in advance to save time before supper; remember, it will store well for several days in the fridge. A tip for cutting a sweet potato into sticks: First cut it crosswise on a diagonal to create oval slices. Then stack a few slices and cut them into sticks.

1 Preheat the oven to 450°F. Line two heavy-duty rimmed baking sheets with parchment paper. Toss the sweet potatoes with 3 tablespoons of the oil and 1 teaspoon of kosher salt in a large bowl. Spread the sweet potatoes in a single layer on the baking sheets and roast, flipping with a spatula once or twice and rotating the pans during cooking, for 22 to 24 minutes, until browned and a bit shrunken.

2 In a small bowl, whisk together the remaining 3 tablespoons of oil and the vinegar, maple syrup, jam, 2 teaspoons of the lime juice, the mustard, and a big pinch of salt. The dressing should have an emulsified, creamy consistency and rich, deep color. Taste and add another teaspoon of lime juice if you like—the flavor should be bright.

3 Put the kale leaves and a pinch of salt in a large bowl. Add 2 tablespoons of the blackberry dressing and toss thoroughly to coat. In a medium bowl, mix the quinoa with 1 tablespoon of the dressing.

4 Arrange the kale loosely on four dinner plates. Sprinkle the quinoa over the kale, dividing it evenly among the plates. Arrange the roasted sweet potatoes on top, then sprinkle each salad with a little more salt, a quarter of the pecans, and a quarter of the berries. Drizzle the remaining dressing over the salads and serve.

ROASTED BRUSSELS SPROUTS, CRISPY SHIITAKES, AND GREEN RICE

WITH CRUNCHY PEPITAS

SERVES 4

12 ounces brussels sprouts, trimmed and cut lengthwise into quarters

¼ cup plus 1 tablespoon extra-virgin olive oil

½ teaspoon kosher salt, plus a pinch

8 ounces large shiitake caps, stemmed and cut into ½-inch-wide strips

1 recipe Green Rice (recipe follows), rewarmed if necessary

½ cup Spicy Roasted Tomatillo Salsa Verde (page 169) or Spicy Lime-Chili Oil (page 83), optional

¼ cup toasted pepitas (pumpkin seeds), pine nuts, or pecans

1 lemon or lime, cut into quarters

⅓ cup sour cream or Lime-Chipotle Sauce (page 164)

This is roasty-toasty comfort food in a bowl for me. I love the deep, earthy flavors and crisp texture of both roasted brussels sprouts and roasted shiitakes, especially when they're nestled into a bowl of my favorite Green Rice. Then I can have fun with the finishes, depending on the mood I'm in and what I've got on hand. I always go with a generous smattering of deeply toasted seeds or nuts (I like pepitas or pecans) and usually a good squeeze of lime and a dollop of sour cream or Lime-Chipotle Sauce. The flavor really amps up with a spoonful of Spicy Roasted Tomatillo Salsa Verde or a drizzle of Spicy Lime-Chili Oil added in. Add tortillas, and this easily converts into burritos.

1 Preheat the oven to 425°F. Line two rimmed baking sheets with parchment paper. In a medium bowl, toss the brussels sprouts with 2 tablespoons of the oil and ½ teaspoon of salt. In another medium bowl, toss the shiitakes with the remaining 3 tablespoons of oil and a pinch of salt. Arrange the brussels sprouts in a single layer on one baking sheet, and arrange the mushrooms on the other baking sheet.

2 Roast the mushrooms, stirring once or twice during baking, until they are golden-brown and crisp, 16 to 18 minutes. Remove the pan from the oven.

Roast the brussels sprouts, stirring once or twice during baking, until they are lightly browned and crisp, 22 to 25 minutes.

3 Place a portion of green rice in each of four serving bowls. Top with the brussels sprouts and then the shiitakes, dividing them evenly among the plates. Spoon 1 tablespoon of salsa verde or 1 or 2 teaspoons of Spicy Lime-Chili Oil (if using) over each serving. Garnish each with seeds or nuts and a lemon or lime quarter (for a generous squeezing). Serve with sour cream or Lime-Chipotle Sauce on the side.

Green Rice

MAKES ABOUT 3 CUPS

1 large garlic clove, peeled

1 quarter-size slice of
fresh ginger

1 small or ½ large jalapeño,
seeded and coarsely chopped

½ cup packed fresh cilantro
(leaves and tender stems)

¾ cup packed baby spinach

1¼ teaspoons kosher salt

1 tablespoon unsalted butter

1 tablespoon extra-virgin olive
oil or grapeseed oil

⅓ cup thinly sliced scallions
(white and light green parts)

1 cup uncooked Texmati rice

There are lots of versions of Mexican *arroz verde* (green rice), but my favorites always feature a good bit of cilantro and spinach. Some have poblano chiles, but mine has just a bit of jalapeño and garlic, plus a little twist from my favorite aromatic, fresh ginger. Although I do wish the bright green puree (everything gets whizzed in a blender first) wouldn't turn a dull green when it cooks, I do love the way it transforms white rice into something earthy and herby that seems to just open its arms to vegetables. I love it with roasted brussels sprouts and shiitakes but also with green beans, okra, corn, and asparagus. It makes a great burrito filling, too, as in the Spicy White Bean Burritos with Green Rice, Pepitas, and Queso Fresco (page 165). Or you can just eat it on its own, straight from the pot!

1 In a blender, combine the garlic, ginger, and jalapeño and pulse until well chopped. (You will need to stop the blender to dislodge the jalapeño pieces a few times.) Add the cilantro, spinach, ¼ teaspoon of the salt, and 1 cup of water. Blend on high until the greens are well chopped.

2 In a medium saucepan, heat the butter with the oil over medium heat. Add the scallions and cook until just softened, 2 to 3 minutes. Add the rice and the remaining 1 teaspoon of salt and cook, stirring, until the rice is fragrant and beginning to toast and crackle, about 2 minutes. Add the contents of the blender plus ⅔ cup of water, stir well, and bring to a boil. Turn the heat to the lowest setting, cover, and cook for 20 minutes. Remove the pan from the heat.

3 Let the covered pan of cooked rice sit for 5 minutes. With a fork, fluff the rice and stir in the green layer on the top. Cover the rice with a paper towel and then the lid again, and let sit 5 more minutes.

AUTUMN FARRO SALAD

WITH QUICK-ROASTED ROOT VEGETABLES, SPINACH, AND LEMON SHERRY DRESSING

SERVES 2

3 tablespoons extra-virgin olive oil

2 tablespoons sherry vinegar

1 tablespoon finely chopped shallots

1 tablespoon honey

2 teaspoons fresh lemon juice, plus 2 lemon wedges

2 teaspoons coarsely chopped fresh thyme

1 teaspoon freshly grated lemon zest

½ teaspoon kosher salt, plus a pinch

1 recipe Quick-Roasted Root Vegetables (see page 83)

1 cup cooked farro (see page 31), reheated if necessary

⅓ cup chopped dried cherries

⅓ cup chopped toasted hazelnuts, pecans, or walnuts

3 cups packed baby spinach

This is it—the warm grain and vegetable salad you'll make again and again, changing it a little with your own favorite ingredients each time you make it. Comforting. Delicious. Just the right balance of grains and roasted vegetables. Bright vinaigrette, crunchy nuts, a bit of sweet dried fruit, a little leafy something. I've become a big fan of farro (see page 31), and it cooks in about 30 minutes. I often cook some over the weekend and use it throughout the week in all kinds of dishes. But you could certainly do the same with barley, short-grain brown rice, or wheat berries and use them in this salad. In a recipe like this, I use the grain in a relatively modest amount so that it doesn't overwhelm the veggies. Everything in balance!

1 In a small bowl, whisk the oil, vinegar, shallots, honey, lemon juice, thyme, lemon zest, and ¼ teaspoon of the salt until emulsified.

2 In a medium bowl, combine the roasted vegetables, farro, cherries, nuts, and the remaining ¼ teaspoon of salt. Toss gently. Add 2 to 3 tablespoons of the dressing and toss gently. Taste and add more dressing or salt if desired.

3 In another medium bowl, toss the spinach leaves with 2 to 3 teaspoons of the dressing and a pinch of salt. Arrange the spinach on two serving plates. Top with the farro mixture and garnish with the lemon wedges.

WARM BROWN RICE, LENTIL, CABBAGE, AND APPLE SALAD

WITH WALNUTS, CRANBERRIES, AND APPLE-DIJON DRESSING

SERVES 2 TO 3

¼ cup grapeseed or mild olive oil, or a combination

2 tablespoons white wine vinegar

1½ teaspoons Dijon mustard

1 teaspoon packed dark brown sugar

½ teaspoon kosher salt, plus a large pinch

1 cup diced yellow onion

2 cups diced green or savoy cabbage

2 cups cooked short- or long-grain brown rice (see page 30)

1 cup cooked lentils, preferably French (or du Puy) or black beluga (see page 237)

1 cup small-diced, unpeeled tart-sweet apple

⅓ cup chopped dried cranberries

⅓ cup chopped toasted walnuts

½ cup fresh parsley leaves

2 to 3 lime wedges

This comforting supper comes together quickly if you've been following our make-ahead mantra and shopping strategies. But even if you make it all from scratch tonight, you can still be done in about 40 minutes. If you're cooking your own lentils for this, choose the smaller black beluga or green French lentils (see page 237); they hold their shape best. (But if you're looking for convenience, consider buying vacuum-packed steamed lentils.) This salad gains flavor as it sits (rice tends to absorb flavors first, then release them), but it also benefits from a fresh squeeze of lime at serving time to bring the flavors out. Feel free to use sliced brussels sprouts in place of the cabbage.

1 In a small bowl, whisk together 3 tablespoons of the oil and the vinegar, mustard, brown sugar, and a big pinch of salt and set aside.

2 In a large (12-inch) nonstick skillet, heat the remaining 1 tablespoon of oil over medium-high heat. Add the onion, cabbage, and ½ teaspoon of salt. Cook, stirring frequently, until the veggies are limp and browned, 5 to 7 minutes. Transfer to a large bowl.

3 If necessary, reheat the rice and the lentils in separate bowls in a microwave for 45 seconds to 1 minute on the high setting. (They don't need to be piping hot.) Add to the bowl with the cabbage and onions. Add the apple, cranberries, walnuts, half the parsley, and all the mustard dressing. Stir well, taste, and season with more salt if necessary. Be aware that the rice and lentils tend to absorb the flavor at first, but then the salad will become more flavorful overall as it sits. Transfer to a serving bowl or bowls and garnish with the lime wedges and the remaining parsley leaves.

QUINOA AND MELTED LEEK-STUFFED ROASTED PORTOBELLOS

MAKES 6 STUFFED MUSHROOMS, SERVES 3 OR 4

6 medium portobello mushrooms caps, stems removed and gills scraped out with a spoon

4 to 5 tablespoons extra-virgin olive oil

½ teaspoon kosher salt, plus more to sprinkle mushroom caps

2 tablespoons unsalted butter

2 cups sliced leeks, well rinsed

2 teaspoons lightly chopped fresh thyme

2 ounces goat cheese, at room temperature

1½ cups cooked quinoa (see page 235), any color

Freshly ground black pepper

2 to 3 tablespoons drained and chopped oil-packed sun-dried tomatoes

¼ cup plus 2 tablespoons finely grated Parmesan cheese

Roasted portobello mushrooms are such an easy, delicious, and filling protein for vegetarians that I feel almost silly reminding you about them. But I do love them with a grain stuffing, and this quinoa version with leeks and goat cheese is so tasty that you'll definitely want it in your repertoire. Also, it provides a good opportunity to learn a few tips for cooking portobellos well. (They're unpleasant when undercooked.) Start with a hot oven (425°F), brush the mushrooms with oil to help transfer heat to the flesh, and arrange them stem-side up to allow juices to pool in the cap. Give the mushrooms plenty of time to cook through; they'll shrink with moisture loss and gain lots of flavor. If you don't have cooked quinoa already on hand, remember it takes only 12 minutes with the "pasta" method (see page 235), and you can start it when you pop the mushrooms in the oven.

1 Preheat the oven to 425°F. Line a rimmed baking sheet with parchment paper. Brush both sides of the portobello caps with the oil. Arrange the caps, stem-side up, on the prepared baking sheet. Season the inside of the caps with a sprinkle of salt. Bake for 23 to 25 minutes, until the mushrooms are shrunken and well browned (juices will be bubbling inside). Remove the baking sheet from the oven and keep the mushrooms on the pan. Set the oven to broil and use an oven mitt to carefully move an oven rack to the top position.

2 In a large saucepan, heat the butter over medium-low heat. Add the leeks and ¼ teaspoon of the salt. Stir and cover. Cook, uncovering frequently to stir, until the leeks are completely wilted and starting to brown, about 10 minutes. Add the thyme, goat cheese, quinoa, the remaining ¼ teaspoon of salt, and several grinds of black pepper. Stir until well incorporated and the quinoa is hot. (Don't overcook it, or the cheese will begin to stick to the pan.) Stir in the sun-dried tomatoes. Remove the pot from the heat.

3 Divide the quinoa mixture evenly among the mushroom caps, mounding it slightly. Sprinkle each stuffed cap with 1 tablespoon of the Parmesan. Put the filled baking sheet under the broiler and broil for 1 to 2 minutes, until the cheese is just melted and has turned a pale golden color. Serve warm.

PARSNIPS AND CREMINIS

WITH WHEAT BERRIES AND LEMON-MISO BUTTER

SERVES 2

2 tablespoons grapeseed or olive oil

½ pound parsnips, trimmed, peeled, and cut into ¼-inch-thick sticks or half-moons

6 ounces cremini mushrooms, cut into quarters if small, into sixths if large

½ teaspoon kosher salt

2 teaspoons minced fresh ginger

1 teaspoon minced fresh garlic

¼ cup sliced scallions (all parts)

1¼ to 1½ cups cooked wheat berries or short-grain brown rice (see page 30), rewarmed if necessary

1 recipe Lemon-Miso Butter (page 39)

Here's another great way to turn cooked grains into supper using our little three-ingredient flavor booster, Lemon-Miso Butter (page 39). For a classic fall combination, we're pairing the earthy and sweet flavors of mushrooms and parsnips with a bit of garlic and ginger. The addition of wheat berries to this mix ensures a lot of pleasantly chewy texture and nutty flavor. (Short-grain brown rice can stand in for the wheat berries.) The Lemon-Miso Butter melts to coat all three. I like a balance of wheat berries and veggies, but you could always add more grain if you like. If you're not a parsnip fan, use carrots instead. You may not need all the Lemon-Miso Butter—save any extra to toss with sautéed veggies another night.

1 In a large (12-inch) nonstick stir-fry pan, heat the oil over medium-high heat. Add the parsnips, mushrooms, and salt. Cook, stirring frequently, until the parsnips are well browned and tender and the mushrooms are well browned and shrunken, about 8 minutes.

2 Add the ginger, garlic, and 3 tablespoons of the scallions, and cook, stirring, until softened and fragrant, about 1 minute.

3 Remove the pan from the heat and stir in the wheat berries and three quarters of the Lemon-Miso Butter. Stir until the butter has just melted and coated the grains. Taste, and add more Lemon-Miso Butter if desired.

4 Transfer to a serving dish and garnish with the remaining 1 tablespoon of scallions.

SPICY STIR-FRIED GREEN BEANS

WITH CASHEWS AND 10-MINUTE FARRO

SERVES 2

1 tablespoon low-sodium tamari

1 tablespoon white (shiro) miso

1 tablespoon mirin (rice wine)

2 teaspoons fresh lemon juice

2 teaspoons packed brown sugar

1 teaspoon Asian chili-garlic paste

½ teaspoon toasted sesame oil

½ teaspoon cornstarch

2 tablespoons grapeseed or vegetable oil

¾ pound slim green beans, trimmed

½ teaspoon kosher salt

2 teaspoons minced fresh garlic

2 cups cooked quick-cooking farro (see page 31), rewarmed if necessary

½ cup coarsely chopped roasted, lightly salted cashews

Sometimes looks aren't everything! The thing about stir-fried green beans is that they get very brown and shrively, and then if you go and put this brown sauce on them—well, sorry guys, but boy, are they delicious! If you've ever had a dish with stir-fried green beans at a Chinese restaurant, you know what we're dealing with here: really yummy stuff. The saucy beans would work nicely with brown rice, too, but I've found that quick-cooking farro (see page 31) is a fast alternative for this simple dish. With some roasted cashews on top, this is a straightforward and filling supper.

1 Have ready two shallow serving bowls or one small platter. In a small bowl, whisk together the tamari, miso, mirin, lemon juice, brown sugar, chili-garlic paste, sesame oil, cornstarch, and 3 tablespoons of warm water and set aside.

2 In a large (12 inch) nonstick stir-fry pan or skillet, heat the grapeseed oil over medium-high heat. When the oil is hot, add the green beans and salt. Cook, stirring and tossing frequently with tongs, until the beans are very well browned in many places and have lost their stiffness, 12 to 14 minutes. (Do not undercook!)

3 Add the garlic and cook, stirring, until fragrant, about 30 seconds. Remove the pan from the heat and stir in the tamari mixture. Quickly portion the farro into the bowls or spoon onto the platter (or, if you like, do this step while cooking the green beans, and cover to keep warm). Immediately pour and scrape the contents of the stir-fry pan over the farro. (You don't want to hold the sauce in the stir-fry pan for long, as it will continue to thicken.) Top with the cashews and serve right away.

57

VEGGIES + BEANS

IN my worldview of legumes, there are beans, and then there are chickpeas (also known as the Great and Powerful Oz of legumes). It's like one of those comical maps where the place you live is drawn huge, and everything else looks like it is going to fall off the horizon. On my legume map, chickpeas loom large, and poor beans—and their friendly neighbor, lentils—look like ghost towns on the edge of the prairie. But I'm exaggerating, really; while I do think that chickpeas have some exceptionally versatile properties, I've come to appreciate quick-cooking lentils in a big way. I also bow down to the undeniable convenience and versatility of canned beans, and to the nutritional wonder of beans of all sorts. I've also grown shell beans in my garden, and oh, what a lovely thing they are.

Just so we're all on the same map: Legumes (Fabaceae) are a huge family of plants that have two distinguishing characteristics: they produce pods (many with edible seeds), and they grow roots that have the unique ability to "fix" nitrogen in the soil, making soil more fertile once the plants are tilled under. Many legumes, such as clover and vetch, are grown as cover crops on farms to improve soil, but other legumes used for food crops (called "pulses") are an important source of nutrition (protein, B vitamins, minerals) worldwide. Pulses include dried fava beans, lima beans, adzuki beans, chickpeas (aka garbanzo beans), lentils, black-eyed peas, kidney beans, black beans, pigeon peas, dried peas, navy beans, cannellini beans, and many more. Soybeans and peanuts are also legumes. Although they are in the legume family, English peas and green beans, which are primarily sold fresh or frozen, are considered vegetables.

As cooks, we're lucky that all these legumes are grown, harvested, packaged, and delivered to us in ways that are easy to prepare. So, how do we make the most of them for veggie suppers?

Tips and Strategies for Beans and Other Legumes

DRIED LENTILS ARE CHEAP AND QUICK.

You can now buy lentils three ways: dried, canned, or vacuum packed. Although canned and vacuum-packed steamed lentils are conveniently ready to use in recipes, they are my least favorite choices. I'm just not crazy about the texture of canned lentils, and dried lentils cook so quickly anyway, so the time savings isn't dramatic. (Canned beans, which offer a big time savings over dried, are another story.) Vacuum-packed lentils, which are found in the produce section (of some groceries), do have a better texture than canned lentils, and because they last (unopened) in the fridge for several months, they're a good addition to your larder for making a quick warm salad some night.

Dried lentils, my top choice, cook in only around 20 minutes. And they are inexpensive. If you're not sure that you like lentils, I think you're more likely to warm up to them if you cook them yourself.

The most common lentils are "regular" brown and green. (You will see them in bulk bins or in the dried bean department in plastic bags.) They are fine for soups and anything saucy, but they cook up rather inconsistently and easily become mushy. There are two varieties of smaller lentils that I want you to

look for instead: black beluga lentils (high in anthocyanins) and green-blue French or du Puy lentils. These little jewels cook up quickly, maintain their shape well, and offer a firm texture and pleasing peppery flavor that marries beautifully with citrusy vinaigrettes, leafy greens, and tangy cheeses. I have found both black and French lentils in bulk bins at natural groceries as well as in specialty packaging at regular grocery stores.

There is one more lovely lentil you'll want to track down: The red lentil, popular in Indian and Asian cuisines, is actually sold as a dal, or split lentil, so it cooks much more quickly and almost immediately loses its shape. (Don't try to use it in salads.) It's ideal for soups (such as Spiced Red Lentil and Sweet Potato Soup with Turmeric, Coconut Milk, and Cilantro, page 229) and also makes a very tasty porridge-like dish that takes quite well to spices and condiments (Red Lentils and Roasted Root Veggies with Spicy Lime-Chili Oil, page 82). Look for it in both bulk bins and specialty packaging.

Do not confuse split peas (yellow and green) with lentils. Until you learn to identify the varieties, pay close attention to labeling and signage.

KEEP CANNED BEANS HANDY.

Because our main goal is to cook delicious veggie suppers every night, it just makes sense to keep canned beans around. I certainly do. In fact, to keep things simple, all the bean recipes in this chapter call for canned beans. In addition to being convenient, they often have a more consistent texture than those we cook ourselves.

You need to be a savvy canned-bean shopper, though, because brands vary a lot. Look for organic beans with no preservatives and preferably no or little added salt. Also, many manufacturers of canned foods are still using cans lined with a material containing BPA (bisphenol A). Two that do not are Eden and Westbrae Natural brands. These brands are great choices because they also offer organic, low-sodium beans. Always rinse canned beans before using.

There's no reason why you can't stock up on canned beans and still cook your own beans from time to time. I especially enjoy cooking dried beans when I get a hold of some delicious heirloom beans (try mail-order sources like Rancho Gordo or Alma Gourmet) or some locally grown shell beans that have been recently dried (these are especially creamy). One of my favorite beans, the lovely skinny French flageolet bean, is really only available as a dried bean, and the flavor and texture makes it well worth seeking out and cooking yourself.

You can cook any bean at home following the chickpea-cooking method on page 236. If you need to estimate equivalents, know that a half-pound (8 ounces) of most dried beans will yield about 3 to 3½ cups when cooked—more than plenty for most recipes in this chapter.

The practice of soaking beans overnight continues to be debated. Some foodies are now quick to say it isn't necessary, but this is one case where I side with the health experts, who advise that soaking beans makes them more digestible and removes some of the phytic acid that can prohibit mineral absorption. And there's no doubt that soaked beans cook a bit more quickly than unsoaked. You can soak beans for as little as six hours and as long as twenty-four hours, so you've got a big window for getting around to cooking them. Another option to consider: why not cook small batches of beans rather than a lot at one time? This feels more manageable to me, and I don't find that cooked beans keep much longer than three, maybe four, days in the fridge anyway. A small batch is usually all I need in that time period.

AND . . . REMEMBER THAT HOME-COOKED CHICKPEAS ROCK.

Now that I've told you how much I like the convenience of canned beans, I am going to flip around (bear with me) and tell you that where chickpeas are concerned, home cooking wins out over canned in my kitchen. I do keep canned chickpeas in my pantry, and I will certainly use them in a pinch. But I have gotten into a regular habit of cooking a batch of chickpeas every week, and here's why: they're incredibly versatile. I know that probably seems obvious—yes, you've had them in soups, salads, and dips. But maybe you didn't know that chickpeas, unlike other beans, can also be sautéed and roasted (see page 236) until brown and crisp.

When I realized this, I was ecstatic. That roasty-toasty flavor adds another level of satisfaction to a legume that is already so high in fiber and protein that it is literally one of the most filling vegetarian ingredients you can cook with.

Because I use chickpeas so much, I like to start out with ones I've cooked myself so that the nutty flavor and firm-but-creamy texture is at its best. Chickpeas you've cooked yourself also last longer (up to 5 days in the fridge, if stored separate from the cooking liquid) than leftover canned chickpeas, which can start to get squidgy in only a few days.

In addition to being high in fiber, chickpeas are rich in iron, folate, and other minerals, and have been associated with all kinds of health benefits, from lowering cholesterol to helping weight loss to stabilizing blood sugar.

Shopping for dried chickpeas can be a little tricky. Theoretically, you should be able to find them packaged in plastic bags along with the other legumes in the bean section of your grocery, but sometimes they are conspicuously absent. So when you see them, buy them. (They are almost always available in natural grocery stores that stock beans and grains in bulk bins.) Dried chickpeas keep very well, so buy a couple of pounds at a time and store them in a large glass cookie jar or in mason jars.

KNOW THE LEGUMES ARE NOT IN CHARGE.

In these recipes, I've kept the amount of beans (and chickpeas and lentils) to a moderate proportion. In other words, the recipes are not all about the beans. This is similar to my approach with grains: I like to let the vegetables and the other ingredients—nuts, herbs, greens, and dressings—dance gracefully with the legumes. This way I don't feel like a cowboy or a forage animal; I deserve better, and so do the beans!

I mention this—using small amounts of legumes—so that you might do the same when improvising on your own. If you're ever in need of a very quick supper, stir-fry or sauté vegetables and add a handful (maybe two handfuls, but not an entire can) of beans or chickpeas or lentils to the mix. The filling factor will instantly double. Just remember that legumes (especially beans and lentils) like to absorb flavors, so avoid blandness by treating them to a nice dunk or toss in something saucy or dressy.

For the Pantry

The following pantry lists include a broad selection of the most versatile beans and legumes you can stock, but start with four or five varieties in cans (get two cans of each) and three or four varieties of dried (including chickpeas and a couple of types of lentil). Start with your favorites. Black beans are always at the top of my list. I use them far more frequently than any other canned bean because they do the tortilla dance so well (see quesadillas and more in the next chapter) while also slipping easily into salads and soups. I love white beans, too, but have a preference for smaller navy beans over larger white beans like Great Northern and cannellini; I always have small white beans on hand. I stock pink beans and black-eyed peas, too.

But you should make your own picks, and because both canned and dried beans and other legumes have a shelf life of one to two years, you don't have to worry about buying something new and different and not using it right away. You'll have plenty of time to try it. When stocking your bean "accessories" (see page 122), know that beans love three things above all others: tomatoes of any kind, hearty herbs such as rosemary, thyme, and oregano, and alliums, especially garlic and scallions. They also enjoy warm spices like cumin and coriander, creamy fresh cheeses like goat cheese and queso fresco, and umami acids like balsamic vinegar and tamari.

The Legumes

IN THE CAN

Aduki (adzuki) beans

Black beans

Black-eyed peas

Chickpeas (garbanzo beans)

Great Northern beans

Cannellini beans

Pink beans

Pinto beans

Small red beans

Small white beans (navy beans)

ON THE SHELF (DRIED)

Black beans

Black beluga lentils

Brown or green (regular) lentils

Chickpeas (garbanzo beans)

Cranberry or other heirloom beans

Flageolet beans

French or du Puy green lentils

Navy beans (small white beans)

Pinto beans

Red lentils

Accessory Ingredients

Balsamic vinegar

Canned tomatoes (I like Muir Glen brand)

Cayenne, ground chipotle pepper, other types of ground chilis

Fresh cilantro

Fresh garlic

Fresh ginger

Fresh tomatoes

Goat cheese

Greens, such as spinach, chard, and arugula

Ground coriander

Ground cumin

Hearty herbs (dried or fresh), such as thyme, rosemary, oregano, and bay leaves

Low-sodium tamari

Scallions

Shallots

Sherry vinegar

Sun-dried tomatoes

Yogurt

SUGAR SNAP, SPRING ONION, AND CHICKPEA STIR-FRY

WITH CUCUMBER-YOGURT SAUCE

SERVES 2 TO 3

1 teaspoon honey (preferably local)

1 teaspoon fresh lime juice

1 teaspoon low-sodium tamari

2 tablespoons grapeseed or vegetable oil

One 15-ounce can chickpeas, drained, rinsed, and dried

1 teaspoon kosher salt

1½ cups sugar snap peas, trimmed and sliced in ½-inch-wide pieces on a diagonal

½ cup thickly sliced spring onions, scallions, or red onions (½-inch-thick slices)

1 cup packed baby spinach

¼ teaspoon ground cumin

¼ teaspoon ground coriander

¼ teaspoon red pepper flakes

½ cup Cucumber-Yogurt Sauce with Lime and Herbs (recipe follows) or 2 tablespoons unsalted butter, melted

2 tablespoons roughly chopped or torn fresh mint or cilantro leaves

In early summer, when the sugar snaps are on the vine and the first "spring" onions (which look like fat scallions!) are ready to pull, I love to feature the two in a quick stir-fry with chickpeas and a bit of spinach. When I'm in a hurry, I finish the dish simply with melted butter, lime, and honey—delicious. More often, for a fresher yet slightly more complex dish, I skip the butter and take just a few more minutes to make my Cucumber-Yogurt Sauce with Lime and Herbs (page 65). It offers a nice cooling contrast to the warm stir-fry and, with the hints of mint, coriander, and cumin working together, makes this a Middle Eastern supper to savor. (If you are not making the yogurt sauce, you will need the butter for rounding out the flavor and lending moistness to the sauté.)

1 In a small bowl, whisk together the honey, lime juice, and tamari and set aside.

2 In a large (12-inch) nonstick stir-fry pan, heat 1 tablespoon of the oil over medium-high heat. When the oil is hot, add the chickpeas and ¼ teaspoon of salt. Cook, stirring frequently, until golden and spotted with brown, 5 to 6 minutes. Using a slotted spoon, transfer the chickpeas to a plate. Take the pan off the heat for a few seconds.

3 Return the pan to the heat and add the remaining 1 tablespoon of oil. When the oil is hot, add the sugar snap peas, spring onions, and ½ teaspoon of salt. Cook, stirring frequently, until the peas and onions are lightly browned, about 4 minutes.

4 Return the chickpeas to the pan. Add the spinach, cumin, coriander, red pepper flakes, and the remaining ¼ teaspoon of salt. Cook, stirring, until the spinach is wilted and the spices are fragrant, about 1 minute. Drizzle the lime-honey mixture over all, stir, and remove the pan from the heat. Stir in the herbs and the melted butter (if using). Transfer to serving plates and garnish with a generous serving of the yogurt sauce (if using).

Cucumber-Yogurt Sauce with Lime and Herbs

MAKES 1⅓ CUPS

½ cup plain, full-fat Greek yogurt, excess liquid drained off

2 teaspoons fresh lime juice

½ teaspoon packed freshly grated lime zest

2 teaspoons honey, or 1½ teaspoons agave nectar

2 teaspoons chopped fresh mint or cilantro, or a combination

Pinch of kosher salt

1 cup finely diced peeled, seeded cucumber

This super-easy sauce is what I call a "spoon" sauce: you spoon it over grilled or stir-fried veggies. Nothing gets pureed here, so the cucumber dice lend some body, and the lime and honey bring a lively flavor. It tastes very fresh, so it's a natural in spring and summer. I like pairing it with the stir-fry, but it is also great with grilled or roasted eggplant slices, stir-fried green beans, Bibb lettuce and tomato salads, or simply with grilled naan.

In a medium bowl, whisk together the yogurt, lime juice, lime zest, honey, mint and/or cilantro, and salt. Stir in the cucumber until well incorporated. If not using right away, store covered in the fridge for up to 1 day.

WHITE BEANS AND ARTICHOKE HEARTS

WITH CHARD, LEMON, THYME, AND BREAD CRUMBS

SERVES 3

2 tablespoons unsalted butter

2 teaspoons minced fresh garlic

1 scant cup coarse fresh bread crumbs (from 1 English muffin)

½ teaspoon kosher salt, plus a large pinch

1 tablespoon extra-virgin olive oil

One 9-ounce package frozen artichoke hearts, thawed or defrosted in the microwave (1½ to 2 cups)

2 cups stemmed and thinly sliced Swiss chard leaves

One 15-ounce can small white beans (navy beans), drained and rinsed

2 teaspoons roughly chopped fresh thyme

1 teaspoon freshly grated lemon zest

Freshly ground black pepper

¼ cup heavy cream

¼ cup coarsely grated Parmesan cheese

This yummy ragout with a crown of crispy bread crumbs is much like a gratin, only unbaked. Just a little bit of cream and cheese brings the sautéed artichokes, chard ribbons, garlic, and white beans together in a happy marriage. Lemon zest, thyme, and fresh black pepper add a bright and herby edge. Serve this on a cool late-spring evening when the temperature has dropped and you want something warming. Well-thawed frozen artichokes actually brown up quite well in the sauté pan, so they're a great choice here. Keep a package in your freezer. (Certainly, if you luck out in finding baby artichokes at your grocer, you can prep and use them in this.) If chard isn't available, stir in baby spinach instead.

1 In a medium (10-inch) nonstick skillet, melt 1 tablespoon of the butter over medium heat. Add ½ teaspoon of the garlic and cook, stirring, just until softened, about 30 seconds. Add the bread crumbs and a big pinch of salt and cook, stirring, until the bread crumbs are golden, about 3 minutes. Remove from the heat and set aside.

2 In a small (3- to 4-quart) Dutch oven (preferably nonstick), heat the remaining tablespoon of butter with the oil over medium heat. When the butter has melted, turn up the heat to medium-high and add the artichokes. Cook, stirring, until they have released most of their moisture and are browned in spots all over, 4 to 5 minutes. Add the chard, the remaining 1½ teaspoons of garlic, and ½ teaspoon of salt, and cook, stirring, just until the chard is mostly wilted, about 1 minute. Add the white beans, thyme, lemon zest, and several grinds of black pepper. Stir to combine. Add the heavy cream and reduce the heat to medium-low. Cook, stirring, just until the cream bubbles and thickens slightly, 30 seconds to 1 minute.

3 Remove the Dutch oven from the heat and stir in the Parmesan. Transfer to a serving platter and garnish with the sautéed bread crumbs.

BABY POTATO, GREENS, GARLIC, AND CHICKPEA HASH

SERVES 2

10 baby red potatoes, preferably yellow-fleshed (about 10 ounces)

2¾ teaspoons kosher salt

3 tablespoons unsalted butter

1⅓ cups cooked or canned chickpeas, drained and rinsed

Generous 1 tablespoon minced fresh garlic

3 cups stemmed and chopped or sliced tender greens, such as Swiss chard, spinach, broccoli leaves, or young kale

Freshly ground black pepper

Hot sauce or vinegar of your choice

¼ cup sour cream

2 to 3 teaspoons chopped fresh chives

A simple, comforting supper with just a few ingredients, this dish was inspired by a freshly dug batch of Red Gold potatoes from the garden. Nutty-tasting yellow-fleshed Red Golds are delicious, but of course not required, in this recipe—any baby potato will do! The potatoes get boiled first, then crushed and sautéed with the other ingredients for a delicious crispy finish. I also love that this recipe showcases another tasty way to use chickpeas as a protein: in a rustic "hash." Sautéing the chickpeas until golden, as I mentioned in the introduction, is the trick to giving them extra flavor. It even works with drained canned chickpeas. Choose your favorite tender greens for this, and be generous with the garlic, too.

1 Put the potatoes and 2 teaspoons of the salt in a large saucepan and cover with a generous amount of water. Bring to a boil, reduce the heat to low, and simmer until just tender, about 25 minutes. Drain.

2 Melt 2 tablespoons of the butter in a large (12-inch) nonstick skillet over medium heat. Add the chickpeas and cook, shaking or stirring, until golden brown, about 5 to 7 minutes. Add the garlic and cook, stirring, until fragrant, about 30 seconds. Add the greens and ¼ teaspoon of the salt and cook, tossing or stirring, until wilted, 1 to 2 minutes.

3 Move the greens and chickpeas to one side of the pan and add the remaining 1 tablespoon of butter. Let it melt and then add the whole boiled potatoes. Using a potato masher or spatula, crush the potatoes into large pieces (you don't want to mash them completely, just break them up), then sprinkle them with the remaining ½ teaspoon of salt and several grinds of black pepper. Increase the heat to medium-high and stir everything together. Press down on the mixture with a spatula and cook until the bottom is somewhat browned, 3 to 5 minutes. Flip the hash over in pieces and cook again until the other side is somewhat brown, 2 to 3 minutes.

4 Remove the hash from the pan and taste for seasoning. Add more salt and pepper and a splash or two of hot sauce or vinegar. (You can also serve the hash with a bottle of hot sauce alongside it instead.) Garnish with the sour cream and chives and serve right away.

LAYERED BLACK BEAN, ZUCCHINI, CORN, AND AVOCADO SALAD

IN A GLASS

MAKES 6 PORTIONS

FOR THE DRESSING

5 tablespoons olive oil

2 tablespoons plus 2 teaspoons fresh lemon juice

1 tablespoon plus 1 teaspoon finely chopped crystallized ginger, or 2 teaspoons fresh ginger plus 1 teaspoon sugar

1 teaspoon minced fresh garlic

1 teaspoon honey

½ teaspoon freshly grated lemon zest

½ to 1 teaspoon seeded and minced fresh serrano or jalapeño pepper

Pinch of kosher salt

continued opposite

I know the ingredient list is long, but there's no cooking involved here. It's actually fun to layer all those ingredients in glasses—and they look so jaunty when you're finished. You can plan to make these little salads when friends are coming over (assemble them up to an hour ahead), or you can always just toss everything together in one bowl as a quick weeknight alternative. Either way, it's one tasty bean salad, partly because the dressing features one of my favorite pantry ingredients: crystallized ginger. If you don't have crystallized ginger, use fresh ginger and a bit of sugar.

1 Place 6 water or wine tumblers, "old-fashioned" cocktail glasses, or other wide and relatively short glasses (about 8 to 10 ounces) on your work surface. (Alternatively, choose a 6- to 8-cup deep glass bowl, preferably straight sided.)

2 *Make the dressing:* In a small bowl, whisk together the olive oil, lemon juice, crystallized ginger, garlic, honey, lemon zest, serrano pepper, and salt.

3 Put the black beans, zucchini, cherry tomatoes, avocados, and corn each in separate small bowls. Toss each with 2 to 3 teaspoons of the dressing and a good pinch of salt.

FOR THE SALADS

One 15-ounce can black beans, drained and rinsed

1 cup diced zucchini (about 4 ounces)

1½ cups halved or quartered red and yellow cherry tomatoes

1 medium-large ripe-but-firm avocado, cut into ½-inch dice (about 1 cup)

1¼ cups fresh raw corn kernels (from about 2 large ears)

Kosher salt

⅓ cup coarsely chopped fresh herbs (any combination of basil, mint, cilantro, parsley, chives, Thai basil, etc.)

⅓ cup sliced scallions (light and dark green parts)

⅓ cup toasted sliced almonds, toasted pepitas, or toasted pine nuts

6 fresh herb sprigs or edible flowers (optional)

4 *Assemble the salads:* Spoon the beans into the bottoms of the glasses, distributing the entire amount evenly among the glasses. Sprinkle the beans with a small bit of the chopped herbs, a few scallions, and some of the nuts. Spoon the zucchini into the glasses, distributing the entire amount evenly. Sprinkle the zucchini with small amounts of herbs, scallions, and nuts. Continue layering on cherry tomatoes, the avocado, and the corn, sprinkling each layer with herbs, scallions, and nuts as you go. Spoon any remaining dressing over the salads.

5 Garnish each glass with an herb sprig or edible flower (if using). Let the salads sit a few minutes for the flavors to mingle and serve at room temperature.

GRILL-ROASTED BELL PEPPERS

WITH LENTIL SALAD AND GOAT CHEESE

MAKES 4 PEPPERS; SERVES 2

4 ounces fresh goat cheese

2 blocky red, yellow, or orange bell peppers of about the same size

1½ cups cooked French (or du Puy) lentils or black beluga lentils (see page 60)

½ teaspoon kosher salt, plus a pinch

2 tablespoons extra-virgin olive oil

2 tablespoons red wine vinegar

1 tablespoon finely chopped shallots

1 teaspoon Dijon mustard

2½ tablespoons chopped fresh parsley, plus 4 small sprigs

1 cup baby greens, such as baby arugula, mizuna, kale, or lettuce (optional)

We all love the sweet, smoky flavor of roasted peppers, but you might not realize how easy it is to roast peppers in a covered gas grill. It's much less cumbersome than using a gas flame or a broiler, and the heat blasting on all sides roasts the peppers evenly. Any way you roast them, sweet bell peppers are a classic pairing with herby lentils and cool fresh cheeses. I like to serve a simple lentil salad draped over a roasted pepper half that's been dolloped with a bit of goat cheese. Every bite is tangy, sweet, and delicious. (And it is especially nice if everything is still a bit warm.) It does take some time to roast, cool, and peel the peppers, but go ahead and roast a bunch while you're at it, and use the rest in salads and grain dishes later in the week. This recipe is easily doubled.

1 While the goat cheese is still cold, crumble it and loosely divide it into 5 portions. Allow to come to room temperature.

2 Heat a gas grill to high heat. Immediately (no need to preheat the grill) put the whole peppers on the grill grate and lower the lid. Grill the peppers, turning every few minutes with tongs, until they are well blistered and mostly but not entirely blackened, 10 to 15 minutes. Transfer the peppers to a big bowl and cover tightly with foil or plastic wrap. Let them sit for 10 or 15 minutes, until cool enough to handle.

3 Working over a strainer set inside a bowl, peel the skins off the peppers. Put the peppers on a cutting board and leave the skins in the strainer. Cut the peppers in half lengthwise, leaving the stems on if possible. Working over the strainer again, gently remove the seeds with your fingers. Reserve the strained juices in the bowl.

4 If the lentils are cold, put them in the microwave for about 1 minute to gently warm them. Transfer the lentils to a medium bowl and season with ½ teaspoon of salt. In a small bowl, whisk together the oil, vinegar, shallots, mustard, a pinch of salt, and the reserved pepper juices. Pour the dressing over the lentils and stir. (The mixture will be liquidy; that's OK.) Stir in 2 tablespoons of the chopped parsley and let the lentil salad sit for a few minutes, then stir again.

5 Place half of the baby greens (if using) on each of two serving plates. Put 2 pepper halves on each plate. Put 1 portion of the goat cheese in each of the 4 pepper halves and pat it flat. Spoon a generous amount of lentil salad over the peppers and garnish with the remaining portion of cheese and the remaining ½ tablespoon of chopped parsley and parsley sprigs.

GREEN BEAN, CORN, RED PEPPER, AND BLACK-EYE PEA SAUTÉ

WITH PEANUT DRESSING

SERVES 3

1 tablespoon low-sodium tamari

1 tablespoon plus
1 teaspoon fresh lemon juice,
plus 3 lemon wedges

2 teaspoons unsulphured
molasses

¼ cup plus 1 tablespoon finely
chopped ("ground") roasted,
lightly salted peanuts

2 tablespoons grapeseed or
olive oil

½ cup diced yellow onion

⅓ cup diced red bell pepper

½ teaspoon kosher salt,
plus a pinch

1½ cups sliced green beans (cut
into ¾-inch lengths)

1 cup fresh corn kernels

Freshly ground black pepper

1½ teaspoons minced
fresh garlic

One 15-ounce can black-eyed
peas, drained and rinsed

¼ cup sliced chives

1 to 2 cups arugula (optional)

You may wonder how black-eyed peas and peanuts wander into a New England cook's repertoire, but the truth is that I spent an impressionable amount of time in the South when I was growing up. And every New Year's, my family would visit Colonial Williamsburg, where we'd eat New Year's Eve dinner at the King's Arms Tavern. The meal always began with peanut soup. Of course, peanuts show up in savory Thai and Vietnamese dishes as well as in African cuisines, and black-eyed peas are actually grown all over the world, too. (Both legumes are highly valued for their protein, fiber, and folate.) So keep an open mind about this unusual sauté, which can also double as a salad when served over arugula. A lemony tamari-peanut dressing is tossed with warm vegetables and beans, and everything comes together harmoniously. For finely chopped, or "ground," peanuts, use a food processor.

1 In a small bowl, whisk together the tamari, lemon juice, molasses, and 1 tablespoon of water until the molasses dissolves. Stir in ¼ cup of the finely chopped peanuts and set aside.

2 In a large (12-inch) nonstick skillet, heat the oil over medium-low heat. Add the onion, pepper, and ¼ teaspoon of the salt. Cook, stirring occasionally, until the onions are softened and just starting to brown, 4 to 6 minutes.

3 Turn the heat to medium-high and add the green beans and ¼ teaspoon of the salt. Cook, stirring, until the beans are somewhat shrunken and browned in places, 5 to 6 minutes. Add the corn kernels, the remaining pinch of salt, and several grinds of black pepper. Cook, stirring frequently, until the corn is slightly shrunken, 2 to 3 minutes. Add the garlic and the black-eyed peas and cook, stirring, until the garlic is fragrant and the beans are warm.

4 Remove the skillet from the heat and immediately pour in the tamari-peanut dressing. Stir well. Arrange the arugula (if using) on a serving platter or three plates and top with the bean-veggie mixture, or spoon the mixture directly onto the platter or plates. Garnish with the chives and the remaining 1 tablespoon of peanuts. Serve with the lemon wedges.

STIR-FRIED BROCCOLI AND BLACK BEANS

WITH ORANGE, GINGER, AND SHALLOTS

SERVES 3

1 large navel orange, washed

2 tablespoons fresh lemon juice

1 tablespoon low-sodium tamari

1 tablespoon packed dark brown sugar

1 tablespoon minced crystallized ginger

1½ teaspoons white (shiro) miso

3 tablespoons plus 1 teaspoon vegetable oil, plus more if needed

1 cup thinly sliced shallots (about 2 large shallots)

1 large garlic clove, thinly sliced

½ teaspoon kosher salt, plus a pinch

5 cups broccoli florets

One 15-ounce can black beans, drained and rinsed

A kicky garnish of sizzled orange zest strips and shallots adds texture and flavor to this easy stir-fry. I love cooking broccoli in my bowl-shaped nonstick stir-fry pan (mine is made by Circulon) because it has plenty of surface area for the broccoli to have direct contact with the heat and brown up while the bowl shape traps moisture and helps the broccoli to steam at the same time. The addition of black beans and a flavorful sauce enhanced with orange, lemon, crystallized ginger, and miso turns this stir-fry into a surprisingly bright and filling supper. The dish is fairly saucy, so you could certainly serve it with a little brown rice or other grain if you like, but it isn't necessary.

1 Using a vegetable peeler (Y-shaped is the easiest to use), peel 6 or 7 wide, long strips of orange zest from the orange. Stack the strips and slice them into thin julienne pieces. Cut the orange in half and use a juicer to extract the juice.

2 In a small bowl, whisk 3 tablespoons of the orange juice and the lemon juice, tamari, brown sugar, crystallized ginger, and miso until the miso dissolves. Set aside.

3 Heat 2 tablespoons of the oil in a large (12 inch) nonstick stir-fry pan over medium-high heat. When the oil is hot, add the orange zest strips, shallots, garlic, and a pinch of salt. Cook, stirring frequently, until the zest is curled and the shallots are limp and shrunken, about 2 minutes. Use a slotted spoon to transfer to a plate. Set aside.

4 Return the pan to medium-high heat and add 1 tablespoon of the oil. Add the broccoli and ½ teaspoon of salt. Cook, stirring frequently, until the broccoli is browned and shrunken, 7 to 9 minutes. Add the black beans and cook, stirring, for 30 seconds. Reduce the heat to medium-low. Give the orange juice mixture a stir and scrape it out of the bowl, over the broccoli and beans. Stir, then immediately remove the pan from the heat and transfer the stir-fry to a serving platter. Garnish with the zest-shallot mixture and serve hot.

INDIAN CURRY

WITH CHICKPEAS, CAULIFLOWER, SPINACH, TOMATOES, AND COCONUT MILK

SERVES 2 TO 3

3 tablespoons grapeseed or vegetable oil

One 15-ounce can chickpeas, drained, rinsed, and dried

¾ teaspoon kosher salt, plus a pinch

3 cups cauliflower florets (1- to 1½-inch pieces, cut so that most have a flat side)

1 cup sliced yellow onion (about 1 medium-large onion, cut lengthwise)

1 tablespoon minced fresh garlic

1 tablespoon minced fresh ginger

1½ teaspoons Asian chili-garlic paste

2 teaspoons curry powder

2 teaspoons packed dark brown sugar

½ teaspoon ground cumin

3 cups packed baby spinach

½ cup canned crushed tomatoes

1 cup canned full-fat coconut milk (preferably organic), well stirred

¼ cup finely chopped fresh cilantro

One night I set out to cook a comforting Indian curry that would have all the things I love in it, starting with sautéed chickpeas and cauliflower and ending with a slightly creamy coconut-tomato sauce. In between, a mix of ginger, garlic, and curry spices (as well as fresh spinach) would provide backbone. I decided to use my handy stir-fry pan, because it is great at both sautéing and simmering. After a little chopping, I started cooking. Fifteen minutes later, I was so happy: I loved it! (The leftovers were delicious, too.) So I pass this treat on to you. You'll want to use curry powder that is fresh and has a pleasing aroma, so give it a sniff.

1 In a large (12-inch) nonstick stir-fry pan, heat 1 tablespoon of the oil over medium-high heat. When the oil is hot, add the chickpeas and ¼ teaspoon of salt. Cook, stirring occasionally, until the chickpeas are golden and browned in spots, 5 to 6 minutes. Transfer the chickpeas to a plate.

2 Return the pan to medium-high heat and add 1 tablespoon of the oil. When the oil is hot, add the cauliflower and ½ teaspoon of salt. Stir, cover, and cook, uncovering to stir occasionally, until the cauliflower pieces are browned in spots (they will be softened but still crisp), about 5 minutes. (If the cauliflower is browning too quickly, reduce the heat to medium. If your pan does not have a lid, use a baking sheet or the bottom of a large skillet.) Transfer the cauliflower to the plate with the chickpeas.

3 Return the pan to medium-high heat and add the remaining 1 tablespoon of oil, the onion, and a pinch of salt. Cook, stirring, until the onions are browned in spots but haven't lost all their stiffness, about 3 minutes. Add the garlic, ginger, chili-garlic paste, curry powder, brown sugar, and cumin. Stir well to combine, and fry the spices for 30 seconds. Add the spinach, tomatoes, and coconut milk and stir well to incorporate the spices with the liquids and to soften the spinach. Add the cooked cauliflower and chickpeas and simmer, stirring, for 1 minute. Stir in the cilantro and remove the pan from the heat. Serve hot or very warm in two or three bowls.

ROASTED CHERRY TOMATO, BUTTERNUT SQUASH, AND WARM LENTIL SALAD

WITH CITRUS MOJO DRESSING

SERVES 3

8 to 9 ounces ripe cherry tomatoes, cut in half

2 tablespoons extra-virgin olive oil

Kosher salt

10 to 12 ounces butternut squash, peeled and cut into ½-inch dice

2 cups cooked lentils (see page 237)

⅓ to ½ cup fresh corn kernels, blanched or microwaved for 30 seconds, or frozen corn, thawed

1 tablespoon plus 1 to 2 teaspoons fresh lime juice

1 tablespoon plus 1 teaspoon orange juice

1 teaspoon minced fresh garlic

2 to 3 tablespoons chopped fresh cilantro

Colorful, yes. Wicked flavorful? You bet. Proof that lentils don't have to be all about the brown and the earthy, this bright salad has a spirited Cuban dressing of lime juice, orange juice, cilantro, and garlic. Combined with deep, roasty flavors from the veggies, it makes a satisfying meal that I can devour standing up, right from the mixing bowl. (Just sayin'. Not that that's ever happened, of course.) For this salad (and, you may have noticed, almost every lentil dish!) I am especially fond of using the small black beluga or green French lentils, but I've also made it with success using vacuum-packed steamed lentils. If you plan to cook your own lentils (see page 237), feel free to do so a day or two ahead and keep them, covered, in the fridge until you're ready to make the salad.

1 Preheat the oven to 450°F. Line a heavy-duty rimmed baking sheet with parchment paper. In a medium bowl, toss the squash with 1 tablespoon of the olive oil and a big pinch of salt. In another medium bowl, gently toss the cherry tomatoes with the remaining 1 tablespoon of olive oil and a big pinch of salt.

2 Spread the squash in a single layer over one half of the prepared baking sheet. Bake for 5 minutes. Remove the baking sheet from the oven and carefully tip the bowl of cherry tomatoes onto the empty side. (If most of the halves can be cut-side up, that's ideal.) Bake for 22 to 24 more minutes, until the squash is tender and browned and the cherry tomatoes are shrunken and a bit charred around the edges. (You can flip the squash once during cooking with a metal spatula, but don't mess with the cherry tomatoes.) Let the veggies cool for 10 minutes or so on the baking sheet.

3 If the lentils are cold, microwave them for 45 seconds to 1 minute to take the chill off. Put the lentils, corn, 1 tablespoon plus 1 teaspoon of the lime juice, the orange juice, the garlic, a big pinch of salt, and 1 to 2 tablespoons of the cilantro into a large bowl. Toss gently but thoroughly. Taste, then add more salt and/or the remaining 1 teaspoon of lime, if needed. (Be aware that all the flavors will build over time.)

4 Using a metal spatula, gently scrape the cherry tomatoes and squash off the baking sheet and into the bowl with the lentil mixture.

(Don't worry if some of the tomatoes fall apart; just be sure to scrape the bits off the pan—they are full of flavor.) Toss gently again.

5 Transfer the warm salad to a serving dish or three serving bowls and garnish with the remaining 1 tablespoon of cilantro.

WARM CANNELLINI BEAN RAGOUT

WITH OLIVES, ROSEMARY, AND GREENS

SERVES 3

2 tablespoons extra-virgin olive oil

1 cup diced yellow onion

½ cup small-diced carrot

2 teaspoons chopped fresh garlic

Generous 2 teaspoons chopped fresh rosemary

Pinch of kosher salt

One 19-ounce can cannellini beans, drained and rinsed

1 cup chopped tomato (about 1 medium tomato)

2 cups stemmed and very thinly sliced collard greens or kale

¼ cup chopped pitted Kalamata olives

2 teaspoons balsamic vinegar, plus more if needed

This easy bean stew is so straightforward to make and easy to eat that you'll find yourself taking leftovers for lunch and then making another batch for the freezer. The classic flavor profile (onions, carrots, garlic, tomatoes) gets a total kick in the pants from a generous addition of pitted Kalamata olives and fresh rosemary. Look for the 19-ounce cans of cannellini beans (larger white beans), but if you can't find that size, simply measure out 2 cups of drained canned or home-cooked beans. Very thinly cut your greens (I like collards in this) for the nicest texture.

1 In a small (3- to 4-quart) Dutch oven, heat the oil over medium heat. Add the onion, carrot, and a pinch of salt. Cook, stirring, until the veggies are soft and beginning to brown, 6 to 8 minutes. Add the chopped garlic and rosemary and sauté until fragrant, about 30 seconds. Add the cannellini beans, tomato, and ½ cup of water. Stir and bring to a simmer. Cover, reduce the heat to very low, and simmer for 10 minutes, stirring once or twice during cooking.

2 Uncover the pot, stir in the collards, and continue to cook, uncovered, on low heat until the liquids are reduced and the mixture is somewhat thickened, 5 to 8 minutes. Stir in the olives and vinegar and cook for 1 minute more. Taste for seasoning and add more vinegar if you like. Portion into three bowls.

RED LENTILS AND ROASTED ROOT VEGGIES

WITH SPICY LIME-CHILI OIL

SERVES 3 OR 4

2 tablespoons grapeseed or olive oil

1 cup diced yellow onion

1¼ teaspoons kosher salt

1 cup diced plum tomatoes (about 2 large tomatoes)

1 to 2 teaspoons minced fresh garlic

½ teaspoon ground coriander

½ teaspoon ground cumin

1 cup red lentils

1 recipe Quick-Roasted Root Vegetables (page 83)—I like a combination of sweet potatoes, butternut squash, and beets

2 to 3 tablespoons Spicy Lime-Chili Oil (recipe follows)

1 to 2 tablespoons coarsely chopped fresh cilantro or parsley

Dried red lentils are the quickest-cooking legume in town—an excellent choice for a weeknight. Tender in less than 15 minutes, they become almost porridge-like, and yet they are anything but bland. In this dish, I cook them with a little bit of onion and tomato and add a spice boost with ground coriander and cumin. (Be sure your spices are fresh and potent. Ground spices contain volatile oils that dissipate over time, so older spices can taste flat or stale.) These lentils get topped with quick-roasted root veggies and a drizzle of Spicy Lime-Chili Oil (page 83), so they deliver flavor on many levels. If you really want to emphasize the veggies in this dish, make 1½ batches of Quick-Roasted Root Vegetables (page 83), which will yield about 3 cups. Another time, you could replace the roasted root veggies with sautéed greens or roasted eggplant. The spicy oil keeps for several days in the fridge, so make it (and the roasted veggies) ahead if you like.

1 In a medium (5- to 6-quart) Dutch oven, heat the oil over medium-low heat. Add the onion and ¼ teaspoon of salt, cover loosely, and cook, uncovering to stir occasionally, until lightly golden, 6 to 8 minutes. Uncover, add the tomatoes and cook, uncovered, stirring, until they lose their moisture and shape and begin to form a paste, 5 to 7 minutes. Add the garlic, coriander, and cumin and cook, stirring, until fragrant, about 30 seconds.

2 Add the lentils and 4 cups of water. Increase the heat to high and bring to a boil, then reduce the heat to low, cover the pot loosely, and simmer, stirring and scraping the bottom of the pan frequently to prevent sticking, until the lentils are tender and the mixture is thick and porridge-like, 12 to 15 minutes. Add the remaining 1 teaspoon of salt and continue simmering, loosely covered, for 3 or 4 minutes. Remove the pot from the heat.

3 Spoon the flavored lentils into three or four shallow serving bowls and, dividing the remaining ingredients evenly among them, top with the roasted veggies, drizzle with the spicy oil, and garnish with the cilantro.

Spicy Lime-Chili Oil

MAKES ¼ CUP

¼ cup grapeseed or olive oil

1 tablespoon freshly grated lime zest

2 teaspoons minced fresh garlic

2 teaspoons red pepper flakes

I love making simple infused oils in a skillet. For the tiny amount of work they require to prep and make, they sure do return a lot of flavor. I particularly love this spicy combination of lime zest, garlic, and plenty of red pepper flakes. Try it drizzled over cooked lentils (see page 237), beans, eggs, or toast.

In a small skillet, heat the oil over medium-low heat. Add the lime zest, garlic, and red pepper flakes and stir together. Heat the oil until bubbling and the garlic is just beginning to color a bit, 2 to 3 minutes. Remove the skillet from the heat and let the oil steep and cool in the pan for 15 minutes.

Quick-Roasted Root Vegetables

MAKES ABOUT 1¾ CUPS

3 to 3½ cups small-diced, peeled butternut squash (½-inch dice) and/or small-diced, unpeeled beets, sweet potatoes, potatoes, and/or turnips

2 to 2½ tablespoons extra-virgin olive oil or grapeseed oil

Generous ½ teaspoon kosher salt

The secret to cooking root vegetables quickly is to cut them into relatively small, even pieces (basically dice) and then roast them in a fairly hot oven. Make sure to use a rimmed baking sheet and spread the veggies out so that they've got plenty of room for air to circulate around them. (If piled on top of each other, they'll steam.) I love to use this method for potatoes, sweet potatoes, turnips, beets, and even butternut squash (never mind that it isn't a root!). If you wind up cooking these veggies a lot, as I do, buy an oven thermometer and check to see if your oven is running true to temperature. Many ovens run high or low, so you might need to compensate with your time or temperature setting. (And then call the appliance repair folks!) To double this recipe, use two baking sheets.

Preheat the oven to 425°F. Line a heavy-duty rimmed baking sheet with parchment paper. In a bowl, toss the vegetables with the oil and salt. Transfer to the baking sheet and spread in a single layer. Bake for 15 minutes, flip the veggies over using a spatula, and continue baking for another 12 to 15 minutes, until the veggies are tender and nicely browned around the edges.

BRICKYARD RED CHILI RICE AND PINK BEANS

WITH ROASTED TOMATOES

SERVES 4

FOR THE RICE

1½ teaspoons chili powder

½ teaspoon ground cumin

½ teaspoon ground coriander

½ teaspoon cane sugar

⅛ teaspoon ground cinnamon

1 teaspoon kosher salt,
plus a large pinch

1 tablespoon unsalted butter

½ cup diced yellow onion

2 teaspoons minced fresh garlic

1 tablespoon tomato paste

1 cup uncooked white
Texmati rice

continued opposite

Red means flavor, so we've got red rice, red tomatoes, and red (well, pink) beans all together here in this fun and delicious take on rice and beans. The rice is easy to make, with spices you've probably got in your pantry (plus a little tomato paste), and the beans get their depth of flavor from a batch of quick-roasted plum tomatoes. Combining the beans and rice with lots of crunchy toasted pecans makes a super-comforting supper. This recipe takes longer to put together than many of our veggie suppers, but it makes up for it by being so versatile: You can use it as a burrito filling, or simply embellish a bowl of it with diced avocado and sour cream or queso fresco. (A squeeze of lime and cilantro never hurt either.) You could also just make the rice and fold in Quick-Roasted Root Vegetables (page 83) or top it with sautéed greens. The rice can be made ahead and reheated.

1 *Make the rice:* In a small bowl, stir together the chili powder, cumin, coriander, sugar, cinnamon, and 1 teaspoon of salt and set aside.

2 In a medium saucepan, heat the butter over medium-low heat. When the butter has melted, add the onion and a big pinch of salt. Cover and cook, uncovering to stir occasionally, until the onion is translucent and beginning to brown, about 5 minutes. Uncover the pan and continue cooking until the onion is lightly browned, 3 to 4 minutes. Add the garlic and cook, stirring, until fragrant, about 30 seconds. Add the chili powder spice mixture and cook, stirring, until very fragrant and well incorporated, about 1 minute. (Use a silicone spatula to smoosh the spices against the bottom of the pan to fry them a bit.) Add the tomato paste and stir and scrape until well incorporated. Add the rice and stir until the spice paste coats the rice. Add 1¾ cups of water, stir, and increase the heat to high. Bring to a boil, then immediately reduce the heat to very low, cover, and simmer for 20 minutes.

3 Remove the pan from the heat and let sit 5 minutes. With a fork, fluff the rice and stir in the red layer on the top. Cover the rice with a paper towel, return the lid to the pan, and set aside.

FOR THE BEANS

1 pound plum tomatoes
(about 5 tomatoes)

2 tablespoons olive oil

Pinch of kosher salt

2 teaspoons minced fresh garlic

¼ teaspoon red pepper flakes

One 15-ounce can pink beans or
pinto beans, drained and rinsed

¼ to ½ teaspoon
balsamic vinegar

¾ cup coarsely chopped
toasted pecans

4 *Make the beans:* While the rice is cooking, roast the plum tomatoes: Preheat the oven to 450°F. Line a heavy rimmed baking sheet with parchment paper. Cut the tomatoes in half lengthwise and scoop the seeds out. Cut them in half again (so they are in lengthwise quarters) and toss with 1 tablespoon of the oil and a pinch of salt. Arrange them in one layer on the prepared baking sheet (ideally, with most of them cut-sides up) and bake for about 25 minutes, until shrunken and quite brown on the bottom. Remove from the oven and let cool for a few minutes. Pop the roasted tomatoes off the parchment paper onto a cutting board and roughly chop into bite-size pieces.

5 In a medium (10-inch) nonstick skillet, heat the remaining 1 tablespoon of oil over medium-low heat. Add the garlic and red pepper flakes and cook until softened and fragrant, about 1 minute. Add the beans, the chopped roasted tomatoes, and ⅓ cup of water. Cover loosely and cook, uncovering occasionally to stir and mash some of the beans lightly, until the liquid has mostly reduced, 4 to 5 minutes. Stir in ¼ teaspoon of the vinegar. Taste, and season with more salt and/or the remaining ¼ teaspoon of balsamic vinegar if needed.

6 Fluff up the rice with a fork again, then turn out into a mixing or serving bowl and add all the bean-tomato mixture and half of the pecans. Stir well to combine. Serve garnished with the remaining pecans.

LENTILS AND SPINACH

WITH BLUE CHEESE, CRISPY SHIITAKES, AND BALSAMIC GLAZE

SERVES 4

1 tablespoon olive oil

½ pound stemmed mature spinach, torn into bite-size pieces (about 8 cups)

½ teaspoon kosher salt

Generous ½ cup crumbled good-quality blue cheese, such as Stilton

1⅓ cups cooked French (or du Puy) lentils or black beluga lentils (see page 237), rewarmed

1 to 2 tablespoons Balsamic Glaze (recipe follows)

1 recipe Quick-Roasted Crispy Shiitakes (recipe follows)

I love this simple combination of complex flavors. Four layers—sautéed spinach, cooked lentils, creamy blue cheese, and roasted shiitakes—form a sort of rustic, warm, composed salad, dressed with nothing more than a good drizzle of sweet-tart balsamic glaze. It's just a great example of how much "umami" you can get from a vegetable dish. (If you don't like blue cheese, try Brie or Camembert.) Yes, you will have to make a few of its components, but none of them take too long, and you can do a lot ahead of time: cook the lentils, make the balsamic glaze, and wash and stem the spinach, for example. The shiitakes are at their best when not too long out of the oven. These portions are on the smaller side; you can certainly divide this into 3 servings instead of 4, if you wish, or serve it with grilled bread.

1 In a large (12-inch) nonstick skillet, heat the olive oil over medium heat. Add the spinach and salt. Cook, stirring, until the spinach is just wilted but still has some body (it will weep less if not overcooked), about 2 minutes. Transfer to a plate.

2 If necessary, drain the spinach and pat it dry. Arrange equal portions on 4 small plates. Top with the blue cheese and lentils, divided equally among the plates. Drizzle with the balsamic glaze and garnish with the crispy shiitake mushrooms.

Balsamic Glaze

**MAKES ABOUT 3½
TABLESPOONS**

⅓ cup balsamic vinegar

2 tablespoons packed dark
brown sugar

You can buy balsamic glaze, but it is much better to make your own, as commercial varieties can contain gluten and other unnecessary ingredients. By simply simmering balsamic vinegar with a bit of brown sugar for a very short amount of time, you get a velvety (but not too thick) syrup to drizzle on beans, roasted veggies, and more. The mixture will thicken much more as it cools, so follow the recipe to avoid over-reducing.

1 Combine the vinegar and the brown sugar in a skillet or small saucepan and stir well. (The reduction will take a little longer in a small, straight-sided saucepan.) Put on medium-high heat and bring to a simmer, stirring and scraping down the sides of the pan almost constantly. Cook just until the mixture is viscous and slightly syrupy, about 2 minutes (a spatula will leave a path where you scrape the bottom). It should have reduced by between ⅓ and ½ of its original volume.

2 Remove the skillet from the heat and let the glaze cool for 5 minutes. Transfer to a heat-proof container and allow to cool completely. Keep, covered, at room temperature or in the fridge for several weeks.

Quick-Roasted Crispy Shiitakes

MAKES ABOUT ½ CUP

4 to 5 ounces large fresh shiitake caps, stemmed and cut into ½-inch-thick slices (about 2½ cups of sliced shiitakes)

2 tablespoons vegetable or olive oil

Pinch of kosher salt

Shiitake mushrooms have a particularly strong umami flavor (meaty and funky), so every vegetarian cook finds creative ways to use them. Roasting intensifies the flavor even further and also shrinks them, so when you slice shiitakes thin and roast them, you wind up with some pretty addictive little nubbins. Use these as a garnish on soups, grain and bean dishes, and pasta, and, of course, in egg sandwiches (such as the English Muffin Egg Sandwich with Spinach, Avocado, Cheddar, Crispy Shiitakes, and Pickled Jalapeños, page 196).

Preheat the oven to 425°F. Line a rimmed baking sheet with parchment paper. In a medium bowl, toss the sliced shiitakes with the oil and salt and spread out on the baking sheet. Bake until shrunken, golden-brown, and crisp, 12 to 16 minutes, depending on the size and thickness of the mushrooms.

Avocado, Orange, Endive,
and Radicchio Salad with Roasted
Chickpeas • 94

ROASTED CHICKPEAS • 95

Sugar Snap Pea, Cabbage,
Edamame, and Peanut Slaw with
Spicy Peanut Sauce and Tofu • 97

Hoop House Dreams Salad
with Farmhouse Vinaigrette • 98

FARMHOUSE VINAIGRETTE • 100

PITA CRISPS • 100

Grilled Romaine Hearts,
Grilled Potatoes, and Green Beans
with Creamy Blender
Caesar Dressing • 101

CREAMY BLENDER CAESAR DRESSING • 103

Grilled Peach, Red Onion,
and Arugula Salad with Grilled
Croutons and Sun Gold
Tomatoes • 104

Farmer's Supper with Garden Lettuce,
Focaccia, Artisan Cheese, Quick
Pickles, and Walnuts • 106

ROSEMARY ROASTED WALNUTS • 107

Warm Fall Salad with
Maple-Vanilla Roasted Delicata
Squash and Pears • 108

Pan-Braised Fingerlings with
Mellow Garlic-Olive Dressing and
Tuscan Kale Salad • 110

Roasted Carrot, Bell Pepper,
and Red Onion Salad with Endive,
Radicchio, and Carrot Top–Pecan
Pesto Dressing • 112

CARROT TOP–PECAN PESTO • 113

Rosemary Roasted Cauliflower
and Frisée Salad • 115

Chopped Winter Salad of Escarole,
Arugula, Blue Cheese, Pecans,
and Roasted Grapes • 116

VEGGIES + LEAVES

LEAFY green vegetables were my first culinary love. They were the first things I planted in my first vegetable garden. Heck, they were the subject of my first recipe story for a food magazine! I will never tire of their stunning beauty in the field and their endless flexibility in the kitchen.

That probably explains why I think of leafy greens as something so special that they deserve their own chapter. I know I said our strategy is to pair vegetables ("Veggies +") with workhorse whole foods like grains and eggs—and now here we are, pairing vegetables with, um, vegetables. But it's only partly my fault. I wouldn't have chosen leafy greens as one of our staple categories just for their beauty, or for sentimental reasons. (Well, not *entirely*.) The fact is, they have serious nutritional cred (antioxidants, vitamins, protein), and, more important from a cook's point of view, leafy greens are the most versatile vegetables—maybe the most versatile food—on the planet. If you want to build a delicious and satisfying vegetarian meal, you simply can't go wrong by starting with greens. And because of their unique texture and mineral-y flavor, they automatically offer the perfect contrast to the denser, fruitier, more traditional vegetables we can pair them with. Leafy greens are that frilly, twirling skirt you wear with the denim jacket. (And they work with a linen blouse or a cotton T-shirt, too.)

One of the reasons I'm calling this chapter "+ Leaves" rather than "+ Greens" is that I want to shine a little spotlight on the way these beautiful vegetables look, because the shape, size, thickness, and texture of an individual leaf can actually offer us the best clues about how to prepare that green. (See "Take a Visual Clue" on page 90.) In this chapter, we'll depend on greens to lend freshness, structure, and texture to our veggie suppers. In other words, we're going to blow up the salad concept: warm, cool, hot, composed, scattered, layered, grilled—all fun. While there are even more ways to use greens (often cooked) in other chapters—where they pair nicely with grains, eggs, noodles, and broths—here is where we let the leaves star in all their three-dimensional leafy wonder.

Tips and Strategies for Leaves

Start with a plan. Our strategy for building fresh veggie suppers with greens is simple: Get familiar with the wide variety of leafy greens; include one or two greens from each of our pantry categories (see page 93) on your weekly shopping list; be choosy when you're at the market; and get into the habit of immediately washing and storing leaves for maximum longevity. Then, be open to creativity. But whatever you do, don't let a weekly shopping trip go by without at least one purchase of fresh greens.

TAKE A VISUAL CLUE.

Shopping for greens at the grocery store can be frustrating, to say the least. Often our choices are limited, and sometimes the leafy greens are so randomly labeled that trying to match up your shopping list with what you see in front of you can put you in a state of total confusion. Say we've got our hearts set on making a warm salad. Wouldn't it be nice if we didn't have to worry about whether the thing we're staring at is actually frisée or curly endive or escarole or some other funky new frilly green lettuce, and simply understand that this pale head with the sturdy crisp white stems and ruffly lime green leaves is just the thing to stand up to a little heat and to catch a tasty vinaigrette in all its tiny swales and minnow-y curves? You can gain this confidence if you start looking at the leafy greens themselves for visual clues about cooking them—and then taking them home, tasting the leaves individually, and using them in different ways.

Consider kale. With so many varieties and sizes now available to us, shopping for it can be a puzzle—especially if you're cooking from a recipe that doesn't specify what kind or size of kale to use. However, by simply looking at the leaves (and touching them if you can—thickness is important), you can get a pretty good sense of how they'll best be cooked.

Finely lobed (sometimes oak leaf–shaped) kale with thin, relatively flat leaves and a floppy disposition is not tough or rubbery, so you know right away that it will work in a salad. The size of the leaf doesn't necessarily matter here; delicate varieties like this (including the beautiful purple-veined Red Russian kale) will be tender not only at one or two inches long (when it is labeled "baby kale") but also at four or five inches long (I'd call that "teenage" kale). If the leaf is relatively thin and fragile between your fingers and the stem is still quite thin, you can use these longer leaves in salads and in quick stir-fries, too. So buy a bunch. (If you have the chance to taste a leaf, even better. It will be sweet and nutty.)

On the other end of the kale spectrum, deeply ruffled or curly kale with thick leaves, very thick stems, and a stiff posture (good in flower arrangements!) will nearly always have a tough, rubbery texture. You will need to braise or simmer it to get it tender, but you can also slice it very thin or chop it fine, which will break down some of the fibers, making it ready for a quick sauté or a hearty, well-dressed salad. (For this use, the stems always need to be removed first.) The good news about mature kale is that it has a lot of flavor, so if you want to make a soup, for example, look for those large, thick leaves.

Unfortunately, you also have to pay attention to freshness when shopping for greens. It would certainly be nice if we could buy all our leafy greens at farmers' markets, but it's probably not practical for many of us. That's too bad, because locally grown greens that have been recently harvested retain more of their nutrients than older, well-traveled ones. Plus farmers' markets offer so much more variety. So, if you can make it to a farmers' market occasionally, that's great. And if you're lucky enough to have a winter market in your area, definitely pay it a visit, because many farmers are now growing greens nearly year-round in hoop houses, and cool-weather greens are the tastiest.

Meanwhile, back at the grocery store, slimy greens make me sad. If you were with me in the produce aisle, given the two options, you might be surprised that I'd actually steer you toward that dry-as-a-bone, wilty bunch of unpackaged

greens in the fresh greens section and away from the plastic box with a sell-by date of tomorrow or yesterday. I applaud the efforts of the produce companies to try to make more varieties of salad greens available to us in these plastic bags and boxes, but by the very nature of that packaging, the greens wind up spending far too much time in transit and on the shelf. They rot from the center of the box or bag, so it's an unpleasant surprise to open one up and find the bad stuff inside. On the other hand, although that bunch of greens in the fresh section does desperately need a soak in water, it is probably nowhere near as old as the boxed greens. After a bit of resuscitation, it could be perfectly fine for cooking, and it might have some flavor, too.

I do, however, understand the convenience of the boxes and bags (really I do!), and because I want you to cook with more greens, I'll offer one more observation and a suggestion. The packages with only one kind of green (baby arugula, baby kale, etc.) seem to hold up better than boxed salad mixes. (Salad mixes suffer in part because the lettuces are often torn or cut before being mixed, which starts the deterioration process early.) For this reason, I suggest making your own, custom salad mix: Buy one whole head of lettuce—green leaf or red leaf or romaine or Bibb—and then buy a box of arugula or baby spinach for mixing in. Add a small head of radicchio or an endive or two, and you've got the makings of a simply fine salad mix. And if you want to fancy up that salad mix on any given week, you can layer on flavor and textures by adding some more greens from the pantry lists on page 93.

WASH. SPIN. STORE.

When you get that head of lettuce home, cut an inch or so off the stem, then separate the leaves, wash them in tepid water, and spin them dry. (I love my OXO salad spinner.) Put them in a paper towel–lined zip-top bag or two, and they will keep for a week. This takes extra time when you get home, but you will be happy on Tuesday when you reach for that bag and the work is already done. You'll be even happier on Friday when you reach for the bag again and that lettuce is still good. This actually may be the single most important part of our leaves strategy! The last thing we want to do is waste food and money (and time going back to the grocery store) because of spent greens. Buying fresh greens in the first place will help with their longevity, but storing greens properly can give them up to five extra days.

GROW.

In addition to the grocery store and the farmers' market, there is one other option for procuring beautiful greens: grow them yourself. Don't laugh! I can tell you in all honesty, with much dirt under my boots, that they are the easiest of all vegetables to grow. So if you have even a spark of interest, go for it. A planter or large pot outside your back door will do; a small garden bed is even better.

For the Pantry

So let's get to the fun stuff: all the varieties of leafy greens we can play with. Don't freak out when you look at the following lists of greens. I do not expect you to keep all these leafy wonders hanging around in your fridge all the time. My intentions are to give you options—to open up the world of leafy possibilities!—and then to help you zero in on a few choices every week.

I've organized the greens by how you'll prepare them. That's what we really care about, after all. When making veggie suppers, it doesn't matter whether a green is technically a lettuce or a *Brassica*, but whether its texture and flavor are right for the type of dish we want to make.

Tender salad greens are ones you'll eat raw most often, and sometimes lightly cooked.

Tender cooking greens are heartier than tender salad greens; they require only a very short cooking time. (Think spinach and Swiss chard.) Use the smaller leaves in salads.

Hearty cooking greens, such as the thickly ruffled mature kale we talked about on page 91), need to be either cooked longer or sliced or chopped to be enjoyed, most often cooked.

For fun, I've also included a list of "Bonus Salad Greens"—from pea shoots to purslane.

As usual, I've included a short list of my favorite "accessory" pantry ingredients. When I think of leafy greens, I think of bright and sweet ingredients as the best partners: vinegars, citrus, all kinds of dried and fresh fruits, and even a bit of jam or chutney for dressings are all wonderful, especially when contrasted with aged cheeses, toasty nuts, or salty olives.

The Leaves

TENDER SALAD GREENS

Mild

Bibb or Boston lettuce

Green and red romaine or baby romaine lettuce

Green leaf lettuce

Market or garden loose-leaf, oak leaf, or frilly lettuces

Mini-lettuces, including Little Gem and Ruby Glow

Red leaf lettuce

Assertive

Arugula

Baby kale

Baby mustard greens (purple and green)

Endive

Escarole

Frisée (curly endive)

Mizuna

Radicchio

Tatsoi

TENDER COOKING GREENS

Baby bok choy

Beet greens

Bok choy

Broccoli leaves

Brussels sprout leaves

Napa cabbage

Radish tops

Savoy cabbage

Spinach

Swiss chard

HEARTY COOKING GREENS

Collard greens

Curly kale

Dandelion greens

Green cabbage

Mustard greens (mature)

Red cabbage

Turnip greens (mature)

Tuscan kale

BONUS SALAD GREENS

Bean sprouts

Broccoli sprouts

Celery leaves

Fennel fronds

Mâche

Microgreens

Nasturtium leaves

Parsley and other leafy herbs

Pea shoots and pea greens

Purslane

Watercress

Accessory Ingredients

Aged cheeses

Apple cider vinegar

Apples, peaches, or pears

Balsamic vinegar

Citrus fruits and juices

Dried fruits

Extra-virgin olive oil

Fresh berries

Fruit jam, jelly, or chutney

Grapeseed oil

Nuts (all)

Sherry vinegar

White balsamic vinegar

White wine vinegar

AVOCADO, ORANGE, ENDIVE, AND RADICCHIO SALAD

WITH ROASTED CHICKPEAS

SERVES 2

1 tablespoon grapeseed oil

1 tablespoon fresh lime juice

1 teaspoon fresh lime zest

1 tablespoon jalapeño (or other hot pepper) jelly

Kosher salt or coarse sea salt

1 large or 2 medium-small endives, cut in half, cored, and leaves separated

½ medium head of radicchio, cored and leaves separated

1 large navel orange, peeled and cut crosswise into thin slices

1 large or 1½ medium ripe-but-firm avocados

¼ cup lightly packed fresh Italian parsley leaves

½ to ⅔ cup Roasted Chickpeas (recipe follows)

For a supper dish that's so simple to prepare, this salad is over-the-top stunning. And the fresh, bright colors belie the fact that it's quite filling, to boot. The roasted chickpeas are a fun twist, providing crunchy texture and toasty flavor that contrast with the cool, creamy avocado and sweet orange. The easy vinaigrette gets a pop, too, from hot pepper jelly. This salad comes together in the time it takes to roast the chickpeas (if you don't already have a stash of them in your freezer). Before you dive in, have fun arranging this on a platter or plates for a pleasing presentation. (Alternatively, you can dice the avocado and slice the radicchio leaves into ribbons instead of leaving them whole to yield bite-size pieces that are easier to eat. Or just chop everything with a knife and fork once you've got it on your plate!) This recipe is for two, but you could easily double it.

1. In a small bowl, whisk together the oil, lime juice, lime zest, jalapeño jelly, and a pinch of salt.

2. Arrange the endive leaves in a ring around the outer edge of a small serving platter or two dinner plates. Tuck or scatter the radicchio leaves in a ring overlapping the endive. Arrange the orange slices over the radicchio. Arrange the avocado slices in the center of the platter or plates. Sprinkle with some salt and the parsley leaves. Spoon the vinaigrette over it all, and garnish with plenty of chickpeas.

Roasted Chickpeas

1 cup cooked chickpeas
(see page 236),
well dried

2 teaspoons grapeseed, peanut,
or other vegetable oil

¼ teaspoon kosher salt, plus
more to taste

Fried and sautéed chickpeas are delicious, but my favorite technique for amping up the flavor and texture of chickpeas is roasting. Roasting gives chickpeas a nutty flavor and crunchy texture. I love to use my own cooked chickpeas for roasting, but you can roast canned chickpeas, too. Either way, just make sure the chickpeas have been rinsed and dried well before tossing with the oil. Cook them to a deep golden brown for the best crunch. Use roasted chickpeas in salads and grain dishes, as a toast garnish, and, of course, for snacking. These are best freshly made, but you can pop any leftovers in the freezer and defrost when you need them.

Preheat the oven to 425°F. Line a rimmed baking sheet with parchment paper. In a small bowl, toss the chickpeas with the oil to coat lightly and season with the salt. Spread out on the baking sheet and roast until well browned and shrunken, 25 to 30 minutes. Let cool for a few minutes and season with more salt, to taste.

SUGAR SNAP PEA, CABBAGE, EDAMAME, AND PEANUT SLAW

WITH SPICY PEANUT SAUCE AND TOFU

SERVES 4

3 cups thinly sliced green cabbage (about ½ small head)

2 cups thinly sliced sugar snap peas (cut at a very sharp angle)

1 cup edamame beans

1 cup chopped roasted peanuts

¾ cup very thinly sliced scallions (white and light green parts, cut at a sharp angle)

3 tablespoons chopped fresh cilantro, plus 4 sprigs for garnish

¼ teaspoon kosher salt

¼ to ⅓ cup plus 3 to 4 tablespoons Spicy Peanut Sauce (page 25), at room temperature

One 14-ounce package extra-firm tofu, pressed and drained

1 cup fresh pea shoots (optional)

Slaw for supper? Of course—especially when delicious Spicy Peanut Sauce (page 25) is involved. When you think of leafy greens, don't forget how versatile raw green cabbage is; it takes only a few minutes to turn it into something delicious. This pretty spring slaw gets a fresh boost from slivered sugar snap peas, edamame, cilantro, and pea shoots (if you like). A bonus of quickly broiled tofu slices makes a lovely base for a mound of it. Chopped roasted peanuts add a crunchy, salty contrast for a supper with great flavor and texture.

1 In a large bowl, combine the cabbage, most of the sugar snap peas, the edamame, the peanuts, most of the scallions, and the chopped cilantro. Add the salt and ¼ cup of the peanut sauce and toss well. Taste, and add a little more peanut sauce if you like.

2 Preheat the oven broiler to high. Line a baking sheet with aluminum foil. Cut the tofu into 8 rectangles, each about ½ inch thick. Arrange the tofu slices on the prepared baking sheet.

Spoon 1 to 2 teaspoons of peanut sauce on top of each slice and spread it to the edges. Broil the tofu until the top is a deep caramel color, 1 to 2 minutes.

3 To serve, arrange 2 slices of tofu on each of four plates (or in shallow bowls), and mound the slaw next to and slightly over them, dividing it evenly among the plates. Garnish with the remaining snap peas and scallions, as well as the pea shoots (if using) and cilantro sprigs.

HOOP HOUSE DREAMS SALAD

WITH FARMHOUSE VINAIGRETTE

SERVES 2

3 cups fresh baby spring greens, including arugula and some lettuce

1 recipe Pita Crisps (recipe follows)

½ cup or more Quick-Roasted Cherry Tomatoes (page 133)

1 medium-large ripe-but-firm avocado

¼ cup or more Lemony Chickpea Hummus (page 139)

12 Kalamata olives, Niçoise olives, or a combination of your favorites

5 to 6 tablespoons mixed toasted nuts (choose two or three kinds: pine nuts, pecans, sliced or chopped almonds, or pepitas)

¼ cup Roasted Chickpeas (page 95)

1 cup fresh pea shoots, pea greens, or pea leaves

1 recipe Farmhouse Vinaigrette (recipe follows)

One of the best things about growing vegetables in a "hoop house" is the chance to harvest baby greens early in the spring. By late April, I might have young arugula, mizuna, several different lettuces, baby kale, baby pea greens, and ruby mustard ready to pick. That's my cue to put together my favorite spring salad—the kind of dish that makes me truly love being a vegetarian, because it has all my favorite goodies in it. I include these make-ahead components not to frustrate you but to inspire you. Once you see how you can create something truly tasty and beautiful by combining a few homemade ingredients with fresh greens, you'll be sold. Next, you'll be making your own signature supper salad. (Remember, the toasted nuts, roasted chickpeas, and pita toasts all freeze well, the dressing keeps in the fridge for weeks, and the roasted tomatoes keep well in the fridge or the freezer.)

1 Choose a 10 x 14-inch or 10 x 12-inch platter. (Round or oval will work fine, too; just arrange the ingredients in circles rather than rows.)

2 With a short edge of the platter closest to you (if using a rectangular one), arrange the spring greens in a wide, mounding strip down the center of the platter. To the left, arrange the pita crisps in an overlapping row along the edge of the plate. Snuggle the roasted tomatoes in a row between the pitas and the greens. Cut the avocado in half and remove the pit; score the flesh if you like, but don't peel it. If you like, cut the halves in half again lengthwise. To the right of the greens, arrange the avocados, a mound of hummus, and the olives in a line down the edge of the plate. Sprinkle the nuts and chickpeas along the right edge of the greens. Scatter the pea shoots over the rest of the greens.

3 Put the salad dressing into a small serving bowl with a small spoon in it. Bring the bowl of dressing and the platter to the table, along with a fork, knife, spoon, and plate for each person. Use the pita crisps to make mini salad sandwiches from all the ingredients, scooping the avocado out of the shell with a spoon, and drizzling dressing on as needed. Or transfer portions of everything onto each plate, drizzle with dressing, and eat with a knife and fork.

Farmhouse Vinaigrette

MAKES 1 CUP

⅔ cup extra-virgin olive oil

¼ cup white balsamic vinegar

2 teaspoons fresh lemon juice, plus more to taste

1 teaspoon freshly grated lemon zest

1 teaspoon local honey

1 teaspoon Dijon mustard

¼ teaspoon kosher salt

Freshly ground black pepper

1 garlic clove, peeled and cut in half

4 sprigs of fresh thyme

This is my "house" dressing for green salads. I always have a jar of it in the fridge. Feel free to substitute maple syrup for the honey and to use your favorite mild vinegar as well. Don't skimp on the lemon zest, which gives this vinaigrette its personality. This recipe is easily doubled.

Combine the olive oil, vinegar, 2 teaspoons of lemon juice, lemon zest, honey, mustard, salt, and several generous grinds of black pepper in a glass jar with a lid. Cover and shake well. (Or whisk together well in a glass measuring cup, then pour into a container with a lid to store.) Taste, and add more lemon juice if desired. Add the garlic clove halves and thyme sprigs and store in the fridge for up to 3 weeks.

Pita Crisps

MAKES 16 TO 24 PITA CRISPS

1 or 2 good-quality pita breads (thick is nice)

Olive oil

Kosher salt

Bring home a package of pita bread, take a few minutes to turn the pitas into "crisps," then pop them in the freezer. You'll be happy to have a stash of these at the ready (they thaw in minutes) for salads, dips, and soups.

Preheat the oven broiler to high. Cut each pita bread into quarters or sixths. Pull them apart so that you get 8 or 12 wedges from each pita. Brush each piece of pita generously with olive oil, sprinkle with salt, and arrange on a rimmed baking sheet. Broil until deeply golden plus brown around the edges, 2 to 3 minutes. Freeze any leftovers.

GRILLED ROMAINE HEARTS, GRILLED POTATOES, AND GREEN BEANS

WITH CREAMY BLENDER CAESAR DRESSING

SERVES 4

2 whole romaine hearts

Olive oil or vegetable oil

2¾ teaspoons kosher salt, plus more for sprinkling

8 baby red potatoes or small fingerling potatoes (about 8 to 10 ounces)

⅔ cup Creamy Blender Caesar Dressing (recipe follows)

½ pound green beans and/or yellow wax beans, tops trimmed

1 lemon, ends trimmed, cut into thin slices (optional)

2 tablespoons whole or roughly chopped Italian parsley leaves

Grilled potatoes + grilled romaine lettuce + creamy Caesar dressing = yum! Kind of a cross between a composed Niçoise salad (green beans and potatoes) and a Caesar salad, this intriguing summer salad is flexible, too: you can blanch the beans or grill them; you can also skip grilling the potatoes and just boil them if you need to. (But I wouldn't—they're grilled with a coating of dressing that makes them extra delicious.) Grilling the lettuce will be a revelation if you've never tried it; it undergoes quite a flavor transformation. Just put the romaine on the grill at the last minute, shortly before serving, because it will wilt rapidly as it cools. The grilled lemons are totally optional (but completely edible!). This is a bold, substantial salad, so enjoy it on a Friday night with friends. Prep and wash the romaine hearts in advance so they will have time to dry.

1 Remove the longest and bulkiest outer leaves from the romaine hearts and trim a sliver off the stem end of each heart. Cut the hearts in half lengthwise. Gently wash any visible dirt away under running water and let the hearts drip dry on towels. (Do this up to an hour in advance if possible, and don't worry if the lettuce doesn't completely dry.) Put the romaine halves on a rimmed baking sheet and brush on all sides with oil. Sprinkle with salt.

2 Put the potatoes in a large saucepan and cover with 2 inches of water. Add 2 teaspoons of the salt and bring to a boil over high heat. Reduce the heat to low and simmer until potatoes are just barely tender, 12 to 14 minutes. Use a slotted spoon to transfer the cooked potatoes onto dish towels to cool. (You can cook the potatoes up to a day in advance and refrigerate when cool.)

3 Preheat a gas grill to medium heat. If you have a grill basket or grill topper, add it to the grill to preheat.

4 When the potatoes are cool enough to handle, cut each in half crosswise and put in a medium bowl. Add ½ teaspoon of the salt and 2 to 3 tablespoons of the Caesar dressing and toss well.

5 In a separate medium bowl, toss the green and/or yellow beans with the remaining ¼ teaspoon of salt and 1 tablespoon

continued →

GRILLED ROMAINE HEARTS, GRILLED POTATOES, AND GREEN BEANS,

continued →

of the Caesar dressing. (Alternatively, cook the beans for 2 to 3 minutes in boiling salted water.)

6 Brush the lemon slices on both sides with a little bit of oil.

7 Arrange the potatoes, cut-side down, directly on the grill grates or on a grill topper. Cook until well marked, about 3 minutes. Using tongs, turn each potato over and grill until the bottoms are browned, about 2 minutes. (Every grill is different and has its hot spots, so some potatoes may be done ahead of others.) Transfer the potatoes to a plate.

8 If grilling your beans, add them to your grill basket or arrange them on a grill topper or (very carefully) directly on the grates. Arrange the lemon slices on

the grill. Cook the beans, turning once, until they are darkened and a bit shriveled, about 4 minutes total. Cook the lemon slices until they are browned on both sides, 2 to 3 minutes total. Transfer the beans and lemon slices to a plate.

9 Arrange the romaine hearts, cut-side down, directly on the grill grates. Cook until well marked, about 2 minutes. Flip over and cook for 1 more minute.

10 Place a romaine half on each of 4 dinner plates. Arrange the potatoes, beans, and lemon slices around the lettuce, distributing the ingredients evenly among the plates, and spoon some dressing over each plate. (You may have some dressing left over.) Sprinkle generously with the parsley and serve warm.

Creamy Blender Caesar Dressing

MAKES ⅔ CUP

2 large garlic cloves, smashed and peeled

1 large egg yolk

2 tablespoons plus 2 teaspoons fresh lemon juice

1 tablespoon Dijon mustard

1 teaspoon packed freshly grated lemon zest

¼ teaspoon kosher salt

½ teaspoon freshly ground black pepper

½ cup extra-virgin olive oil

This lemony Caesar dressing is a variation on one I learned to make at my first cooking job, at Al Forno restaurant in Providence, Rhode Island. The blender method is easy because it automatically emulsifies and thickens the dressing. With plenty of lemon and garlic, this dressing packs a punch that lends a lot of personality wherever it appears, starting with lettuce but not ending there. Try it as a dressing for baby kale, too, or as a dip for grilled broccoli. Or brush it over bread before grilling. It keeps for up to a week, covered, in the fridge, so make a batch ahead, especially during the summer months.

Combine the garlic, egg yolk, lemon juice, mustard, lemon zest, salt, and pepper in a blender. Blend, scraping down the sides as necessary, until the garlic is well chopped and everything is thoroughly combined. With the motor running (and the lid or cover removed), carefully pour in the oil in a slow, steady stream. Blend until the dressing is thick, creamy, and emulsified. If not using right away, store tightly covered in the fridge for up to 5 days.

GRILLED PEACH, RED ONION, AND ARUGULA SALAD

WITH GRILLED CROUTONS AND SUN GOLD TOMATOES

SERVES 4

2 tablespoons balsamic vinegar

2 tablespoons fresh lime juice

2 tablespoons maple syrup

Kosher salt

Four 1-inch-thick slices of ciabatta bread

1 medium red onion, cut crosswise into ½-inch-thick slices (keep slices together)

2 ripe-but-firm peaches or nectarines, cut in half and pitted

Extra-virgin olive oil

1½ cups halved Sun Gold tomatoes or other yellow or colorful cherry tomatoes

4 to 5 cups arugula

3 to 4 tablespoons crème fraîche or sour cream (optional)

This casual summertime supper salad features two of my favorite pairings. First, there's the kicky flavor contrast of sweet summer peaches with brightly acidic vine-ripened tomatoes. Second, there's the fun textural juxtaposition of juicy tomatoes and crunchy grilled bread. The tomato-bread mix is a twist on an Italian panzanella salad, only here it is used a bit more like a garnish for an arugula, peach, and grilled onion salad. (Arugula never had it so good!) A drizzle of balsamic vinegar, lime, and maple syrup brings together all the flavor points in this colorful mix. If you've never grilled peaches before, no worries—it's much easier than it sounds, and quite delicious. You can use nectarines instead if you like.

1 Preheat a gas grill to medium heat.

2 In a small bowl, whisk together the vinegar, lime juice, maple syrup, and a big pinch of salt and set aside.

3 Arrange the bread slices, onion slices, and peach halves on a rimmed baking sheet for transporting them to the grill. Brush both sides of everything generously with olive oil and season with a little salt. (If you like, you can thread the onion rings on metal skewers or metal turkey lacers for easier cooking.)

4 Arrange the bread and onion slices on the grill. Cover and cook until the bread is golden and marked on the bottom, about 2 minutes. Use tongs to turn the bread over, and cook until the other side is golden and marked, about 2 minutes. Remove the bread from the grill. Check the onions to see whether they are beginning to soften up. Once they have grill marks, turn them over and continue cooking until the other side is marked, 3 to 4 minutes more. Remove the onions from the grill and wrap them in aluminum foil to help them finish cooking through.

5 Arrange the peaches (cut-side down) on the grill and cook until grill marks form, 3 to 4 minutes. (Try not to move the fruit for the first 3 minutes.) Rotate the peaches 90 degrees (to make cross-hatch grill marks) and continue cooking for another 2 to 3 minutes. Remove the peaches from the grill. (They do not need to be grilled on the skin side; they will be soft and very warm already.)

6 Cut each slice of grilled bread into 8 to 12 pieces and put the pieces in a large bowl. Add the tomatoes, drizzle with 2 tablespoons of the balsamic mixture, and toss well.

7 Arrange the arugula loosely on a large serving platter (or use 4 dinner plates). Arrange the peach halves over the arugula. Drop the tomato-bread mixture all around the peaches. Separate the grilled onion rings and arrange them over the salad. Season with salt and pepper, and drizzle with as much of the remaining balsamic mixture as you like.

8 If using a platter, bring it to the table with serving spoons to portion out the salad, and with forks and knives for cutting up the peaches. When serving the salad onto plates, garnish each portion with a dollop of crème fraîche or sour cream (if desired), to be tossed in individually for a creamy finish.

FARMER'S SUPPER

WITH GARDEN LETTUCE, FOCACCIA, ARTISAN CHEESE, QUICK PICKLES, AND WALNUTS

SERVES 4

1 loaf of focaccia or 1 French baguette (preferably with a not-too-crunchy crust)

Extra-virgin olive oil

Kosher salt

½ pound artisanal cheese, such as aged blue cheese, or fresh mozzarella, sliced

1 recipe Balsamic Glaze (page 87)

1 recipe Basil "Pesto" Oil (page 13)

¾ cup Quick-Roasted Cherry Tomatoes (page 133), or ½ cup raw cherry tomatoes, cut in half

½ cup Rosemary Roasted Walnuts (recipe follows) or any toasted nuts

¼ cup quick-pickled onions or corn (Quick-Pickled Corn, Jalapeños, and Onions, page 199, optional)

Generous 6 to 8 handfuls of pretty garden lettuce leaves, or combined inner leaves from heads of red leaf, romaine, and Bibb from the market (4 to 5 cups)

Freshly ground black pepper

Taking a page from the British ploughman's lunch (bread, cheese, and pickles), my Farmer's Supper is a totally fun and casual meal to share with friends (maybe friends who've been helping out in the garden!). Like the Hoop House Dreams Salad with Farmhouse Vinaigrette (page 100), this is another great excuse to feature greens and goodies, only this one is inspired by all the pretty lettuces—with names like Speckled Amish and Flashy Green Butter Oak—that I grow in the field in early summer. When they're at their peak, I can't get enough of them. To turn them into something filling while still letting them shine, I make these "lettuce sandwiches" with some of my favorite condiments, such as Quick-Roasted Cherry Tomatoes, Balsamic Glaze, Basil "Pesto" Oil, Rosemary Roasted Walnuts, and Quick-Pickled Corn, Jalapeños, and Onions. I set everything out on a big board (al fresco of course!) with some warm bread. (Toasted or not, focaccia or a baguette is nice here.) I also splurge and pick up a really nice artisanal cheese—from a local farm, if I can. I like a firm, aged blue cheese here, but a creamy washed-rind cheese would be nice, too—or have both!

1 Split the focaccia or baguette in half horizontally and then cut into rectangles or squares. If you like, brush each piece generously with oil and season with salt, then grill or broil. (Follow the method on page 238.) If desired, top some of the bread pieces with the cheese slices and return to the grill or broiler to melt.

2 Arrange six small serving bowls. Put the balsamic glaze, basil oil, cherry tomatoes, walnuts, pickled onions, and some salt each in a separate bowl. Arrange the filled bowls, the pieces of bread or toast, the cheese, the lettuce leaves, a pepper grinder, and a bottle of olive oil on a large board or several boards, with small serving utensils and a small stack of plates alongside.

3 Make open-faced or closed sandwiches. Stuff them with plenty of garden lettuce drizzled with balsamic glaze and basil oil, sprinkled with sea salt, and topped with a few slices of cheese, some pickles, and the roasted walnuts.

Rosemary Roasted Walnuts

MAKES ABOUT 1 CUP

1 tablespoon unsalted butter

1 cup walnut pieces

1 teaspoon chopped
fresh rosemary

½ teaspoon kosher salt or
fine sea salt

A version of these nuts appeared in an issue of *Gourmet* magazine many years ago in an article written by the wonderful Laurie Colwin. I remember that my mom, my sister, and pretty much everyone I knew who liked to cook adopted them as a classic appetizer to serve with drinks. (I like everything salty and roasted.) These days I like them best as a savory condiment. They're especially good with blue cheese or in a winter salad.

Preheat the oven to 375°F. Line a rimmed baking sheet with parchment paper. Melt the butter in the microwave or in a small saucepan. Put the walnut pieces in a small bowl and drizzle the butter over them. Add the rosemary and salt and toss gently but thoroughly. (A small silicone spatula works well for this.) Scrape the walnuts and any seasonings onto the prepared baking sheet. Roast until golden brown, 13 to 15 minutes. Let cool completely. Store in an airtight container at room temperature for a few days or in the freezer for several weeks.

WARM FALL SALAD

WITH MAPLE-VANILLA ROASTED DELICATA SQUASH AND PEARS

SERVES 4

1 tablespoon extra-virgin olive oil or grapeseed oil, plus more for brushing

2 medium delicata squashes (about 1½ pounds)

2 medium ripe-but-firm pears (about 1 pound)

Kosher salt

3 tablespoons unsalted butter

3 tablespoons maple syrup

2 teaspoons vanilla extract

¼ teaspoon ground cardamom

6 cups mixed fall greens, such as baby spinach, radicchio, and frisée or endive

Freshly ground black pepper

2 tablespoons diced shallots

1 tablespoon plus 1 teaspoon white balsamic vinegar

Garnishes (choose one or more of the following):

⅓ to ½ cup coarsely grated or diced aged Cheddar

⅓ cup Rosemary Roasted Walnuts (page 107) or other toasted nuts

3 tablespoons dried cranberries

Yep, it's as good as it sounds. Roasted pears and roasted delicata squash are simply delicious together—especially when drizzled with a maple-vanilla-cardamom glaze (stolen from my very first cookbook, *Fast, Fresh & Green*) and served alongside a bevy of bold fall greens tossed with a warm shallot vinaigrette. This takes a bit of time to put together, but there's a lot of flavor payoff, so make this when friends are coming over. At least you don't need to peel the squash! You can choose some or all of the garnishes, but if you've got time, do make the Rosemary Roasted Walnuts—they make the perfect salty counterpart to the sweet and tangy stuff.

1 Preheat the oven to 450°F. Line two rimmed baking sheets with parchment paper. Brush the parchment with oil. Cut the squashes in half lengthwise and scoop out the seeds with a serving spoon. Turn the halves over, cut-side down, on a cutting board. Trim off the ends, then slice the squash halves crosswise into ½- to ¾-inch crescents. Cut the pears in half, scoop out the seeds, trim off the ends, and cut each of the halves lengthwise into 5 or 6 wedges or slices. Arrange the squash in a single layer on one baking sheet. Arrange the pears in a single layer on another baking sheet. Season both with a little salt.

2 In a small saucepan over low heat, melt the butter. Add 2 tablespoons of the maple syrup, 1½ teaspoons of the vanilla extract, the ground cardamom, and a big pinch of salt. Stir and remove from the heat. Brush the mixture all over the squash and pear slices. (Reserve any extra.) Bake the squash and pears for 20 to 24 minutes, flipping them over halfway through cooking if you like, until browned and tender. (The pears may be done before the squash.) If you do flip the slices, brush the top side with any reserved maple butter before continuing to bake.

3 Put the greens into a large heatproof mixing bowl. Season with salt and pepper. In a small skillet, combine 1 tablespoon of the olive oil, the shallots, and a big pinch of salt. Place over medium-low heat and cook, stirring, until the shallots are just golden, 4 to 6 minutes. Add the remaining 1 tablespoon of maple syrup, the vinegar, the remaining ½ teaspoon of vanilla, and a few grinds of black pepper. Cook, stirring, until heated through and

quickly remove from the heat. Stir again and pour over the greens. Toss well.

4 Arrange the pear and squash pieces, overlapping them in a decorative way, around or down the edges of four plates or one platter. Arrange the greens so that they are in a mound in the center of each plate or running alongside the pears and squash. Garnish with cheese, walnuts (or other nuts), and/ or dried cranberries. Serve right away.

PAN-BRAISED FINGERLINGS

WITH MELLOW GARLIC-OLIVE DRESSING AND TUSCAN KALE SALAD

SERVES 3

6 cups stemmed and thinly sliced Tuscan kale leaves (from about 2 bunches)

½ teaspoon kosher salt, plus 2 pinches

3 tablespoons extra-virgin olive oil

1 tablespoon sherry vinegar

1 tablespoon fresh lemon juice

1½ teaspoons black olive tapenade

2 teaspoons honey, or 1½ teaspoons agave nectar

8 large garlic cloves, cut crosswise into 2 or 3 pieces

12 to 14 ounces small fingerling potatoes, cut in half lengthwise

1 to 2 tablespoons roughly chopped fresh mint, to taste

Kale and potatoes make another wonderful warm-salad pairing, and I especially love fingerling potatoes with Tuscan kale. I've discovered over the years that braising, rather than roasting, is the best method for cooking fingerling potatoes. The potatoes don't dry out when cooked this way, and they take on the delicious flavors of whatever they're braised with. The braising doesn't take long. I like to brown the potatoes in oil first and then simmer them in a small amount of liquid until done. It *is* important with this technique not to crowd the pan too tight, which is why I call for 12 to 14 ounces of potatoes (instead of 1 pound) in a medium (10-inch) straight-sided pan. In this recipe, the potatoes are braised with garlic, and then the softened garlic is mashed in the warm pan with an olive tapenade–spiked dressing. The dressing it makes is very tasty on the potatoes and kale, but I must warn you that it is rather rustic looking!

1 Put the kale in a large bowl and season it with a pinch of salt. In a small bowl, whisk together 1 tablespoon of the oil and the vinegar, lemon juice, tapenade, honey, and a big pinch of salt. Drizzle just under half of the dressing over the kale and toss thoroughly. Let sit while you cook the potatoes.

2 In a medium (10-inch) straight-sided sauté pan, heat the remaining 2 tablespoons of oil over medium heat. Add the garlic pieces and sauté just until the pieces begin to turn a light golden brown, 2 to 4 minutes. Sprinkle ½ teaspoon of the salt over the bottom of the pan and arrange the potato halves, cut-side down, in the pan among the garlic

cloves. Cover the pan loosely, leaving the lid partially askew to let a little steam escape, and cook until the bottoms of the potatoes are lightly browned, 5 to 6 minutes. (Rotate the pan occasionally for even browning.)

3 Pour ¾ cup of water into the pan (it will sputter a bit), cover loosely again, and reduce the heat to maintain a moderate simmer. Cook without stirring until the water reduces to just a couple of tablespoons. (Cooking time varies a lot, depending on your stove and pan; begin checking after 8 or 10 minutes, but it may take longer.) Check to see if the potatoes are tender by poking them with a paring knife. If not, add another

¼ cup of water, bring to a simmer, cover loosely again, and cook until the liquid reduces to a couple of tablespoons again, another 3 to 5 minutes.

4 Remove the pan from the heat and gently run a metal spatula under the potatoes to loosen them. Arrange the kale on three plates. Transfer the potatoes to the three plates (leaving the garlic behind in the pan), arranging them in equal portions over the kale. Add the remaining dressing to the warm pan, and use the back of a fork to mash the garlic coarsely and stir into the dressing. Spoon the warm dressing over the potatoes and sprinkle the chopped mint over all.

ROASTED CARROT, BELL PEPPER, AND RED ONION SALAD

WITH ENDIVE, RADICCHIO, AND CARROT TOP–PECAN PESTO DRESSING

SERVES 4

1 pound fresh carrots (tops removed and most of them reserved for the pesto), plus 8 to 12 small sprigs of carrot tops for garnish

1 medium-large red or yellow bell pepper (7 to 8 ounces)

1 medium-large or two small red onions (5 to 6 ounces)

¼ cup plus 1 tablespoon extra-virgin olive oil

½ teaspoon kosher salt

Freshly ground black pepper

½ cup Carrot Top–Pecan Pesto (recipe follows)

1 teaspoon white balsamic vinegar

½ medium head of radicchio, cored and roughly chopped

2 cups arugula

1 medium endive

3 tablespoons coarsely chopped toasted pecans

This delicious warm salad is just the thing to make when you get some lovely carrots with the tops still on from the farmers' market or another nice market. Use the greens to make Carrot Top–Pecan Pesto (page 113), and then roast the roots with peppers and onions, which will caramelize to add sweet flavor. (If you can't use the greens right away, detach them from the roots and store them wrapped in damp cloth in a zip-top bag.) Serve the roasted roots scattered over radicchio, arugula, and endive for colorful presentation. The pesto is fairly thick, so to make a dressing I thin it with a bit more oil and hot water, plus a little vinegar.

1 Preheat the oven to 450°F. Peel the carrots and cut lengthwise into pieces about ½ inch wide and 2 to 3 inches long. Cut the bell pepper into 1½-inch pieces. Peel the onion and cut in half, then cut into ¾-inch wedges, leaving the stem end intact if possible.

2 In a large bowl, combine the carrots, pepper, onion, 3 tablespoons of the oil, salt, and several grinds of black pepper and toss well. Transfer to two 9 x 13-inch baking dishes and arrange in a single layer. (They will be snug, but not too snug.) Bake for 32 to 35 minutes, stirring once or twice, until the carrots are tender and deeply browned and the peppers and onions are softened and browned. Let the veggies cool in the baking dishes for a minute.

3 In a small bowl, whisk the pesto, the remaining 2 tablespoons of olive oil, 2 tablespoons of very hot water, and the vinegar until smooth. (The dressing will still be thick.)

4 Arrange the extra carrot-top sprigs around the edges of a large serving platter. Scatter the radicchio and arugula onto the platter. Cut the endive into quarters, cut out the core, and cut crosswise into 1-inch pieces. Scatter over the other greens. Season with a little salt.

5 Arrange the roasted veggies loosely over the greens. Use a fork or small spoon to scatter as much pesto dressing as you like over the veggies (you may not use it all), and garnish with the pecans. Bring the platter to the table and toss gently together (if you like) right before serving.

Carrot Top–Pecan Pesto

MAKES 1 CUP

1 garlic clove, peeled

2 cups packed carrot tops (leaves and tender stems only), washed and dried (from 1 large or 2 medium bunches of carrots)

½ cup packed fresh parsley or fresh cilantro (leaves and tender stems), or a combination

⅓ cup coarsely chopped toasted pecans

½ cup coarsely grated Parmesan cheese

½ teaspoon kosher salt

Freshly ground black pepper

1 teaspoon white balsamic vinegar

⅓ cup plus 1 tablespoon olive oil

Yes, you can eat carrot tops! I get asked that question a lot. I first made carrot-top pesto for a "root to leaf" story I did for *Vegetarian Times* magazine a few years ago. My latest version features toasted pecans for a great depth of flavor. I like to combine the carrot tops with a little bit of another herb such as parsley (which will keep a bright green color) or cilantro. Covered tightly, this will keep in the fridge for a week. Use it in a roasted vegetable salad, toss it with whole wheat linguine, or mix some with goat cheese to make a great spread for toast. This pesto is a thick one, so depending on how you use it, you may want to thin it a bit with hot water or more olive oil—just take care not to dilute the flavor too much.

In the bowl of a food processor, pulse the garlic clove until minced. Add the carrot tops, parsley, and pecans and process until finely chopped. Add the Parmesan and process to combine. Add the salt, several grinds of black pepper, and 1 teaspoon vinegar. Process to combine. With the motor running, gradually pour the oil through the feed tube in a thin stream. Process until incorporated. The pesto will be quite thick. To store, transfer to a small bowl and top with a piece of plastic wrap. Press the plastic wrap to the surface of the pesto so that it is in direct contact all over, and store in the refrigerator.

ROSEMARY ROASTED CAULIFLOWER AND FRISÉE SALAD

SERVES 2

4 cups very small cauliflower florets

3 tablespoons extra-virgin olive oil

1 tablespoon chopped fresh rosemary

½ teaspoon kosher salt, plus a pinch

4 cups torn leaves of frisée (about 1 small head)

½ teaspoon minced fresh garlic

1 tablespoon white balsamic vinegar

2 teaspoons Dijon mustard

Freshly ground black pepper

½ red apple (such as Pink Lady or Honey Crisp), cut into thin slices

¼ cup Rosemary Roasted Walnuts (page 107)

Crisp nutty nuggets of roasted cauliflower are like vegetable candy, and this pretty and flavorful salad is a great excuse to eat them for dinner! I love curly frisée, especially with a mustard vinaigrette (a classic French bistro combination), and the pale leaves are so perfect for a "winter white" salad. But frisée can be hard to find, so if you need to, improvise with a combination of escarole and endive—or anything that can take the heat of a warm dressing. Fresh rosemary is the perfect bridge, connecting the roasted cauliflower, the warm dressing, and our delicious Rosemary Roasted Walnuts. Enjoy this satisfying supper on a chilly winter evening. Another time, if you happen to have a few cooked French lentils around, they make a great addition to this salad, too.

1 Preheat the oven to 450°F. Line a rimmed baking sheet with parchment paper. In a large bowl, combine the cauliflower, 2 tablespoons of the oil, 2 teaspoons of the rosemary, and ½ teaspoon of the salt and toss well. Transfer to the prepared baking sheet, scraping the bowl with a silicone spatula to include all the rosemary and oil. (Keep the bowl nearby.) Arrange the cauliflower in a single layer. Bake for 22 to 25 minutes, until well browned and crisp.

2 Put the frisée in the reserved mixing bowl and season with a pinch of salt. Place two dinner plates on your countertop.

3 In a small skillet, heat the remaining 1 tablespoon of oil over medium heat. Add the minced garlic and the remaining 1 teaspoon of rosemary and cook until fragrant and just softened, about 1 minute. Remove from the heat and whisk in the vinegar and mustard. Drizzle the hot mixture over the frisée and toss well. Grind a generous amount of black pepper over the frisée and toss again.

4 Mound a lofty portion of frisée in the center of each plate. Arrange the roasted cauliflower around the frisée. Tuck the apple slices into the salad and garnish with the roasted walnuts. Serve right away.

CHOPPED WINTER SALAD

OF ESCAROLE, ARUGULA, BLUE CHEESE, PECANS, AND ROASTED GRAPES

SERVES 4

FOR THE SALAD

2 cups seedless grapes

¼ cup extra-virgin olive oil

1 tablespoon plus ½ teaspoon sherry vinegar

1½ teaspoons maple syrup

Kosher salt

1 large shallot, peeled and cut lengthwise into six wedges, leaving the stem intact

1 tablespoon orange juice

1 teaspoon Dijon mustard

4 cups chopped escarole (inner light parts), well washed

4 cups arugula

½ medium head of radicchio, chopped or sliced

½ cup Stilton or Roquefort cheese, crumbled while still cold

½ cup chopped toasted pecans or walnuts

FOR THE CROUTONS

2 cups small (½-inch) cubes of pumpernickel bread

1 tablespoon olive oil

1 tablespoon unsalted butter, melted

I love chopped salads—they're jaunty and easy to eat, plus you get all the flavors and textures of the salad in every satisfying bite. You might think of a chopped salad as a summertime thing, but winter is a great time for a salad like this one, which has hearty escarole and arugula as its base and blue cheese, pecans, and roasted grapes to fill it out. (Walnuts would work just as well as the pecans.) Croutons are important in this salad for adding both heft and crunchy texture; I've suggested using pumpernickel bread for the croutons, but rye or any whole-grain bread, would work, too. You can make the croutons ahead and keep them in the freezer.

1 Preheat the oven to 425°F. Line a rimmed baking sheet with parchment paper. In a medium bowl, toss the grapes with 2 teaspoons of the olive oil, ½ teaspoon of the vinegar, ½ teaspoon of the maple syrup, and a pinch of kosher salt. Arrange on the prepared baking sheet. In the same bowl, toss the shallots with 1 teaspoon of the oil and a pinch of salt and arrange next to the grapes on the baking sheet. Bake for 25 to 30 minutes, until the grapes have shrunken and are browned in spots and the shallots are well browned. Let the grapes and shallots cool for a few minutes, then coarsely chop the shallots. Lower the oven to 375°F.

2 In a small bowl, whisk together the remaining 3 tablespoons of olive oil, the remaining 1 tablespoon of vinegar, the remaining

1 teaspoon of maple syrup, the orange juice, the mustard, and a big pinch of kosher salt and set aside.

3 Make the croutons: Line a rimmed baking sheet with parchment paper. Put the bread cubes into a medium bowl, drizzle with the olive oil and melted butter, and toss. Season with salt and toss again. Spread the bread cubes on the prepared baking sheet and bake at 375°F for about 12 minutes, until crisp.

4 In a large bowl, combine the escarole, arugula, radicchio, blue cheese, and walnuts and the roasted grapes and chopped shallots and toss well. Add the dressing and croutons and toss to combine. Transfer to four bowls.

VEGGIES + TOAST

THERE'S something inherently calming about eating toast for supper. It's simple and manageable—tidy and compact. You can wrap your head around the whole idea. And then there's just the vaguest notion from childhood that you're getting a special treat. I'm especially fond of toast, because it was one of the first things I mastered in the kitchen. For some reason I was allowed to use the toaster oven before any other cooking equipment, and my specialty was Bubbling Cheese Toast. I think this was basically a slice of American cheese on top of a piece of Pepperidge Farm sandwich bread, broiled. I liked the burnt edges.

Here's a promise: The recipes in this chapter will be significantly tastier and more satisfying than my childhood cheese toast! (Or "toastie," I should call it, as the Brits do.) And yes, these toasts will take a little bit longer to make than the cheese toastie, but in exchange you will truly get supper. You'll have grilled asparagus and roasted vegetables. There'll be avocado toast, and hummus, too. (Yippee!) You'll turn naan into pizza and ciabatta into a salad. You'll come to appreciate how good bread, toasted or grilled to bring out its subtle caramel flavors and crisp texture, is the nearly perfect foil for the juicy, earthy, smoky flavors of vegetables. And you'll never again think of toast as simply the ubiquitous diner-breakfast sidekick. In fact, you'll be making up your own "toasties" soon.

Tips and Strategies for Toast

GOOD BREAD, GOOD TOAST.

Twenty years ago, I couldn't have written a chapter on toast for a cookbook, because good-quality bread wasn't nearly as widely available as it is today. With good bread comes excellent toast—this is why you now see whole cookbooks and entire restaurant menus devoted to the subject of toast! How you define good bread is of course a bit subjective, and unfortunately, food marketers have unscrupulously hijacked the useful term "artisan." The good news is that you have antennae, and you know what you like.

Here on the Island we don't have a great artisan bakery (the best bread is baked in private homes or in small batches and sold at farmers' markets), but all our grocery stores import freshly baked bread from bakeries on the mainland. I'm grateful that I can get a decent ciabatta and a good crusty multigrain, whole wheat, or white peasant loaf nearly any day I look for it. (As a bonus, these loaves are sometimes sliced—maybe a little thinner than I'd like but certainly more accurately and quickly than I can do myself.) When I see challah bread I buy it, and some days I might pounce on an olive loaf or a baguette. Also, we do have a food shop that bakes gluten-free bread several days a week. (If you are avoiding gluten, it's certainly worth your while to track down a bakery like this, which will offer tastier options than the grocery store.)

Generally speaking, at the grocery store, if you steer away from the sandwich bread aisle, where highly refined flours and multitudinous preservatives (not to mention soft, squishy textures) reign, and steer toward the rack where the boules and baguettes have arrived fresh from the local bakery, you will be on the right path to finding good bread. (Though, I have to confess, I'm loath to give up my English muffins. I probably never will!) Look for a nice dark crust, the first sign of a great loaf. (A serious crust in itself helps preserve a loaf until it is cut.) The shape of a boule should be evenly domed, indicating it was properly proofed. If the bread is sliced, look for an airy crumb that's consistently distributed in the loaf. And speaking of boules, a nice, large round or oval loaf is perfect for our toast suppers because it yields long, wide pieces when cut crosswise— lots of surface area for us to top. Because ciabatta ("slipper bread") and some peasant loaves can be narrow, I sometimes cut them on a sharp diagonal to make longer slices.

You will have to wander to the outskirts of the bread aisle in a traditional grocery store to pick up naan and pita bread. I've always loved naan, the traditional Indian flatbread, and I am thrilled it is available in grocery stores now, as it makes a most excellent, quick grilled pizza. (I like Stonefire-brand naan, which comes in two sizes, but Trader Joe's also stocks naan in its freezer section.)

SLICE IT, FREEZE IT.

When you get your naan home, freeze it. When you get your multigrain or your challah home, slice it and freeze it. Hint-hint: freeze bread. I learned this simple trick years ago from my mom, Perky, who enthusiastically pursued bread baking via her James Beard cookbooks. We'd eat a few warm slices of freshly baked cheese bread or cinnamon bread, then she would carefully wrap and freeze the remaining slices for us to eat later. She froze all her sandwich bread, her rolls, everything.

Today my stomach flips a little and my teeth hurt when I see friends stashing bread in the refrigerator. I'm exaggerating. Still, because I feel it is polite not to say anything, I have to endure a bit of internal anxiety all the same: nothing makes bread go stale—and tough—faster than the fridge. (It has to do with a chemical realignment of the starch molecules that happens at cold temperatures but not at freezing temps.) You are better off keeping your bread at room temperature than in the fridge, but then you risk your bread molding before you can eat it all. So, just leave a few slices out (wrap them loosely in plastic) and freeze the rest.

Before freezing your bread, be sure to slice it first, if it hasn't been sliced already. (A long, sturdy serrated bread knife is a purchase you won't regret.) A thickness of about 1/2 inch is fine for denser breads, but a lighter, more airy loaf can be cut a little thicker, say about 3/4 inch. To freeze, wrap two or three slices in a few layers of plastic wrap and put those little bundles in a big zip-top bag. Label it with the type of bread and the date. Then you can pull out just what you need and it will defrost quickly. Bread keeps in the freezer (depending on how cold your freezer is and how frequently it is opened) for several weeks.

GO FOR GOLDEN.

As much as I love toast, I don't own a toaster, or even (sigh) a toaster oven. I am, however, very friendly with my broiler and my grill. (In a pinch, one can always "toast" in a frying pan, too.) The reason that I am happy with the oven broiler and grill is that I most often want to brush oil, or a little melted butter, on one or both sides of a slice of bread before browning it (and it's not a good idea to put fat into a toaster). You can always drizzle oil or melted butter on after toasting instead, but if you do it beforehand, it creates a slightly more interesting texture—sort of a moist/crisp contrast.

Also, if you grill or broil your toast (as opposed to sending it into a deep, dark hole), you can keep an eye on it and manipulate it for even cooking (if necessary) by moving it around with tongs. And you'll definitely want to keep an eye on your toast to get that nice, deep golden color for the best flavor. On the grill, the edges of the bread will begin to get a little charry, which adds a smoky note. Coloring up happens fast, so don't make a telephone call or take a shower while you're toasting!

Broiling bread has one additional advantage: you can make toast, top it, and then return the toast to the broiler to brown the topping or melt the cheese. (For more on toasting and grilling bread, see page 238.)

For the Pantry

With hopes that so many options won't create an overwhelming quandary for you, here are my favorite breads, listed as inspiration as you start your own stash. As with all our veggie-supper pantry lists, the goal here is to get stuff in the door ahead of time so that we need only pirouette in the kitchen to find your supper ingredients. The (freezer) door is wide open for customization, so start sampling your neighborhood bread to find what you like.

I've organized my picks according to what I *usually* have in my freezer and what I *often* have in my freezer. Of course, these are the breads that are featured in the recipes, too. And then I've added a wish list—the kinds of loaves I might score if I arrive early at the farmers' market or stop in at an artisan bakery on a day trip to Boston or Providence. The world of bread is vast, though, so I have no doubt you will expand this list many times over. And last, I've included a short list of favorite accessory ingredients for toast. Not many are needed, as the vegetables themselves, and some delicious homemade spreads we're going to make, will take top billing.

The Breads

(ALMOST) ALWAYS IN MY FREEZER

Challah

Ciabatta

Crusty white peasant bread

Crusty multigrain peasant bread

Crusty whole wheat peasant bread

Naan

OFTEN IN MY FREEZER

French baguette

Pita bread

Sourdough bread

WISH I HAD A BIG ENOUGH FREEZER FOR

Cheese bread

Focaccia

Nut and dried-fruit bread

Olive or rosemary-olive bread

Specialty or ancient-grains bread

Accessory Ingredients

Blue cheese

Extra-virgin olive oil

Feta cheese

Fresh tender and woody herbs

Honey

Maple syrup

Parmesan cheese

Pecans, walnuts, and pine nuts

Sea salt

Unsalted butter

SAVORY FRENCH TOAST

WITH SPINACH AND STRAWBERRY-MAPLE-BALSAMIC SAUCE

MAKES 4 TOASTS; SERVES 4

2 tablespoons unsalted butter

4 large eggs

⅔ cup half-and-half

½ teaspoon coarsely chopped fresh thyme

½ teaspoon freshly grated orange zest

½ teaspoon pure vanilla extract

2 tablespoons plus ½ teaspoon balsamic vinegar

½ teaspoon kosher salt, plus more for sprinkling

Freshly ground black pepper

4 large slices of challah bread (each about 1 inch thick; use the long slices from the middle of the loaf)

2 tablespoons maple syrup (preferably darker grade)

1⅓ cups sliced fresh strawberries (small berries are nice)

2 teaspoons grapeseed or vegetable oil

2 cups packed baby spinach

¼ cup crème fraîche, fromage blanc, ricotta, or whipped fresh goat cheese

2 to 3 tablespoons chopped toasted pecans

I know, I know—it's not like you're going to eat French toast every night, but occasionally you need something fun. This savory version has a custard lightly flavored with thyme, orange, and vanilla and a tangy topping of strawberries heated with maple syrup and balsamic vinegar. A bed of spinach hides under the toast, and a dollop of crème fraîche or ricotta adds a creamy note. For me, challah is the only choice for French toast, because it has a texture that's both tender and strong at the same time. Along with that alluring yeasty flavor, it handles a soak in custard and a fry in the pan better than any bread I know.

1 Cut 1 tablespoon of the butter into 4 equal pieces and return to the refrigerator to keep chilled.

2 In a medium bowl, whisk together the eggs, half-and-half, thyme, orange zest, vanilla, ½ teaspoon of the vinegar, ½ teaspoon of salt, and several grinds of black pepper. Arrange the challah slices in a shallow baking dish in a single layer and pour the egg mixture over them. Let them sit for 10 to 15 minutes, turning over once during soaking.

3 In a small skillet, combine the remaining 2 tablespoons of vinegar with the maple syrup and the strawberries. Heat over low heat, stirring, just until hot. Remove from the heat and stir in the 4 pieces of chilled butter.

4 In a large (12-inch) nonstick skillet, heat the remaining 1 tablespoon of butter and the oil over medium-low heat. Once hot, arrange the soaked challah slices in the pan and sprinkle the tops with salt. Cook until golden brown on the bottom, 4 to 5 minutes. Carefully flip the slices, season with a bit more salt, and cook until the bottom is golden brown, 3 to 5 minutes.

5 Arrange ½ cup of spinach leaves in a small pile in the center of each of four serving plates. (Save several spinach leaves for garnish.) Place 1 piece of French toast atop each serving of spinach. Top each with a dollop of the crème fraîche, garnish with a few spinach leaves, and spoon the warm strawberry sauce over all. Sprinkle with toasted pecans and serve right away.

AVOCADO TOAST

WITH BABY KALE, BLUE CHEESE, PECANS, QUICK-PICKLED RADISHES, AND HONEY

MAKES 2 TOASTS

2 radishes, trimmed and cut into very thin slices

1½ teaspoons fresh lemon juice

Pinch of cane sugar

Kosher salt

1 tablespoon extra-virgin olive oil, plus more for brushing

2 slices of multigrain bread (each about ½ inch thick, preferably oval slices about 6 inches long)

3 tablespoons good-quality blue cheese, like Great Hill Blue, crumbled

1 small ripe-but-firm avocado, cut in half and sliced

1 cup baby kale leaves, preferably a frilly variety like Red Russian

1 to 2 tablespoons finely chopped toasted pecans

Local honey, for drizzling

Don't get me started on this one—I can eat these avocado toasts literally every day for a week, even more. Love. So many good flavors and textures all together, and good looks, too. (Avocado toast deserves special treatment, after all, because it has risen to cult status.) Two fun things here: super-quick "pickled" radish slices (in lemon juice, sugar, and salt) and a drizzle of honey at the finish. With the salty blue cheese, creamy avocado, toasty pecans, and nutty baby kale, this is one satisfying supper. I use my favorite multigrain bread for this toast (the one that's made at a local bakery but sold in the grocery store). It has a dense texture, with delicious nubbins of seeds and grains, making it the perfect foil for the richness of the avocado and blue cheese.

1 Preheat the oven broiler to high. In a small bowl, combine the sliced radishes with ½ teaspoon of the lemon juice, the sugar, and a pinch of salt and toss well. Set aside.

2 In another small bowl, whisk together the remaining 1 teaspoon of lemon juice, 1 tablespoon of the olive oil, and a pinch of salt.

3 Place the bread slices on a small baking sheet and brush one side of each piece generously with olive oil (about 1 teaspoon per slice). Broil until nicely browned. Flip over and broil other side until lightly browned.

4 While the toast is still warm, use a sandwich knife to smear 1½ tablespoons of blue cheese on the olive oil–brushed side of each piece of toast. Arrange the avocado slices over the cheese (half an avocado per piece), season with a bit of salt, and drizzle with a tiny bit of the lemon and oil mixture. In a small bowl, toss the kale with the remaining lemon and oil mixture and mound it on top of the avocado, distributing it evenly between the slices. Drain the radish slices and tuck them among the kale leaves. Sprinkle the pecans over all, and drizzle lightly with honey. (A fork is a great tool for drizzling honey. Gently rewarm your honey if it has become grainy.) Cut the toast slices in half and serve.

CAESAR SALAD TOAST

WITH GRILLED ASPARAGUS, LITTLE GEM LETTUCE, AND CIABATTA

SERVES 4

16 to 20 medium asparagus spears, trimmed to about 6 inches long

2 to 3 teaspoons extra-virgin olive oil

Kosher salt

4 slices of ciabatta or other peasant bread (each about ½ to ¾ inch thick, preferably oval slices about 6 inches long)

⅓ to ½ cup Creamy Blender Caesar Dressing (page 103)

2 heads of Little Gem, Ruby Glow, or other mini-romaine lettuces, leaves separated, or about 16 to 20 leaves of any combination of Bibb, romaine, and/or red-leaf lettuce

¼ cup finely grated Parmesan cheese

This all-in-one salad and toast is just all that, I promise. The creamy, lemony blender dressing bridges the nutty asparagus, crisp toast, and cool lettuce, and together the elements combine in a beautiful and delicious way. Ciabatta is the perfect bread here because of its light, airy, crunchy quality—excellent for capturing the dressing. I created this recipe originally to showcase Little Gem, a lovely mini-head lettuce that has the crispness of a romaine and the sweet, buttery flavor of a Bibb. You will find it (and other mini-lettuces) more and more at farmers' markets, and it also appears in grocery stores under the name Sweet Gem. If you don't see it, no worries. Use Bibb lettuce instead, perhaps mixed with a few inner leaves of a red-leaf lettuce. Grill, broil, or sauté the asparagus for equally great results.

1 Preheat the oven broiler to high or a gas grill to medium-high heat. If your asparagus spears are especially thick, cut them lengthwise down the middle. Toss the asparagus in 2 to 3 teaspoons of oil, just enough to coat, and season with a big pinch of salt. Arrange on a baking sheet if broiling. Arrange directly on the hot grill grate if grilling. Broil or grill (covered) until the asparagus turns bright green and begins to brown and char in places, about 4 to 6 minutes total, flipping or rolling over with tongs halfway through cooking. (Alternatively, to retain a brighter color and slightly firmer texture, you can sauté the asparagus spears with 2 teaspoons of oil in a large skillet over medium-high heat, stirring and tossing, for about 5 minutes total.) Transfer to a plate.

2 Brush both sides of the bread slices with some of the dressing (about ½ to 1 teaspoon per side, depending on the size of your bread slices). Sprinkle one side with salt. Arrange the bread on a baking sheet if broiling. Arrange directly on the hot grill grate if grilling. Broil or grill until golden brown, about 2 minutes per side.

3 Put the lettuce leaves in a large, shallow mixing bowl. Add a pinch of salt and about 1 tablespoon of the dressing. Toss gently with your hands until the leaves are nicely coated. You might want to add 1 to 2 teaspoons more dressing, but take care not to overdress.

4 Put a piece of toast on each of four plates. Arrange a few dressed lettuce leaves next to and just over the toast on each plate. On each plate, drape 4 to 5 asparagus spears over the lettuce and toast. Spoon or brush a little more dressing over the asparagus and garnish each plate with 1 tablespoon of the Parmesan cheese. Serve right away.

GRILLED MULTIGRAIN TOAST

WITH WHIPPED LEMON-THYME FETA, GRILLED SUMMER SQUASH, AND ARUGULA

MAKES 4 TOASTS

3 tablespoons extra-virgin olive oil, plus more for brushing

1 tablespoon chopped fresh parsley or mint, plus more to taste (optional)

2 teaspoons black olive tapenade

2 teaspoons minced fresh garlic

2 teaspoons honey, plus more for drizzling

1 tablespoon lemon juice

¼ teaspoon kosher salt, plus more for sprinkling

¾ to 1 pound summer squash (any kind, any color, including zucchini and pattypans), trimmed and cut into ⅜-inch-thick slices at a sharp angle

4 slices of multigrain bread (each about ½ inch thick and 6 inches long)

1 to 1½ cups baby arugula

6 to 8 tablespoons Whipped Lemon-Thyme Feta (recipe follows), at room temperature

I love to grow a colorful selection of summer squash: bright yellow Golden Arrow zucchini and Sunburst pattypans, deep green Jackpot and Raven zucchini, and the lovely crookneck called Zephyr. And because the flavor of squash is best not long after picking, I like to head straight to the grill when it starts coming in. I pop a few slices of multigrain bread on the grill, too, and with a smear of Whipped Lemon-Thyme Feta (so good—page 130) and a bit of arugula, I've got a satisfying early-summer supper.

1 In a shallow mixing bowl, combine 3 tablespoons of olive oil and the parsley (if using), tapenade, garlic, 2 teaspoons of honey, the lemon juice, and ¼ teaspoon of salt and stir well. Add the squash slices and toss. Let sit, stirring occasionally, about 25 minutes.

2 Brush both sides of the bread slices generously with oil. Sprinkle with salt.

3 Preheat a gas grill to medium-high heat. If the squash slices are small, place a grill topper in the grill to heat so that you won't lose your squash through the grill grates. Arrange the squash directly on the grill grate or on the topper, reserving the marinade. Cook until the bottoms are marked, 3 to 5 minutes. Flip gently with tongs and continue to cook until the bottoms are marked and golden, 2 to 3 minutes. (Cooking times may be a bit longer if using a grill topper.) Transfer the squash to a plate.

4 Arrange the bread slices on the grill and cook until marked and browned around the edges, about 2 minutes. Flip over and cook the other side until marked and brown, about 2 minutes.

5 In a medium bowl, toss the arugula with a pinch of salt and a few teaspoons of the leftover squash marinade.

6 Spread 1½ to 2 tablespoons of the whipped feta on each piece of toast. Arrange the dressed arugula leaves over the feta. (Save several arugula leaves for garnish.) Arrange the squash slices, overlapping, over the arugula. Garnish each piece of toast with 1 or 2 more arugula leaves and drizzle with a little bit of honey, if desired. Cut the toasts in half or, for easiest eating, crosswise into five or six pieces and serve.

Whipped Lemon-Thyme Feta

MAKES 1⅓ CUPS

¼ cup extra-virgin olive oil, plus more if needed

1 large garlic clove, cut into thin slices

¼ teaspoon red pepper flakes

½ pound feta cheese, broken into small chunks

1 teaspoon freshly grated lemon zest

1 tablespoon loosely packed fresh thyme leaves

1 to 2 teaspoons chopped fresh parsley or mint, or a combination (optional)

Bursting with flavor, this multitasking spread is a summer staple in my fridge. I first made it to liven up all the zucchini I always grill when my squash plants start yielding like crazy. But soon I was adding some of the leftover spread to eggs and egg sandwiches, then I smeared it on grilled naan (Grilled Naan "Pizza" with Quick-Roasted Cherry Tomatoes, Whipped Lemon-Thyme Feta, Cucumbers, and Basil, page 131) and tossed it with warm pasta. So yummy! And I discovered that it keeps really well for a week in the fridge. Start with good-quality feta, and crumble it just before putting it into the food processor. (Don't buy pre-crumbled feta, which is generally lower quality and saltier.) Some feta is denser than others, so keep pulsing and processing until you reach a spread-like consistency, and add a little more olive oil if you need to.

1 In a small skillet or saucepan, combine the oil, garlic, and red pepper flakes and place over medium-low heat. Heat, stirring, until the oil is bubbling and the garlic is fragrant, 3 to 4 minutes. Remove from the heat and let cool until almost at room temperature, for 5 to 10 minutes.

2 Put the feta cheese, lemon zest, thyme, and the infused oil into the bowl of a food processor and process, pulsing several times and stopping to scrape down the sides repeatedly, until well combined and lightened in texture. Some fetas will need more processing. If the mixture is still dense, add a bit more olive oil. Add the chopped parsley (if using) and pulse until well mixed.

3 Transfer to a storage container (I like glass for this), cover tightly, and keep in the refrigerator for up to 1 week.

GRILLED NAAN "PIZZA"

WITH QUICK-ROASTED CHERRY TOMATOES, WHIPPED LEMON-THYME FETA, CUCUMBERS, AND BASIL

SERVES 2

2 large naans (4 to 5 ounces each) or 4 small naans (3 ounces each), thawed if frozen

Extra-virgin olive oil

Kosher salt or coarse sea salt

⅔ cup Whipped Lemon-Thyme Feta (page 130)

1 to 1½ cups (1 to 2 recipes) Quick-Roasted Cherry Tomatoes (recipe follows)

1 small or ½ large slicing cucumber, unpeeled, cut into very thin slices

2 tablespoons thinly sliced fresh basil, mint, or oregano, or small whole leaves

I've been a grilled pizza fanatic ever since I learned to make it at my first restaurant job. So I flipped out when I discovered that store-bought naan, tossed on the grill for just a couple minutes (Grilled Naan with Grilled Mushrooms, Blue Cheese, and Spinach, page 140), does an amazing job of approximating thin-crust grilled pizza. No need to make dough and wait for it to proof! I also discovered that grilled naan and my Whipped Lemon-Thyme Feta (page 130) are a great pairing, so when I start harvesting the first cucumbers from the garden, this topping combination is a no-brainer. For the most intriguing flavor, I add a batch (or two) of Quick-Roasted Cherry Tomatoes (page 133), but in a pinch, sliced fresh sandwich tomatoes will do. Naan sizes vary, so use the quantities in this recipe as a guideline.

1 Preheat a gas grill to medium or medium-high heat. If using the larger naans, cut each in half crosswise so that you have four half-moon shaped pieces. Brush the naans with oil on both sides and sprinkle with salt.

2 Put the naans directly on the grill grate and cook just until grill marks appear and the bottom is starting to turn golden, 1½ to 2 minutes. Flip over and cook for 1 more minute. (You want the naan to be grilled enough on the first side to begin losing its flexibility, but not so much that it gets stiff. Leave the second side somewhat soft.) Remove from the grill.

3 While the naans are still hot, spread one side of each piece with 2 to 3 tablespoons of the whipped feta. Arrange an equal portion of the roasted tomatoes (slightly overlapping for a pretty look if you like) over the feta, leaving some of the feta peeking out around the edges. Arrange enough cucumber slices, slightly overlapping, to cover the tomatoes on each "pizza." Sprinkle the cucumber with salt, drizzle with a little olive oil, and garnish each with ½ tablespoon of the fresh herbs. Eat right away.

Quick-Roasted Cherry Tomatoes

MAKES ¾ TO 1 CUP

8 to 10 ounces ripe cherry tomatoes, cut in half (a generous 2 cups of tomato halves)

1 tablespoon olive oil

Large pinch of kosher salt

Roasted tomatoes are my absolute favorite savory flavor boost—for anything. And when I'm in a hurry, the quickest way I can get that flavor is by roasting the smallest tomatoes of all: cherries. You can roast cherry or grape tomatoes of any size, but slightly larger ones work better here. If yours are all very small, reduce the oven temperature to 425°F and the cooking time to 18 to 22 minutes. Best of all, you can store these little flavor bombs for several days in the fridge and use them in everything, from salads to frittatas.

Preheat the oven to 450°F. Cover a heavy-duty rimmed baking sheet with a piece of parchment paper. In a medium bowl, toss the cherry tomatoes with the oil and salt. Arrange the cherry tomatoes, cut-side up, in a single layer on the prepared baking sheet. Bake for 22 to 24 minutes, until the cherry tomatoes are shrunken and a bit charred around the edges. Let cool for 10 minutes or so on the baking sheet before removing them. (If some of the cherry tomatoes stick to the parchment paper, lift up the paper and push the tomatoes off from behind.) Use the roasted tomatoes right away, or store in the fridge for 5 to 6 days or in the freezer for up to 3 months.

DOUBLE TOMATO AND WHITE BEAN BRUSCHETTA SALAD

SERVES 4

3 cups cored and diced, ripe and juicy beefsteak tomatoes (about 1½ pounds)

¾ cup cooked or canned small white beans, drained and rinsed

¼ cup drained and chopped sun-dried or roasted tomatoes (such as Quick-Roasted Cherry Tomatoes, page 133)

¼ cup plus 1 tablespoon extra-virgin olive oil

1 tablespoon plus 1 teaspoon minced fresh garlic

¼ cup thinly sliced fresh basil leaves, plus small leaves for garnish, if you like

1 teaspoon sherry or red wine vinegar

¼ teaspoon kosher salt, plus more for sprinkling

8 slices of French baguette (¾ inch thick and 5 to 6 inches long, cut at a sharp angle)

2 cups baby greens of any sort (kale, arugula, mizuna, spinach, pea shoots, etc.)

Call me a bruschetta freak. Ripe, juicy beefsteak tomatoes + garlic + basil + toasted bread is a nearly perfect combination, as far as I'm concerned. But luckily, bruschetta is a generous dish, too, and it doesn't mind being stretched and reinterpreted a bit. For a filling supper—and a pretty presentation—I add a few white beans to the mix and garnish with baby greens. I also underline the flavor of the tomatoes by adding chopped sun-dried or roasted tomatoes to the fresh mix. (It's a great flavor-building trick—try doing it with salsa, too.) I use diagonal slices of a baguette here, but you could experiment with other breads. No matter what you choose, be sure it's well toasted—or, in this case, grilled. That juicy tomato topping needs a crisp, crusty bread for contrast. I should also say that I'm afraid this recipe is not for the garlic-averse—consider yourself forewarned!

1 Preheat a gas grill to medium heat.

2 In a medium bowl, combine the tomatoes, beans, sun-dried tomatoes, 2 tablespoons of the oil, 2 teaspoons of the garlic, the sliced basil, the vinegar, and ¼ teaspoon of salt and stir well. Set aside.

3 In a small bowl, stir the remaining 2 teaspoons of garlic with the remaining 3 tablespoons of oil. Brush one side of each baguette slice generously with the garlic oil. Sprinkle lightly with salt. Place the baguette slices directly on the grill grate with the oil side down. Cook until golden brown on the bottom, 1½ to 2 minutes. Flip over and cook until the other side is golden, 1 to 2 minutes more.

4 Arrange four plates on your countertop. Sprinkle the greens over or around the plates. Put two grilled baguette slices on each plate, and spoon the tomato-bean mixture evenly over them (you might be left with some extra). Let the salads sit for a few minutes to allow the bread to soak up some of the tomato juices. Garnish with small basil leaves (if using) and serve.

VEGGIES + TOAST

ROASTED EGGPLANT, GOAT CHEESE, PINE NUT, AND PEASANT TOAST

WITH BASIL "PESTO" OIL

SERVES 4

8 ounces globe eggplant (about ½ large eggplant)

2 tablespoons extra-virgin olive oil, plus more for brushing

½ teaspoon kosher salt, plus more for sprinkling

4 large slices of peasant bread or olive bread (each about ½ inch thick)

3 ounces fresh goat cheese

¼ cup Basil "Pesto" Oil (page 13)

3 tablespoons toasted pine nuts

In late summer, when all the colorful eggplants are ripening, there's plenty of fresh basil around, and I'm looking for light suppers with deep flavor, this toast is a staple for me. Combining roasted eggplant, basil, goat cheese, and pine nuts is a no-brainer—these four were made for each other. I give eggplant slices my "quick-roast" treatment so that they're ready in about 25 minutes. Once I toast the bread, I spread the goat cheese on quickly so that it can get nice and creamy between the crunchy toast and the still-warm eggplant slices. (Eat it right away, too!) Feel free to grill the bread rather than broil it if you like.

1 Preheat the oven to 450°F. Line a heavy-duty rimmed baking sheet with parchment paper. Trim the eggplant and score the skin by dragging a fork down it lengthwise all the way around. If the eggplant is large and plump, cut it into quarters lengthwise; otherwise, cut it in half lengthwise. Cut the quarters or halves crosswise into slices about ⅜ inch thick. Put the slices into a medium bowl, drizzle with the olive oil and add ½ teaspoon of salt and toss well. Arrange the slices in a single layer on the prepared baking sheet. Bake for 20 to 22 minutes, flipping the slices over halfway through baking if you like, until the eggplant is tender, shrunken, and lightly browned.

2 Move an oven rack to the top position and preheat the oven broiler to high. Brush the bread slices generously with olive oil on both sides and sprinkle with salt. Arrange on a baking sheet. Broil until the tops are golden brown, about 2 minutes. Flip the slices over with tongs and broil the other side until lightly brown, about 2 minutes.

3 Remove the toast from the broiler and immediately spread one side of each piece with goat cheese, dividing it equally among the slices. Spoon 1 teaspoon of basil oil over the goat cheese on each piece of toast. Top each piece with about 2 teaspoons of pine nuts. Next, arrange the eggplant slices over the pine nuts and goat cheese, and drizzle about 2 teaspoons of the basil oil over the eggplant on each slice.

4 Cut the toast slices in half and serve right away.

WARM CIABATTA TOASTS

WITH LEMONY CHICKPEA HUMMUS AND SAUTÉED VEGGIES

MAKES 2 TOASTS

2 slices of ciabatta (¾ to 1 inch thick and 6 to 7 inches long, cut at a sharp angle)

1 to 2 teaspoons extra-virgin olive oil, plus more for brushing

Kosher salt or sea salt

⅓ to ½ cup Lemony Chickpea Hummus (recipe follows)

1 teaspoon to 1 tablespoon unsalted butter (optional)

1 cup very thinly sliced veggies (choose one or two of the following: kale or collards, brussels sprouts, broccoli raab [tender tops only], broccoli or cauliflower, carrots, peppers, shallots, onions, mushrooms, baby spinach or chard leaves, or whole shishito peppers) (see Note)

1 tablespoon pine nuts or sliced almonds (optional)

¼ teaspoon freshly grated lemon or lime zest (optional)

2 tablespoons Roasted Chickpeas (page 95, optional)

Pea shoots, fresh Italian parsley leaves, or baby greens (optional)

Ciabatta—crisp on the outside, airy and chewy on the inside—is my favorite bread (as you might have already guessed), and I always keep a sliced loaf in the freezer. Then, on a cool night, I can make one of these savory toasts, with my Lemony Chickpea Hummus, a topping of sautéed veggies, and a garnish or two. (There are lots of combos—the choice is yours.) You might not think of pairing hummus with cooked vegetables and warm toast, but hummus is actually delicious as a cool-weather condiment. Try these toasts with a combination of brussels sprouts, shallots, and pine nuts, with a topping of kale and roasted chickpeas, or with any of the combinations suggested here. (Warm hummus is also delicious with melted butter—yes!—especially brown butter, so I've included instructions for making a super-quick batch of "brown-butter nuts" to top the veggies with.) These toasts are also great with Quick-Roasted Cherry Tomatoes (page 133). Any way you make them, these toasts are a compact and satisfying supper. Double or triple the recipe as you like.

1 Move an oven rack to the top position, 4 to 5 inches from the broiler element, and preheat the oven broiler to high. Brush the ciabatta slices generously with oil on both sides and sprinkle with salt. Arrange on a baking sheet. Broil until the tops are golden brown, about 2 minutes. Flip the slices over and toast the other side until golden, 1 to 2 minutes more.

2 If the hummus is chilled, gently warm it: You can warm it on the stovetop in a small covered saucepan over very low heat, uncovering frequently to stir. Alternatively, you can microwave it on high for a few seconds.

3 In a small nonstick skillet, heat 2 teaspoons of oil (or 1 teaspoon of oil and 1 teaspoon of butter, if desired) over medium heat. Add the veggies and a pinch of salt and increase the heat to medium-high. Cook, tossing frequently, until the veggies are limp and browned around the edges, 2 to 6 minutes, depending on the type(s) of vegetable. (Thinly sliced hearty greens need only 1 or 2 minutes to glisten and wilt.) Remove the pan from the heat.

continued →

WARM CIABATTA TOASTS,

continued →

4 If you like, you can use the skillet to make "brown-butter nuts" at this point: Transfer the veggies to a plate, then heat 2 teaspoons of unsalted butter in the skillet over medium-low heat. Add the pine nuts or sliced almonds and cook until lightly browned, 4 to 5 minutes. Remove the pan from the heat.

5 Spread 3 to 4 table-spoons of hummus on each piece of toast. Top with the sautéed veggies and spoon the brown-butter nuts over (if using) and/or sprinkle with the roasted chickpeas. Scatter the lemon or lime zest over all, and garnish lightly with the pea shoots (if using). Serve right away.

Note: The combinations for this dish are endless. Here are some of my favorites:

Lemony Hummus with Sautéed Kale, Brown-Butter Pine Nuts, and Lemon Zest

Lemony Hummus with Broccoli Raab, Onions, and Roasted Chickpeas

Lemony Hummus with Brussels Sprouts, Shallots, and Almonds

Lemony Hummus with Cauliflower, Chard, and Chickpeas

Lemony Hummus with Sautéed Shishito Peppers, Lime Zest, and Parsley

Lemony Chickpea Hummus

MAKES 2¼ CUPS

2 cups cooked chickpeas (see page 236) or canned chickpeas, drained and rinsed

¼ cup tahini (see Note)

⅓ cup freshly squeezed lemon juice, plus more to taste

¼ cup plus 2 tablespoons chickpea cooking liquid or warm water

2 tablespoons extra-virgin olive oil, plus more for drizzling

1½ teaspoons minced fresh garlic

1 teaspoon kosher salt

¼ teaspoon ground cumin

Cayenne

Coarsely chopped fresh cilantro or parsley (optional)

Hummus has a lovely texture and flavor when made from freshly cooked chickpeas (see "How to Cook Chickpeas," page 236), but it is also perfectly delicious when made from canned chickpeas. If you do cook the chickpeas yourself, save a little of the cooking water to make the hummus. I find that a little extra water added at the end of pureeing gives hummus a particularly light and fluffy texture. My friend Eliza (who tested every recipe in this book) created this hummus with a generous measure of lemon and a bit of cumin. You'll love it!

1 Put the chickpeas, tahini, ⅓ cup of lemon juice, ¼ cup of the cooking liquid or water, and 2 tablespoons of the olive oil into the bowl of a food processor and process until well combined. (It will still be a little rough.)

2 Scrape down the sides of the food processor and add the garlic, salt, cumin, and a small pinch of cayenne and process again until smooth. Taste for lemon and salt, and add more if needed. Add the remaining 2 tablespoons of cooking liquid and process until light and fluffy. (Add a little more liquid or water if needed.)

3 To serve, scrape the hummus into a bowl, sprinkle with a pinch of cayenne, and drizzle with olive oil (about 1 to 2 tablespoons). Garnish with cilantro or parsley if desired. If making hummus ahead for toast or another use, scrape the hummus into a refrigerator container and drizzle with olive oil to cover. Cover and keep for up to 1 week in the fridge.

Note: If you are opening up a new can of tahini and the solids are very hard to mix with the liquid, scrape everything out into a food processor or blender and process until well combined and smooth.

GRILLED NAAN

WITH GRILLED MUSHROOMS, BLUE CHEESE, AND SPINACH

SERVES 2

2 teaspoons extra-virgin olive oil, plus more for brushing

1 large garlic clove, sliced

2 to 2½ cups packed baby spinach

Kosher salt

2 large naans (4 to 5 ounces each) or 4 small naans (3 ounces each), thawed if frozen

3 ounces Gorgonzola or other creamy blue cheese, or Brie or Camembert

1 recipe Grilled Maple-Tamari Shiitakes (recipe follows), cut into halves or quarters

½ lemon, cut into wedges (optional)

Once I found out how delicious and easy grilled naan "pizza" is (Grilled Naan "Pizza" with Quick-Roasted Cherry Tomatoes, Whipped Lemon-Thyme Feta, Cucumbers, and Basil, page 131) in the summertime, I wanted to create another topping for naan that would work well in the fall, when I'm still using my grill quite a lot. I knew my Grilled Maple-Tamari Shiitakes (page 141) would be a great place to start, and then I thought of spinach and creamy blue cheese. Turns out, that's a pretty tasty combo. However, if you're not a blue cheese person, you can never go wrong pairing Brie or Camembert with mushrooms. Any cheese that will melt a bit when spread on warm bread is great. If you don't have a grill, you can broil the naan for similar results.

1 In a small skillet, heat 2 teaspoons of oil over medium heat. Add the garlic and cook until sizzling, about 1 minute. Add the spinach and a pinch of salt and toss until wilted, 30 seconds to 1 minute. Remove from the heat. Divide the spinach into 4 portions.

2 Preheat a gas grill to medium or medium-high heat. If using the larger naans, cut each in half crosswise so that you have 4 half-moon-shape pieces. Brush the naans with oil on both sides and sprinkle with salt.

3 Put the naans directly on the grill grate and cook just until grill marks appear and the bottom is beginning to turn golden, 1½ to 2 minutes. Flip over and cook for 1 more minute. (You want the naan to be grilled just enough on the first side to begin losing its flexibility, but not so much that it gets stiff. Leave the second side somewhat soft.) Remove from the grill.

4 While the naans are still hot, dollop or spread an equal amount of cheese on each. Arrange an equal amount of cooked spinach and mushrooms over each. Cut the pizzas into smaller pieces, if you like, and eat right away. Serve with lemon wedges for squeezing over. (If you need to, you can return the naan pizzas to the grill briefly after topping to melt the cheese a bit more. Put them on a baking sheet for easy transport.)

Grilled Maple-Tamari Shiitakes

MAKES ABOUT 20 GRILLED MUSHROOMS

2 tablespoons maple syrup

2 tablespoons
low-sodium tamari

1 tablespoon peanut or
vegetable oil

2 teaspoons toasted sesame oil

1 tablespoon chopped
fresh ginger

2 teaspoons chopped
fresh garlic

8 ounces (about 20 large)
shiitake mushrooms, stems
trimmed off

Marinating and grilling shiitake mushrooms only ups the umami factor in an already deeply flavorful vegetable. Plus, the mushrooms then become versatile ingredients: try using them as a topping for grilled naan, serving them in a salad with somen noodles and Asian greens (page 22), or folding them into a warm grain salad. If you don't have a grill, you can broil these on a baking sheet. Choose the largest shiitake caps you can find; smaller ones can fall through grill grates or overcook.

1 Heat a gas grill to medium heat. Scrape the grill grates clean while the grill is heating up. If you have a grill topper and want to use it, put it on the grill to preheat.

2 Meanwhile, whisk together the maple syrup, tamari, peanut oil, sesame oil, ginger, and garlic in a wide, shallow bowl. Add the shiitake caps and toss. Let sit, stirring and tossing occasionally, while the grill heats up, about 20 minutes (but don't marinate for much longer than 30 minutes).

3 Arrange the mushroom caps, stem side up, directly on the grill grate or on a grill topper. Cover the grill and cook until the bottoms of the mushrooms are darkened or well marked, about 3 to 4 minutes. (Try not to disturb them for the first few minutes, or they might tear.) Use tongs to turn the mushrooms over, and cook until the other side is just golden, 1 to 2 minutes more.

ROASTED BUTTERNUT "SMASH" ON WHOLE WHEAT TOAST

WITH CRANBERRY-CITRUS HERB BUTTER AND CRISPY SHALLOTS

MAKES 2 OR 3 TOASTS

2 cups small-diced, peeled butternut squash (about 9 ounces)

2 tablespoons plus 2 teaspoons extra-virgin olive oil or grapeseed oil, plus more for brushing

Kosher salt

3 tablespoons Cranberry-Citrus Herb Butter (recipe follows), at room temperature

2 large shallots, peeled and cut into thin slices (optional)

2 or 3 slices of whole wheat boule or other peasant bread (each about 6 inches long)

2 tablespoons chopped toasted pecans, toasted pepitas, or Rosemary Roasted Walnuts (page 107)

I'm not a big fan of mashed veggies—mostly because the veggies are usually steamed or boiled first, so their flavor can be a bit wan. But once I figured out that I could mash *roasted* vegetables (especially roasted butternut squash), I was only a step away from putting this delicious stuff on toast. And then, when I mixed roasted butternut squash with my Cranberry-Citrus Herb Butter (page 143) and a few crispy shallots—well, I was all set, I'll tell you! This satisfying and delicious toast is now one of my favorite fall suppers.

1 Position a rack in the middle of your oven and preheat to 425°F. Line a rimmed baking sheet with parchment paper. Toss the squash with a scant 2 tablespoons of the oil and ¼ teaspoon of salt. Arrange in a single layer on the baking sheet and bake, flipping with a metal spatula halfway through cooking, for 26 to 28 minutes, until nicely browned and tender.

2 Immediately transfer the squash to a medium saucepan over low heat and add 4 to 5 teaspoons of the cranberry butter. Toss and stir, then use a handheld masher to gently mash the roasted squash and butter until it roughly holds together. (Some hunks of squash will remain.) Remove the pan from the heat and cover to keep warm if making ahead, or keep the pan on low heat for a few minutes, stirring, if waiting until the toast is done.

3 Cook the shallots (if using): Heat 2 teaspoons of the oil in a small (8-inch) nonstick skillet over medium heat. Add the shallots and a pinch of salt. Cook, stirring, until softened and browned, about 5 minutes. Transfer the shallots to a paper towel–lined plate.

4 Preheat an oven broiler or the broiler in a toaster oven. Brush the bread slices with a small bit of oil on one side and sprinkle with salt. Arrange the slices on a baking sheet. Broil until golden brown on the top side, about 2 minutes. Remove the pan from the oven, turn the slices over, and dot or brush the top of each slice with 1 teaspoon of the cranberry butter. Broil until the top side is lightly browned, about 2 minutes.

5 Spread the warm squash mixture evenly on the toasts. Top with the shallots (if using) and toasted nuts. Serve right away.

Cranberry-Citrus Herb Butter

MAKES ABOUT ⅓ CUP

4 tablespoons unsalted butter, softened at room temperature

¼ teaspoon kosher salt

¼ teaspoon freshly grated orange zest

¼ teaspoon freshly grated lemon zest

2 tablespoons very finely chopped cranberries

1 teaspoon chopped fresh thyme

½ teaspoon seeded and minced fresh jalapeño

Make-ahead "compound" butters are great flavor boosters to keep in your fridge arsenal for amping up veggie suppers. This great fall combination of orange, lemon, cranberry, and thyme is one of the secrets behind delicious roasted butternut toast. But if you keep some in your fridge, you can also toss it with roasted brussels sprouts, add a little bit to cooked rice, or toss noodles with it.

Put the butter in a small bowl. Add the salt and orange and lemon zest. Mash and stir the butter using a small silicone spatula or the back of a spoon. Add the cranberries, thyme, and jalapeño, and continue to stir until the mixture is smooth. Pack into a small bowl, crock, or refrigerator container and cover tightly. Store in the fridge for up to 1 week or the freezer for up to 2 months. Bring to room temperature before using.

CRISPY BROCCOLI AND BUTTERY SPINACH TOAST

WITH PINE NUTS AND PARMESAN

MAKES 2 TOASTS

1 cup very small (¾-inch) broccoli florets

1 tablespoon extra-virgin olive oil, plus more for brushing

Kosher salt

1 tablespoon unsalted butter

4 ounces baby spinach (about 4 cups)

2 slices of sourdough bread (about ½ to ¾ inch thick)

2 tablespoons toasted pine nuts

2 tablespoons grated Parmesan cheese

For green veggie lovers, here's a double whammy: a lovely bed of buttery spinach topped with nuggets of crisp-roasted broccoli. Toasted pine nuts and Parmesan (our favorite spinach partners) nestle in for a completely satisfying and nourishing toast supper. My friend Amy Miller and I had a spinach toast cook-off (don't ask!), and this one was her excellent idea. (We liked both so much that I've included the other in this chapter as well—see Creamy Spinach on Garlic Toast on page 145.) Keep an eye on the little broccoli florets—they take only about 15 minutes to get nicely browned and crisp.

1 Preheat the oven to 425°F. Line a rimmed baking sheet with parchment paper. In a small bowl, toss the broccoli florets with 1 tablespoon of oil and a big pinch of salt. Arrange the broccoli in a single layer on the prepared baking sheet. Bake, flipping or tossing halfway through cooking, for 15 to 18 minutes, until well browned and crisp.

2 In a medium (10-inch) nonstick skillet, heat the butter over medium heat. When the butter has melted, add the spinach and a big pinch of salt. Cook, tossing frequently, until the leaves are wilted, 1 to 2 minutes. Remove from the heat.

3 Preheat the oven broiler to high. Brush both sides of the bread slices with olive oil. Place on a baking sheet and sprinkle with salt. Broil until the tops are slightly golden, about 2 minutes. Flip the slices over and toast the other side until golden, about 2 minutes more.

4 Arrange equal portions of spinach over the two slices of toast. Top with the crispy broccoli florets, then the toasted pine nuts and the grated Parmesan. Cut each piece in half and serve right away.

CREAMY SPINACH ON GARLIC TOAST

MAKES 2 TOASTS

2 slices of boule-style white French peasant bread (about ½ inch thick and 6 inches long)

3 tablespoons half-and-half

½ teaspoon all-purpose flour

⅛ teaspoon freshly grated lemon zest

Pinch of dried thyme

Kosher salt

Freshly ground black pepper

1½ tablespoons unsalted butter

2 teaspoons extra-virgin olive oil

1 teaspoon minced fresh garlic

4 ounces stemmed baby spinach (about 4 cups)

Freshly ground black pepper

¼ cup coarsely grated Parmesan cheese, plus a bit more for garnish

2 tablespoons toasted pine nuts or toasted, thinly sliced almonds

One cold Sunday evening in early December, I came inside as the sun was setting, thinking I wanted something warm and comforting—but not too complicated—for supper. For some reason, I couldn't get creamed spinach out of my head! *Why not creamed spinach on toast?* I thought. *On garlic toast. With a little Parmesan. Yes!* I improvised a bit, and wound up liking my creamy spinach toast so much that it jumped right over into my repertoire department. Turns out it's as good in the spring or fall as it is in wintertime.

1 Preheat the oven broiler to high. Place the bread slices on a rimmed baking sheet.

2 In a small bowl, whisk together the half-and-half, flour, lemon zest, thyme, a big pinch of salt, and several grinds of black pepper. Set aside.

3 In a medium (10-inch) nonstick skillet, heat the butter and oil over medium heat. When the butter has melted, add the garlic and stir. Cook just until the garlic is fragrant and starting to soften, about 30 seconds.

4 Take the skillet off the heat, and brush the top sides of the bread slices with some (but not all) of the garlic, butter, and oil mixture from the pan. Sprinkle with salt. Broil the bread until the top is golden brown, about 2 minutes. Flip the slices over and broil the other side until lightly toasted, about 1 minute. Place the toasts on a board or platter.

5 Return the skillet (with the remaining garlic, butter, and oil) to medium heat. Add the spinach, a generous pinch of salt, and several grinds of pepper. Cook, tossing with tongs, until all the spinach is wilted, 1 to 2 minutes. Turn the heat to medium-low and use a spatula to scrape all the half-and-half mixture into the skillet. Stir constantly as the mixture begins to bubble, and remove the skillet from the heat once the mixture begins to visibly thicken, 30 seconds to 1 minute. Immediately stir in ¼ cup of Parmesan. Spread the creamy spinach onto the pieces of toast and garnish with the toasted nuts and a bit more Parmesan. Cut in half and eat right away.

VEGGIES + TORTILLAS

T A DA! Proof that veggie suppers are not only delicious but fun, too: the tortilla. Yes, we are shamelessly jumping on the taco bandwagon. But listen, it's not such a big stretch to think of tortillas as a major pantry staple. Tortillas—first handmade by the Aztecs and then for centuries by Mexican women—have been, and still are, a product of huge cultural, economic, and culinary importance for Mexico. The fact that tortillas have gone global—and that here in the United States we now have good tortillas available to us everywhere (more on that to come)—means that vegetarians can celebrate. What was traditionally a vehicle for slowly cooked and chopped meat is also a perfect host for vegetables, beans, rice, herbs, and sauces in endless combinations.

Those sauces are key. In fact, while you might see authentic tacos filled with everything from crispy fried grasshoppers to battered fish, you will rarely see a real taco that isn't offered with at least one saucy, freshly made condiment to top it off. That's why, for most recipes in this chapter, we'll start with the tortillas—turning them into tacos, quesadillas, burritos, tostadas, and tortilla soup—but we'll finish with a little sauce, from Plum Tomato-Fresh Ginger Salsa (page 157) and Spicy Roasted Tomatillo Salsa Verde (page 169) to Lime-Chipotle Sauce (page 164) and Quick Savoy-Kale Slaw (page 161). We'll get lots of satisfaction (and fun) from their mingling with the other flavors and textures and even temperatures. True to our strategy, many of these sauces can be made ahead of time.

As a bonus, they also turn out to be versatile condiments that can be used in all kinds of veggie suppers, especially egg dishes.

In the middle, between the tortilla and the sauce, we'll showcase fillings that are so satisfying—including beans and rice, avocados (both of which are complete proteins), eggplant, mushrooms, corn, and cabbage—that these recipes wind up being some of the best for transitioning to a vegetarian diet. So, while you're enjoying your veggie suppers, you could be working on converting a family member, too.

Tips and Strategies for Tortillas

THE LESS PROCESSED, THE BETTER.

I did say that there are some very good tortillas on the market, but unfortunately, there are some truly awful products, packed with preservatives and artificial ingredients, right there with them. (Do not, under any circumstances, buy "wraps.") Tortillas were meant to be eaten freshly cooked, so short of making them yourself, it would be best to get tortillas from a local tortilla factory, if you have that kind of luck. Your next-best bet is a good Mexican-style brand such as Maria and Ricardo's or El Milagro, if you see them.

Most often, you will be faced with choosing from other national brands and a grocery store brand. The best thing you can do is to look at the ingredient label. A corn tortilla may be white or yellow, but either way it should have only four ingredients: stone-ground corn, water, lime, and maybe salt. Some will have many more ingredients; there are even corn tortillas now that contain wheat gluten, which is just ridiculous considering what a great gluten-free food corn tortillas are (usually). The added gluten may be an attempt to give corn tortillas more structure, but if I want structure, I'll get a (wheat) flour tortilla. (I happen to really prefer the maizy flavor of a good corn tortilla, while I appreciate the flexibility of a flour tortilla.)

Unfortunately, many of the flour tortillas on the market are full of ingredients designed to soften and preserve them, so once again, you'll need to compare labels and make the best choice you can. Organic flour tortillas from Whole Foods Markets (365 Everyday Value brand) and Maria and Ricardo's are among the ones with the shortest ingredient lists. Ultimately, you'll have to take tortillas home and cook with them to compare their flavors and textures. Make note of brands you like so that you can buy them again.

CHOOSE FROM THREE MAIN SIZES.

As best I can tell (and I say this because, again, labeling and standards are not very consistent), the most widely available tortillas in this country come in three sizes: small, or taco-size (about 6 inches); medium, or fajita-size (about 8 inches); and large, or burrito-size (about 10 inches). You may also see "burrito" tortillas that are 12 inches. Sometimes, however, the small, taco tortillas (the most common form of corn tortillas) can be closer to 5 inches, and a medium tortilla might measure just 7 inches. So, while the following recipes call for 6-, 8-, and 10-inch tortillas, you may need to improvise with what you can find.

FREEZE TORTILLAS.

Once you find tortillas that you like, buy a variety of sizes and store them in your freezer. Pop the whole bag into a large zip-top freezer bag for an extra layer of protection from freezer burn. Tortillas defrost quickly, but you can also transfer a few into your refrigerator every so often. Most tortillas will keep well in the fridge for a couple of weeks.

PICK YOUR WARMING—AND CRISPING—METHODS.

Although there are a few brands of uncooked tortillas on the market, the majority of tortillas available to us are already cooked, so most of the time what you will be doing at home is reheating, or warming, your tortillas. (There are several good ways to heat tortillas, depending on whether you want them steamy or a bit toasty—see page 239.) But, for fun, a couple of recipes here call for fried tortillas (that is, tostados and tortilla strips). For the crispiest fried tortillas, you'll need to use enough oil so that the tortilla is just submerged (for shallow frying), but you can also crisp a tortilla nicely in a skillet with just a small amount of oil. It won't have quite that perfectly crunchy texture that falls apart when you bite into it, but it will be pleasantly crisp. When we make quesadillas, we'll pan-fry them in only a very small amount of oil and butter—a good example of how a tortilla can take on some flavor and a bit of crispness without being deep-fried.

IN BETWEEN THE TORTILLA AND THE SAUCE, BE JUDICIOUS.

A great burrito can be a bodacious thing, but it's amazing how fast you can overfill a tortilla, loading it up too much before rolling. (Fortunately, you'll find good directions for rolling and folding burritos in the recipe for Spicy White Bean Burritos with Green Rice, Pepitas, and Queso Fresco on page 165.) Likewise with a quesadilla: you don't want so much filling and cheese that the top and bottom tortillas can't come within kissing distance of each other. And, when you're spooning filling into a little corn taco, remember you will still need to top it with a forkful of slaw, a smattering of pepitas, and maybe a little Lime-Chipotle Sauce. Plus you're going to need to pick it up with your hands! This is why tacos were originally designed to be snacks. Use a light hand—you can always have another.

For the Pantry

As I already mentioned, because you can freeze tortillas, it doesn't hurt to stock up on a few different sizes of both corn and flour tortillas. And that is all you need to do here. I am not a proponent of flavored tortillas or wraps, so in this case our pantry requirements are very simple.

Our list of tortilla "accessories" for the pantry is a bit longer, and it includes a few ingredients you might not be familiar with. The first is *queso fresco*, a mild, fresh cow's-milk cheese that has a pleasantly creamy but crumbly texture. This unaged cheese feels light and adds a nice texture and creamy freshness to tacos and tostados. It is now available in many major groceries, but if you can't find it, use a smaller amount of feta cheese or fresh goat cheese, though it is tangier than queso fresco.

One of my favorite Mexican ingredients is pepitas, or hull-less pumpkin seeds. (They are harvested from a particular type of pumpkin that produces hull-less seeds, so don't try to shell regular pumpkin seeds to get them!) Flat, green, and oval-shaped, they are especially delicious lightly toasted until puffed and golden. (They do start to pop when toasted, so keep an eye on them—see "How to Toast Nuts" on page 237.) I store pepitas in the freezer because, like many seeds with high concentrations of good fats, they have a shorter shelf life than most nuts.

Last, you might already have canned chipotles (smoked jalapeños in a thick, rich tomato sauce called adobo) in your pantry. The big question is always what to do with the rest of the can after using only one pepper or a bit of sauce. Just transfer all the remaining contents into a small food storage container and freeze. Whatever amount you need in the future can usually be gently pried out with a knife or spoon, without even defrosting.

The Tortillas

Small (taco-size, 6-inch) corn tortillas and flour tortillas	Medium (fajita-size, 8-inch) flour tortillas	Large (burrito-size, 10-inch) flour tortillas

Accessory Ingredients

Avocados	Chili powder	Monterey jack cheese
Canned beans	Fresh chile peppers	Pepitas
Canned chipotles in adobo	Fresh cilantro	Pine nuts
Canned (vegetarian) refried beans	Fresh garlic	Queso fresco
Cheddar cheese	Ground chipotle pepper	Sour cream and/or Greek yogurt
	Limes	

LITTLE GREENS QUESADILLAS

WITH CHEDDAR, SCALLIONS, AND TOMATOES

MAKES 4 SMALL QUESADILLAS

3 tablespoons plus 2 teaspoons unsalted butter

¼ cup thinly sliced scallions or spring onions (white and light green parts)

⅓ cup cooked chickpeas (see page 236), drained and rinsed

¼ teaspoon kosher salt, plus a pinch

1 teaspoon minced fresh garlic

4 cups loosely packed, thinly sliced Tuscan kale (stemmed)

¼ teaspoon balsamic vinegar

⅓ cup drained and thinly sliced sun-dried tomatoes or Quick-Roasted Cherry Tomatoes (page 133)

3 tablespoons lightly chopped toasted pine nuts (optional)

1½ cups extra-sharp aged cheddar

8 small (taco-size, 6-inch) corn tortillas

¼ cup sour cream

¼ cup Spicy Roasted Tomatillo Salsa Verde (page 169, optional)

When life gives you extra greens, make quesadillas! Here's one of my favorite combos—Tuscan kale, garlic, scallions, sun-dried tomatoes, and cheddar. Plus a few chickpeas for extra heartiness. But really, you can chop or slice any hearty green, sauté it with some aromatics, and it will make a great quesadilla filling. I like the flavor of corn tortillas with greens, but flour tortillas are good here, too, and they cook up a bit crisper. I also like using the smallest, taco-size tortillas to make "little" quesadillas. You can add an extra southwestern kick with a garnish of Spicy Roasted Tomatillo Salsa Verde (page 169) if you like, and for a change-up, replace half (but not all) of the cheddar with fresh goat cheese.

1. In a medium (10-inch) nonstick skillet, heat 1 tablespoon of the butter over medium heat. Add the scallions, chickpeas, and a pinch of salt and cook, stirring, until both are lightly browned, 5 to 6 minutes. Add the garlic and cook, stirring, until fragrant, just a few seconds. Add the kale and ¼ teaspoon of salt and cook, stirring, until the greens are wilted, about 1 minute. Remove the pan from the heat, sprinkle the kale mixture with the vinegar, and stir.

2. Transfer the kale mixture to a medium bowl and let cool a few minutes. Add the tomatoes and pine nuts (if using) and stir well. Divide the mixture into 4 roughly equal portions.

3. Wipe the skillet clean and return it to medium-low heat. Add 1 teaspoon of the butter; when it has melted, add 1 tortilla to the pan. Sprinkle with a generous 2 tablespoons of cheese, top evenly with a quarter of the veggie mixture, sprinkle with about 2 tablespoons more cheese, and top with a second tortilla.

4. Press the top tortilla down gently and cover the pan. Cook until the bottom is lightly golden, 2 to 3 minutes (1 to 2 minutes for flour tortillas), then carefully flip with a spatula, adding another 1 teaspoon of the butter to the pan, and cook until the bottom is golden brown, about 2 minutes. Don't be tempted to turn the

continued →

LITTLE GREENS QUESADILLAS,

continued →

heat up—you want time to let the cheese melt.

5 Transfer the quesadilla to a wooden cutting board. Let the pan cool for a minute, then return it to the heat. Repeat the process to assemble and cook three more quesadillas. Let the last quesadilla cool for at least a few minutes before cutting.

6 Slice the quesadillas into wedges. Garnish with the sour cream and salsa verde (if using) and serve warm.

CRISPY TORTILLAS

WITH WATERCRESS, PEAS, AVOCADO, SPROUTS, AND SMOKY CHILI BROTH

SERVES 3 OR 4

1 tablespoon vegetable or grapeseed oil, plus more for frying (about 1½ cups)

½ cup finely chopped yellow onion

Kosher salt

2 teaspoons chopped fresh garlic

1½ teaspoons chili powder

½ teaspoon smoked paprika

1 tablespoon tomato paste

4 small (taco-size, 6-inch) corn tortillas, cut into thin strips (¼ to ½ inch wide)

4 cups tender watercress sprigs (discard tougher stems)

¾ cup frozen peas, thawed, or fresh peas, blanched or microwaved for 30 seconds

1 large or 1½ medium avocados, cut into large dice or 1-inch wedges

2 radishes, cut into very thin slices (optional)

Generous 1 cup pea shoots or pea greens

4 lime wedges

For this updated riff on tortilla soup, springtime lends some lovely greenery in the form of both watercress and pea greens. Of course, it's the crispy fried tortilla strips that really make this fun and texturally interesting, but a lightly smoky (red!) chile broth provides a nice contrasting backdrop to the greenery, too. For the most satisfying "soup," be sure not to skip the avocado and peas. The four portions are light here; for a slightly heartier supper, make three portions out of this recipe, and add a few black beans to the mix as well. Frying the tortilla strips is a bit time-consuming, but you can do it ahead if you like; they hold well at room temperature for several hours. You can make the broth a day ahead, too. If you can't find the pea shoots or greens for garnish, you can use some more watercress instead.

1 In a large saucepan, heat 1 tablespoon of oil over medium-low heat. Add the onion and a pinch of salt and cook, stirring, until lightly golden, about 5 to 7 minutes. Add the garlic, 1 teaspoon of salt, the chili powder, and the smoked paprika. Cook, stirring rapidly, until fragrant and combined, about 30 seconds. Add the tomato paste and stir well. Add 4 cups of water and stir well, scraping the bottom of the pan and whisking to incorporate. Bring the broth to a boil, reduce the heat to low, and gently simmer, uncovered, for 10 minutes. Remove the pan from the heat. (If making ahead, let cool then cover and store in the fridge for up to 1 day.)

2 Line a plate or tray with paper towels. Pour enough oil into a medium saucepan to cover the bottom of the pan by 1 inch. Heat the oil over medium to medium-high heat until a tortilla strip sizzles when dipped into the oil. Once the oil is hot, add 8 to 10 of the tortilla strips and use tongs to scrunch them up a bit to make them wavy. Fry until the strips are lightly golden brown, anywhere from 30 seconds to 2 minutes. Transfer to the paper towel–lined plate or tray. Sprinkle with salt. Repeat the process to fry the remaining tortilla strips.

3 Arrange four shallow soup bowls on your work surface. (If you have made the broth ahead, reheat it.) Divide the watercress

into four portions and add to bowls. Put an equal portion of peas in each bowl. Pour the broth over the vegetables, then mound an equal portion of tortilla strips in the center of each bowl. Add the avocado and radishes (if using). Garnish each bowl with a mound of pea shoots and a lime wedge and serve right away.

FAIRY TALE EGGPLANT TACOS

WITH PLUM TOMATO–FRESH GINGER SALSA

MAKES 4 TO 5 SMALL TACOS

1 tablespoon plus 2 teaspoons grapeseed or vegetable oil

10 to 12 ounces Fairy Tale (petite) eggplants or Japanese eggplants

5 small (taco-size, 6-inch) flour or corn tortillas

Generous ½ teaspoon kosher salt

½ cup thinly sliced red bell pepper

½ cup thickly sliced scallions (½-inch-thick slices, white and light green parts)

1 teaspoon minced fresh garlic

1 teaspoon minced fresh ginger

15 to 20 sprigs of fresh cilantro, or small mint or parsley (or a combination)

1 large or 1½ medium ripe-but-firm avocados, halved and cut into thin slices

½ cup Plum Tomato–Fresh Ginger Salsa (recipe follows)

For such a simple sauté, this taco filling delivers great flavor. I love to use my little "Fairy Tale" eggplants here; the creamy white flesh gets tender so quickly, and the flavor is mild and delicious. (Plus they're quick to prep.) Slim Japanese eggplants are also nice here, and of course you could really use any eggplant. Just cut the bigger varieties into smaller pieces, as they take more heat and time to cook through. A little red bell pepper, a few scallions, plus a hit of ginger and garlic to pair with the fresh, gingery salsa complete this bright combination. Avocados (surprisingly good with eggplant) offer a rich and creamy counterpoint. This filling is enough for up to five tacos. You can double it by making two batches ahead of time and combining to reheat. You can make the salsa a day ahead, too.

1 Trim the caps from the eggplants. If using Fairy Tale eggplants, cut them in half lengthwise. If they are longer than a few inches, cut the pieces in half crosswise as well. If using Japanese eggplants, cut them in half lengthwise and then crosswise into 1/2-inch-thick half-moons. (Cut any other eggplants into 1-inch pieces about 1/2 inch thick.)

2 Warm the tortillas (see page 239).

3 In a large (12-inch) nonstick skillet, heat the oil over medium-high heat. Add the eggplant pieces and a generous 1/4 teaspoon of salt and cook, stirring, until the eggplant is well browned and softened, 5 to 7 minutes. Add the bell pepper, scallions, and 1/4 teaspoon of salt and cook, stirring, until the scallions are browned in spots and the peppers are limp, 3 to 4 minutes. Add the garlic and ginger and cook, stirring, until fragrant, about 30 seconds. Remove the pan from the heat and transfer the eggplant mixture to a serving bowl.

4 Put the tortillas, cilantro, and avocado slices on separate plates or a serving board or platter, and spoon the salsa into a serving bowl. Place on the table with the eggplant mixture and some serving utensils and self-serve.

Plum Tomato–Fresh Ginger Salsa

MAKES 2 CUPS

1½ cups cored, seeded, and small-diced ripe plum tomatoes

2 tablespoons chopped fresh cilantro

1 tablespoon extra-virgin olive oil

1 tablespoon orange juice

2 teaspoons red wine vinegar, plus more to taste

1 teaspoon maple syrup

2 teaspoons minced fresh ginger

1 teaspoon minced fresh garlic

1½ teaspoons seeded and minced fresh serrano pepper

¼ teaspoon kosher salt, plus more to taste

Chopping up a batch of this easy, fragrant salsa is one more reason to love late summer. Fruity tomatoes and zingy ginger have a great affinity for each other, so consider this a gingery riff on a simple, fresh summer salsa. It's meant to be a bit loose and saucy (not ultra-chunky), which makes it great for spooning onto tacos and grilled veg. For an even saucier version, puree everything in the food processor. (In that case, you can rough-chop the tomatoes rather than dicing them. Pureeing will intensify the ginger, garlic, and other flavors.)

In a medium bowl, stir together all the ingredients. Taste, and add more vinegar or salt if necessary. (The flavor will strengthen as it sits.) Transfer the salsa to a bowl for serving. Store any leftovers in the fridge, covered, for up to 3 days.

CRISPY TOSTADOS

WITH BEEFSTEAK TOMATO, CORN, ICEBERG, AND AVOCADO "STACKS"

MAKES 4 TOSTADOS

Vegetable or peanut oil, for frying (⅓ to ½ cup)

4 small (taco-size, 6-inch) flour tortillas

Kosher salt

1 recipe Lime-Chipotle Sauce (page 164)

1½ cups Quick Savoy-Kale Slaw (page 161) or thinly sliced iceberg lettuce

4 thick slices of large, ripe beefsteak tomatoes (if the tomatoes are not large, use 8 thick slices)

Freshly ground black pepper

1 large or 2 small ripe-but-firm avocados, cut in half and sliced

1 cup fresh corn kernels

½ cup loosely packed fresh cilantro sprigs or basil leaves

½ cup queso fresco

¼ cup toasted pepitas (pumpkin seeds)

These fun and pretty stacks of quintessential summer goodies come together pretty easily—even with a little time spent at the stove frying the tortillas. Showcase your biggest ripe beefsteak tomatoes here, and use the freshest sweet corn. A layer of shredded iceberg lettuce is nice, but a bit of Quick Savoy-Kale Slaw is even better. The crisp tortillas do eventually get soft under all those goodies, so sometimes I start eating with a knife and fork and then fold up the remainder.

1 Fry the tortillas: Spread a few layers of paper towels on a cutting board, tray, or other surface near your stove. Pour enough oil into the bottom of a medium (10-inch) heavy-duty skillet to cover the bottom by about ¼ inch. (Alternatively, use a 12-inch stir-fry pan.) Heat the oil over medium-high heat until shimmering. (Watch carefully and do not overheat the oil—if it is beginning to smoke, it is too hot.) Carefully add 1 tortilla and cook until the underside is golden brown, 10 to 20 seconds. The tortilla will puff up or bubble—that's OK: use tongs to press gently down on the middle of the tortilla to keep the entire bottom surface in contact with the oil, but don't worry about deflating the bubble. Use the tongs to turn the tortilla over and cook the other side until golden, another 10 to 15 seconds. Transfer the tortilla to the paper towels. (Gently poke a hole in one side to deflate any large bubble slightly.) Repeat the process to fry the remaining 3 tortillas. If you pause during the frying, remove the skillet from the stove so that the oil does not overheat; reheat it when ready to fry again.

2 Place each tortilla on a plate and sprinkle with salt. Spread a small amount (a scant 1 teaspoon) of the Lime-Chipotle Sauce onto each tortilla. Arrange a quarter of the slaw on the tortilla. Center 1 large slice of tomato (or 2 smaller slices) on top of the slaw and sprinkle the tomatoes with salt and pepper. Arrange the avocado slices on top of the tomatoes. Dollop a small amount of the Lime-Chipotle Sauce onto each tostado. Top with an equally divided amount of fresh corn, cilantro, queso fresco, and pepitas (in that order), centering each ingredient to give the tostados some height. Serve with a knife and fork (and napkins!) and eat right away.

GRILLED PORTOBELLO TACOS

WITH QUICK SAVOY-KALE SLAW AND QUESO FRESCO

MAKES 6 SMALL TACOS

4 large portobello mushroom caps, stems removed and gills scraped out with a spoon

Extra-virgin olive oil or grapeseed oil, for brushing

Kosher salt

6 small (taco-size, 6-inch) flour or corn tortillas

2 to 3 cups Quick Savoy-Kale Slaw (recipe follows)

½ cup crumbled queso fresco (about 2 ounces)

1 recipe Lime-Chipotle Sauce (page 164)

12 to 16 sprigs of fresh cilantro (optional)

What a great pairing! The deep, smoky, umami flavor of grilled portobellos gets a totally fresh and bright contrast from a super-quick slaw that features both cabbage and kale (plus lime and cilantro). One of my favorite taco fillings, this is the one to serve to your nonvegetarian friends. I love the slightly salty, fresh taste of *queso fresco*, but a little bit of feta or goat cheese could stand in. Don't forget the super-fast Lime-Chipotle Sauce to finish. This is a straightforward recipe that delivers a lot of bang for the effort. If you don't have a grill, broil or roast the mushrooms.

1 Preheat a gas grill to medium-high heat. Brush the portobellos generously with oil on both sides and season with salt. When the grill is hot, arrange the mushrooms, stem side up, directly on the grill grates, cover the grill, and cook until well marked on the bottom, 5 to 7 minutes. (Rotate the caps halfway through cooking if you like.) Carefully turn the caps over (liquid will have pooled in the caps, so there may be flare-ups when it pours out). Continue grilling until the edges of the bottom are brown, about 3 minutes. Transfer to a cutting board and let cool for a few minutes. Slice thin.

2 Warm the tortillas (use the grill if you like—see page 239). Put the warm tortillas, sliced portobellos, slaw, queso fresco, Lime-Chipotle Sauce, and cilantro sprigs (if using) into or on separate serving bowls, plates, and/or boards and arrange on the table or on a countertop, then self-serve. Place a few slices of mushroom along the bottom of a tortilla and top with slaw, a little bit of crumbled queso fresco, and a drizzle of the sauce to finish.

Quick Savoy-Kale Slaw

MAKES 4 CUPS

3 cups packed, very thinly sliced
savoy cabbage or green cabbage
(about 8 ounces)

1 cup very thinly sliced young or
baby kale leaves (about 1 ounce)

2 tablespoons plus 1 teaspoon
fresh lime juice

1 tablespoon cane sugar

3 tablespoons chopped
fresh cilantro

½ teaspoon kosher salt

I never get tired of the brilliantly easy alchemy of combining
cabbage, lime juice, sugar, and salt. The easiest slaw on the planet
also takes well to the occasional surprise ingredient: in this case,
it's slivered or baby kale. (Another time, you could experiment with
adding thinly sliced radishes, scallions, jicama, apples, or pears.)
I find this slaw particularly delicious in Grilled Portobello Tacos,
but I think you'll find it's easy to sneak into any taco. The longer it
sits, the softer it will get. I like to use it after just about 15 minutes,
when it is still a bit crunchy; however, I've also enjoyed leftovers
that were stored in the fridge overnight, so it is quite flexible.

In a large bowl, combine the
cabbage, kale, lime juice,
sugar, cilantro, and salt and
toss well. Let sit, tossing well
every few minutes, for about
15 minutes. Let sit longer,
tossing and tasting every few
minutes, if you like.

SPICY EGG TACOS

WITH SALSA VERDE, SHARP CHEDDAR, AND PICKLED VEGGIES

MAKES 8 TACOS, SERVES 4

8 medium (fajita-size, 8-inch) flour tortillas

6 large fresh eggs

Splash of milk, cream, or water

Large pinch of kosher salt

Freshly ground black pepper

1 tablespoon unsalted butter

2 cups coarsely grated extra-sharp cheddar cheese

3 to 5 tablespoons Spicy Roasted Tomatillo Salsa Verde (page 169), at room temperature, or store-bought salsa verde

8 inner or small leaves of baby romaine or Bibb lettuce

½ cup or more quick-pickled corn (Quick-Pickled Corn, Jalapeños, and Onions, page 199)

⅓ cup or more quick-pickled onions (page 199)

1 ripe avocado, cut in half and sliced

8 to 16 sprigs of fresh cilantro (leaves and tender stems only), or to taste

I've worked over the egg sandwich quite a bit—it's my standby comfort food. I'm pretty partial to a griddled English muffin for my sandwich "wrapper" (English Muffin Egg Sandwich with Spinach, Avocado, Cheddar, Crispy Shiitakes, and Pickled Jalapeños, page 196), but I also love to mix things up by turning my egg sandwich into an egg taco. Either way, something spicy is essential—a bit of heat, as well as a little acidity, cuts the richness of a scrambled egg. So my Mexican-inspired egg tacos have this one-two punch: a spicy homemade salsa verde on the bottom and homemade veggie pickles as a garnish. Both the salsa and pickles are great make-aheads to keep in the fridge, but you can buy a good salsa verde for an easy alternative.

1 Warm the tortillas in a hot oven and keep them wrapped in foil (see page 239).

2 Crack the eggs into a medium bowl. Add the milk, salt, and a few grinds of black pepper and whisk until well combined.

3 In a large (12-inch) nonstick skillet, heat the butter over medium heat. When the butter is bubbling, tilt the pan to coat the bottom. (You want your pan to be well heated all over, or the eggs will stick.) Add the egg mixture and let sit for about 1 minute. Use a silicone spatula to gently fold the outside edges toward the middle, and let the insides run out. Sprinkle with ¼ cup of the cheese. Let cook, undisturbed, for 1 minute, then fold the outside edges in again. Flip the eggs over, break into large pieces with your spatula, and cook until just starting to brown lightly on the bottom but still a bit glossy on the top, 30 seconds to 1 minute. Remove the pan from the heat.

4 Arrange the warm tortillas on a large cutting board or work surface or on serving plates. Spoon 1 to 2 teaspoons of salsa verde (thinned with water if you like) down the middle of each tortilla and top with a lettuce leaf. Sprinkle the remaining cheese over the lettuce leaves, dividing it equally among the tacos. Top each with a portion of eggs, a sprinkling of pickled corn and/or a few pieces of pickled onion, 1 or 2 slices of avocado, and 1 or 2 sprigs of cilantro. Fold up, and serve right away.

TWO-POTATO, RED ONION, AND BELL PEPPER TACOS

WITH LIME-CHIPOTLE SAUCE

MAKES 6 SMALL TACOS, SERVES 2

6 small (taco-size, 6-inch) corn tortillas

3 tablespoons extra-virgin olive oil

2 cups small-diced, unpeeled sweet potato (about 8 ounces, or 1 small sweet potato)

2 cups small-diced red potatoes (about 8 ounces, or 2 medium potatoes)

1 teaspoon kosher salt

1 cup small-diced red onion

¾ cup small-diced red bell pepper

2 teaspoons minced fresh garlic

½ to 1 teaspoon seeded and minced fresh jalapeño or serrano pepper

1 recipe Lime-Chipotle Sauce (recipe follows)

6 to 12 baby lettuce leaves

12 small sprigs of fresh cilantro

So satisfying, this sweet potato and red potato sauté is one of my favorite taco fillings. The root veggies, onions, and peppers gently caramelize in the pan, then get finished with a hit of garlic and fresh chile. Tucked into a warm corn tortilla with a drizzle of quick-to-make Lime-Chipotle Sauce, their flavors are deep and comforting. One skillet holds only enough veggies to fill about 6 tortillas, but if you wanted to serve this for friends, you could either use more skillets and/or make a batch or two ahead. (It holds well and reheats easily in the microwave.)

1 Warm the tortillas in a hot oven and keep them wrapped in foil (see page 239).

2 In a large (12-inch) nonstick skillet that has a lid, heat the olive oil over medium heat. When the oil is hot, add the sweet potatoes, red potatoes, and the salt. Stir and cover loosely. Cook, uncovering to stir occasionally, until the vegetables have shrunken a bit and are beginning to brown, about 12 minutes (listen for a gentle sizzle—if the vegetables are browning too fast, drop the heat a bit). Uncover, add the onion and bell pepper, and stir. Cook, uncovered, stirring more frequently (and adjusting the heat as necessary), until the potatoes are tender and nicely browned and the onions and peppers are well-softened, about 12 minutes more. Add the garlic and jalapeño. Cook, stirring, until fragrant, about 30 seconds. Remove the pan from the heat and let cool for a few minutes. Taste, and add more salt if you like.

3 Spoon the Lime-Chipotle Sauce into a serving bowl. Arrange the pan of vegetables, the bowl of sauce, the lettuce, the cilantro, and the warm tortillas in your serving area. Assemble tacos with a lettuce leaf on the bottom, some veggies and 2 sprigs of cilantro next, and a small spoonful or drizzle of sauce over the top.

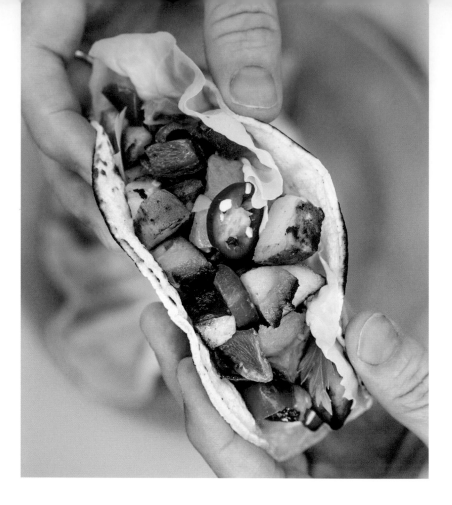

Lime-Chipotle Sauce

MAKES ½ CUP

¼ cup mayonnaise

3 tablespoons Greek yogurt

1 tablespoon plus 1 teaspoon
fresh lime juice

½ teaspoon freshly grated
lime zest

½ to 1 teaspoon minced canned
chipotle in adobo, or 1 teaspoon
sriracha sauce plus ¼ teaspoon
dried chipotle powder or
smoked paprika

Pinch of kosher salt

I like this spicy drizzling (or dipping) sauce on just about any kind of taco, but especially one that has potatoes or mushrooms in it. It's got that great combination of smoky heat and cool creaminess, and it's so quick and easy to make, you can't go wrong. I like to use canned chipotle in adobo sauce for this, but a good substitute is some sriracha hot sauce and either ground chipotle pepper or smoked paprika. This sauce does keep in the fridge for a couple of days, but be aware that it tends to get spicier as it sits. You can always stir in an extra 1 or 2 tablespoons of yogurt to reduce the spiciness if you like.

In a small bowl, whisk together all the ingredients. Let sit for 1 minute. Taste, and adjust seasonings as you like. Transfer to a small serving bowl.

SPICY WHITE BEAN BURRITOS

WITH GREEN RICE, PEPITAS, AND QUESO FRESCO

MAKES 5 BURRITOS

1½ teaspoons packed dark brown sugar

1 teaspoon ground cumin

1 teaspoon ground coriander

1 teaspoon paprika

½ teaspoon cocoa powder

1 teaspoon kosher salt, plus 2 pinches

¼ teaspoon ground chipotle pepper

Large pinch of ground cloves

2 tablespoons extra-virgin olive oil

1 cup diced yellow onion

2 cups seeded and diced plum tomatoes

2 teaspoons minced fresh garlic

1 teaspoon seeded and minced jalapeño

One 15-ounce can small white (navy) beans or pinto beans, drained and rinsed

¼ cup chopped fresh cilantro, plus 15 to 20 sprigs

5 large (burrito-size, 10-inch) flour tortillas

continues on page 166

To my mind, the best burritos contain both beans and rice, plus a nice portion of veggies. The addition of crunchy and creamy things is important, too. For this warm and hearty combo, I make a spicy white bean and tomato filling on the stovetop while I'm cooking a batch of my Green Rice. There's a little time investment here for these hearty results, but you can break up the prep by making the beans or the rice, or both, a day before you plan to make the burritos. (Or plan to eat these over two nights.) When it comes time to assemble the burritos, I add avocado slices, a squeeze of lime, crunchy toasted pepitas (some crunch is key), crumbled *queso fresco*, and a few cilantro sprigs. (There's lots of protein in this one!) Folding and rolling a burrito can be a little tricky, so follow the instructions here, then cut the burrito on the diagonal for easiest serving and eating.

1 In a small bowl, stir together the brown sugar, cumin, coriander, paprika, cocoa, 1 teaspoon of the salt, the chipotle, and the ground cloves. Set aside.

2 In a large (12-inch) nonstick skillet, heat the olive oil over medium heat. Add the onion and a pinch of salt and cook, stirring, until golden, 6 to 8 minutes. Add the tomatoes and a pinch of salt and cook, stirring, until the tomatoes are very broken down and paste-like and the pan is quite dry, 10 to 12 minutes. Add the garlic and jalapeño and cook, stirring, until softened, about 1 minute. Add the spice mixture and cook, stirring well, until well combined and darkened in color. Add the beans and 1 cup of water and stir, scraping the bottom of the pan. Bring to a gentle simmer and cook until the liquids have reduced to just a few tablespoons, about 5 minutes. Remove the pan from the heat. (You can remove the pan while the mixture is still slightly soupy like this; the beans will absorb extra liquid as they cool.) Stir in the chopped cilantro. Taste, and season with more salt if you like.

3 Warm the tortillas in a hot oven and keep them wrapped in foil (see page 239).

continued →

SPICY WHITE BEAN BURRITOS,

continued →

2½ cups cooked Green Rice (page 50), reheated if necessary

1 cup crumbled queso fresco (about 5 ounces)

¼ cup toasted pepitas

1 avocado, cut in half and sliced

½ lime

4 Place 1 tortilla on your work surface. Spoon ½ cup of the warm rice onto the lower center of the tortilla, forming a rough shape a little bigger than a deck of cards (with the long side facing you). Put a portion of the bean mixture on top of the rice. Top with one-fifth of the queso fresco, some of the pepitas, a few sprigs of cilantro, a few avocado slices, and a small squeeze of lime.

5 Wrap the burrito: Start by folding up the bottom (the side closest to you); then fold the two sides in, keeping the filling layered and compact. Then roll the whole burrito tightly over the rest of the tortilla to close it. Cut the burrito in half on a sharp diagonal and arrange the two halves on a plate. Repeat with the remaining tortillas and fillings.

TOSTADOS OF REFRIED BEANS AND SPICED SWEET POTATO FRIES

WITH SALSA VERDE

MAKES 4 TOSTADOS

1½ teaspoons kosher salt, plus more for sprinkling

½ teaspoon cane sugar

¼ teaspoon ground cumin

¼ teaspoon ground coriander

¼ teaspoon ground cinnamon

¼ teaspoon paprika

8 ounces sweet potato, unpeeled, sliced on a diagonal and cut into batons, or "fries," about 2 inches long (about 1 large sweet potato)

2 tablespoons grapeseed oil, plus more for frying

4 small (taco-size, 6-inch) flour tortillas

¾ cup (vegetarian) canned refried beans, heated and kept warm in a covered saucepan

3 to 4 tablespoons crumbled queso fresco or sour cream (or both)

⅓ cup Spicy Roasted Tomatillo Salsa Verde (recipe follows) or store-bought salsa verde

3 to 4 tablespoons toasted pepitas (pumpkin seeds)

Comfort, spice, crunch, and sauce—it's all here in one delicious and satisfying tostado supper. Roasted sweet potatoes and beans are such a friendly pair that you could use this filling in tacos or quesadillas, too, any time you're not up for frying tortillas. I do like crunchy tostados, and that basically means submerging the tortilla in a little bit of bubbling oil. You can pan-fry them in less oil if you'd rather; they'll be tasty, though a bit more chewy, less crunchy. For this filling, I hijacked the spiced sweet potato fries from my first cookbook, *Fast, Fresh & Green*. The spices, along with some bright heat from the salsa verde, contrast nicely with the mild beans. Add a bit of sour cream or *queso fresco* for a creamy note. Once your tostado is assembled, you can cut it into quarters to eat, or allow it to soften for a minute or two and then just fold it up like a taco.

1 In a small bowl, stir together 1 teaspoon of the kosher salt and the sugar, cumin, coriander, cinnamon, and paprika. Set aside.

2 Preheat the oven to 425°F. Line a large heavy-duty rimmed baking sheet with parchment paper. In a medium bowl, toss the sweet potatoes with 2 tablespoons of the oil and ½ teaspoon of the salt. Spread out in a single layer on the prepared baking sheet and bake, flipping over halfway through cooking, for 22 to 24 minutes, until lightly browned and tender. Remove from the oven and sprinkle with some of the salt mixture (you may have some left over).

3 Fry the tortillas: Spread a few layers of paper towels on a cutting board, tray, or other surface near your stove. Pour enough oil into the bottom of a medium heavy-duty (10-inch) skillet to cover the bottom by about ¼ inch. (Alternatively, use a 12-inch stir-fry pan.) Heat the oil over medium-high heat until shimmering. (Watch carefully and do not overheat the oil—if it begins to smoke, it is too hot. You may need to drop the heat to medium.) Carefully add 1 tortilla and cook until the underside is golden brown, about 10 to 20 seconds. The tortilla will puff up or bubble—that's OK: use tongs to press gently down on the middle of the tortilla to keep the entire bottom surface in contact with the oil, but don't worry about deflating the bubble. Use the tongs to turn the

continued →

TOSTADOS OF REFRIED BEANS AND SPICED SWEET POTATO FRIES,

continued →

tortilla over and cook the other side until golden, another 10 to 15 seconds. Transfer the tortilla to the paper towels. (Gently poke a hole in one side to deflate any large bubbles slightly.) Repeat the process to fry the remaining 3 tortillas. If you pause during the frying, remove the skillet from the stove so that the oil does not overheat; reheat it when ready to fry again.

4 Arrange the fried tortillas on a board and sprinkle with salt. Spread 2 to 3 tablespoons of the refried beans on top of each tortilla. Top with a portion of the spiced sweet potato fries. Sprinkle with queso fresco or dollop with sour cream. Spoon a few teaspoons of salsa verde over all, and top with pepitas. Cut into quarters or fold in half to eat.

Spicy Roasted Tomatillo Salsa Verde

MAKES 2 CUPS

1 pound tomatillos, papery husks removed, cut in half (about 5 or 6 tomatillos)

2 small yellow onions, peeled and cut into quarters

2 medium jalapeños, stemmed

4 large garlic cloves, cut in half

3 tablespoons extra-virgin olive oil

½ teaspoon kosher salt, plus a large pinch

⅔ cup packed fresh cilantro (leaves and tender stems)

2 tablespoons fresh lime juice

1 to 3 tablespoons water

¼ cup minced scallions (white and light green parts), optional

You can certainly buy salsa verde, but making this Mexican condiment at home is a kick—and it's easy. I adapted mine from a recipe by my friend (and former boss) Martha Holmberg, whose awesome cookbook, *Modern Sauces*, has a primo spot on my cookbook shelf. This salsa winds up being pretty spicy with its whole jalapeño, but that makes it perfect for pairing with mild ingredients like eggs (Spicy Egg Tacos with Salsa Verde, Sharp Cheddar, and Pickled Veggies, page 162) and rice. It's a good excuse to get friendly with tomatillos, too.

1 Preheat the oven to 450°F. Line a rimmed baking sheet with parchment paper. In a medium bowl, combine the tomatillos, onions, jalapeños, garlic, oil, and ½ teaspoon of the salt and toss well. Spread out on the prepared baking sheet and bake for 10 minutes. Use tongs to flip the vegetables over, and continue roasting for 10 to 12 minutes, until the vegetables are well softened and brown. (The tomatillos should be collapsed, and the onions and garlic should be well browned.) Remove from the oven and let the vegetables cool on the pan for 15 minutes or so.

2 Transfer the roasted vegetables to the bowl of a food processor, being sure to scrape in all the browned juices from the pan as well. Add the cilantro, lime juice, and a big pinch of salt. Pulse until the salsa is well blended but still a bit chunky. Add 1 to 3 tablespoons water to thin a bit and process again. (Do not overprocess.) Transfer to a bowl and stir in the scallions (if using). If not using right away, tightly cover with plastic wrap and store in the fridge for up to 5 days. Bring to room temperature and thin with a little water if necessary before using.

ROASTED BUTTERNUT SQUASH AND BLACK BEAN QUESADILLA

WITH FRESH CORN AND PEPPER JACK

SERVES 2 TO 3

3 tablespoons unsalted butter

1 small or ½ medium red onion, diced (about ¾ cup)

Kosher salt

1 cup fresh corn kernels (from about 1½ ears of corn)

1 teaspoon minced fresh garlic

½ teaspoon freshly grated lime zest

1 recipe Quick-Roasted Root Vegetables (choose all butternut squash, page 83)

1 to 2 tablespoons chopped fresh cilantro

½ cup cooked or canned black beans, drained and rinsed

½ teaspoon adobo sauce from a can of chipotles in adobo (optional)

4 medium (fajita-size, 8-inch) flour tortillas

1½ cups grated Pepper Jack cheese

One of my favorite late summer/early fall vegetable combos is butternut squash, fresh corn, and black beans. And these three just happen to make a great quesadilla filling together, especially when mixed with Pepper Jack cheese, a hit of chipotle and lime, and garlic and onions, too. I like to quick-roast the squash first for extra flavor and a nice, soft texture. (You can roast it a day ahead if you like, and store it, covered, in the fridge.)

1 In a medium (10-inch) nonstick skillet, heat 1 tablespoon of the butter over medium-low heat. Add the onion and a pinch of salt, and cook, stirring, until softened and golden, 6 to 8 minutes. Add the corn and a pinch of salt and cook, stirring, until the corn looks slightly shrunken and glistening, 2 to 3 minutes. Stir in the garlic and the lime zest and cook until softened and fragrant, about 30 seconds. Stir in the black beans and the adobo (if using) until well combined.

2 Transfer the veggie-bean mixture to a medium bowl. Add the roasted squash and cilantro and stir well.

3 Wipe the skillet clean and return it to medium heat with ½ tablespoon of butter. (Alternatively, you can switch to a 12-inch skillet, which will give you a little more room for flipping over the quesadilla.) When the butter has melted, add 1 tortilla to the pan. Sprinkle with a quarter of the cheese, top evenly with half of the veggie mixture, sprinkle with another quarter of the cheese, and top with a second tortilla.

4 Press the top tortilla down gently with a spatula and cover the pan. Cook until the bottom is golden brown and the cheese has melted, 2 to 3 minutes. Carefully flip with a spatula, adding 1/2 tablespoon of the butter to the pan, and cook the quesadilla until the bottom is golden brown, about 2 minutes.

5 Transfer the quesadilla to a wooden cutting board. Let the pan cool for a minute, then return it to the heat. Repeat the process to assemble and cook the second quesadilla. Let the second quesadilla cool for a few minutes before cutting.

6 Slice both quesadillas into wedges and serve warm.

SPICED CAULIFLOWER, CHICKPEA, AND BROWN RICE BURRITO

WITH ARUGULA

MAKES 4 BURRITOS

2 cups cooked short-grain brown rice (see page 235)

1 cup cooked chickpeas (see page 236) or canned chickpeas, drained and rinsed

4 large (burrito-size, 10-inch) flour tortillas

Double recipe Spiced Cauliflower Sauté (page 194), reheated if necessary

⅓ cup or more chopped toasted pecans or toasted sliced almonds

⅓ cup Lime-Chipotle Sauce (page 164)

1 large or 2 small avocados, cut in half and sliced

1 to 1½ cups loosely packed arugula, or 20 to 30 small sprigs of fresh cilantro

I've included this comforting burrito recipe as an example of how you can put together a hearty supper quickly if you max out our make-ahead strategy. I love short-grain brown rice, so I often keep a batch of it on hand; if I reheat it with some chickpeas or other beans, I've got the instant base for a burrito. This one gets a big helping of flavor from a Spiced Cauliflower Sauté and our Lime-Chipotle Sauce. Avocados, arugula (or cilantro if you prefer), and toasted pecans bring richness and depth. Go ahead and assemble all four burritos, even if you don't plan to eat them all tonight. You'll have delicious leftovers tomorrow. (Wrap in foil and reheat in a moderate oven.)

1 In a medium bowl, stir together the rice and the chickpeas. Reheat in a microwave on high for 2 minutes or in a medium saucepan, covered, over low heat.

2 Warm the tortillas (see page 239).

3 Place 1 tortilla on your work surface. Spoon about ½ cup of the warm rice and ¼ cup of the chickpeas onto the lower center of the tortilla, forming a rough shape a little bigger than a deck of cards (with the long side facing you). Put a portion (one quarter) of the cauliflower sauté on top of the rice and chickpeas.

Sprinkle with a quarter of the pecans. Add a generous spoonful of Lime-Chipotle Sauce and several arugula leaves or sprigs of cilantro. Top with a portion of avocado slices and a bit more Lime-Chipotle Sauce if desired.

4 Wrap the burrito: Start by folding up the bottom (the side closest to you); then fold the two sides in, keeping the filling layered and compact. Then roll the whole burrito tightly over the rest of the tortilla to close it. Cut the burrito in half on a sharp diagonal and arrange the two halves on a plate. Repeat with remaining tortillas and filling.

VEGGIES + EGGS

RUMOR has it that as a baby, I would eat eggs only if my big sister Eleanor fed them to me, in my high chair. After that, as a young girl, I disdained eggs altogether (except for my Dad's special, buttery "Grandpa egg"—and in popovers). Fast-forward, oh, a few years, and I am living on a small farm with more than five hundred laying hens. You could say I got friendly with eggs. More than friendly. Now, I pretty much bow down to them in gratitude for what they give in the way of a quick, delicious supper (especially in August on a busy small farm). And that's not even considering breakfast or lunch.

And here's the honest truth: a farm-fresh egg really is all that it's hyped up to be. It starts out with one big advantage over grocery store eggs: youth. While a grocery store egg is usually anywhere from three to six weeks old (but can be more), eggs you buy at a farmers' market are usually no more than a few days old, and a farm-stand egg could be just a few hours old. And youth is kind to eggs: their yolks are plump, and their whites are firm and bouncy.

Next to freshness, the factor that most affects the flavor and texture of an egg is the hen's diet.

All laying hens eat some grain, but a hen that spends time outdoors, either on pasture or in a fenced area of soil and scrub, augments her diet with bugs, seeds, and leafy things. Her eggs will usually have a yellower yolk, from the beta-carotene in her forage. Studies have also shown that farm eggs are higher in vitamin D and omega-3 fatty acids than eggs of factory hens. The flavor is deeper and richer as well.

I'm sharing all this with you not because I want to put you off completely from grocery store eggs, but because I've developed a passion for farm eggs. (And you *can* get decent eggs at the grocery store now.) Oddly enough, even after all the eggs I've handled, I still feel like I'm opening a present when I open up a carton of fresh eggs. I think of all the possibilities, and the comfort and nourishment and fun that lies ahead in the cooking and eating of those goodies. Hard to put a price on, really.

Tips and Strategies for Eggs

BE A CHOOSY EGG SHOPPER.

Despite the confusing labeling of eggs ("free-range," "all-natural," "cage-free," "pastured"), there actually are things to look for on an egg carton that will steer you toward good eggs. Above all, look for either the "Animal Welfare Approved" logo or the "Certified Humane: Raised and Handled" label—these identify farms that have passed a rigorous set of standards for keeping laying hens. "USDA Organic" eggs are your next-best bet (these birds are not caged), especially if you want eggs from hens on a GMO-free diet. (Non-GMO feed grain is still very expensive in this country because so much of our soy and corn crop is genetically modified. This is why organic eggs cost more.) Beyond that, choose identifiable national brands as opposed to generic, cheap eggs; they will have some quality standards, but without third-party certification (such as Animal Welfare Approved), there is a lot of wiggle room here (and potentially deceptive marketing—see confusing labeling above). You should also keep an eye out for local eggs in your grocery store, because many groceries are now buying them directly from farmers.

And last, as I recommend with any ingredient, do a taste comparison of different brands to see what you like. You might even want to try some organic eggs next to some typical factory eggs. (You will notice a difference, I promise.) And with this one ingredient, try not to be lured by the lowest price—a great egg that's slightly more expensive is worth it. Even if a dozen organic eggs cost six dollars, that's still only fifty cents for a powerhouse of nutrition and only a dollar for a great start to an entire veggie supper.

DON'T UNDERESTIMATE AN EGG.

The astonishing thing about eggs is their unique ability to do double duty. On the one hand, they can be a delicious and filling major player. (Think scrambled eggs, fried eggs, baked eggs, and hard-cooked eggs.) But, just as gracefully, they can play a completely different, supporting role as binder, leavener, custard maker, candlestick maker. (OK, just kidding about that last one.) But really, what other ingredient in our veggie-supper larder has two distinct personalities?

It's good to remember this, because it has gotten frightfully trendy to just throw an egg on everything. That's not such a terrible sin, as a fried or poached egg does pair well with many things. But if that's all you did, you'd be missing out on some of the brilliant alchemy that happens when eggs meet cream or milk and, sometimes, flour or cheese. Custard, batter—two words that scream, "Add some veggies (and maybe some herbs and spices) to me, and you've got supper!" I never get tired of manipulating egg custards and batters into new dishes, from bread puddings to frittatas to savory pancakes.

So for our veggies suppers, we'll make sure we take eggs in both directions. Say you've got some fresh brussels sprouts—you could pair them with potatoes and a fried egg in a delicious hash (page 188), or combine them with custard in a warming bread pudding (page 202).

GRAB A WHISK, A BOWL, AND A NONSTICK SKILLET (OR TWO).

If you've been scrambling eggs with a fork or combining batters with a wooden spoon, I think you'll be surprised at how much easier and more efficient it is to beat eggs with a balloon whisk. A balloon whisk is simply a handheld whisk with a bulbous shape that incorporates air when mixing. It is worth going to a good kitchen store and buying one with sturdy tines and a solid handle that feels comfortable in your hand, as you will have it for years to come.

While you're at it, make sure you've got a good set of nesting mixing bowls that are wider than they are deep, and keep them in a convenient spot in your work area. (I find deep bowls are awkward to work in.) For mixing eggs (and most things), I like wide stainless-steel bowls that range in volume from 2 cups to 6 quarts.

Now, if you are an egg freak like me, you might go ahead and get a nonstick skillet in all three of the most common sizes (8-inch, 10-inch, and 12-inch), if you don't already have them. But if you are on a budget (also like me!), you will probably want to purchase these piecemeal. I recommend buying yourself a heavy, ovenproof 10-inch nonstick skillet first, because you can use it to make everything from frittatas to puffy pancakes to scrambled eggs.

For complete versatility in making egg suppers, stock up on a few baking dishes, too. Single-serving ramekins are great for make-ahead bread puddings and for simple baked eggs, and a standard 9 x 12-inch baking dish can be great for one large bread pudding or other baked egg dish.

For the Pantry

Depending on the size of your household, you'll want to have one or two dozen eggs on hand pretty much all the time for making veggie suppers. Keep the eggs in their original carton or keep them well covered, because eggs have porous shells and can absorb refrigerator odors. The porous shells also allow air and moisture to escape as an egg ages, so if the eggs are kept covered, they will stay fresher a bit longer. All grocery store eggs (and most farm eggs for sale at markets) will have been washed, and because washing removes the protective "bloom" that covers an egg when it is laid, all washed eggs must be refrigerated. Even if you buy unwashed eggs from a farmer, I still advocate refrigerating them, as you won't lose any quality in doing so.

The recipes in this chapter all call for large (hen) eggs, which weigh 2 ounces on average. (The USDA says a carton of large eggs should weigh 24 ounces total, but within the carton, eggs can vary a bit in weight.) If you are buying eggs from a local farm, you may have a range of sizes—some huge, some small. For most of our veggie-supper recipes, slight variations in egg size won't matter too much. However, for the custards and pancake batters designed to fit into a pan with a specific volume, it's best to stick with eggs that are all consistently large (2 ounces).

Even though our egg pantry list has only one ingredient in it, our egg "accessories" are fun to stock because eggs have so many natural partners, from cheese to fresh herbs to spices.

The Eggs

1 or 2 dozen fresh large eggs (preferably certified humanely raised, organic, and/or local)

Accessory Ingredients

All-purpose flour	Dijon mustard	Goat cheese
Black pepper	Feta	Hot sauce
Butter	Fresh chile peppers	Leeks
Cheddar cheese	Fresh cilantro	Milk
Chives	Fresh mint	Parmesan cheese
Citrus zest	Fresh parsley	Scallions
Cream		Thyme

FRESH EGG SALAD TOASTS

WITH ARUGULA AND SLICED TOMATOES

SERVES 4

6 hard-cooked eggs (see page 238), peeled

2 tablespoons mayonnaise, plus more for brushing

1 tablespoon grainy Dijon mustard

½ teaspoon kosher salt, plus more for sprinkling

¼ teaspoon freshly ground black pepper (or several grinds)

1 tablespoon finely sliced fresh chives

4 thick slices of peasant bread (preferably ½ inch thick and 5 to 6 inches long)

Extra-virgin olive oil, for brushing (optional)

2 cups arugula

2 medium ripe tomatoes, cored and sliced

My best friend, Eliza, and I started cooking together as toddlers. First it was mud pies, then it was the Easy-Bake Oven. We both grew up to become cooks, and now Eliza tests all my recipes. When we were little, I wouldn't eat egg salad, but it was on the menu a lot at her house. So when I wanted to do an egg salad toast for this book, naturally I asked Eliza for her recipe. And guess what: now I love it! With a bit of grainy Dijon mustard and some fresh chives in the salad, and with spicy arugula and juicy tomatoes paired with crunchy artisan bread, it all works deliciously. Another really great thing: the salad keeps in the fridge for 2 to 3 days. Make it one night and then have a super-quick supper the next.

1 Slice the eggs with a knife or with an egg slicer. Put them in a medium bowl and mash them with a fork until coarsely mashed. Add 2 tablespoons of mayonnaise, the mustard, ½ teaspoon of salt, and the pepper and stir until just combined. Fold in most of the chives, reserving a few for garnish.

2 Preheat the oven broiler to high. Brush both sides of the bread slices with a little mayonnaise or olive oil. (Mayonnaise creates a slightly crisper toast.) Arrange the bread slices on a baking sheet and sprinkle with a little salt. Broil until the tops are lightly golden, about 2 minutes. Flip the bread slices over and broil until the other side is lightly golden, about 2 minutes more.

3 If the toasts are very large, you can cut them in half. Arrange the toasts on a platter or individual serving plates and top evenly with equal portions of arugula leaves, reserving some for garnish. Top each toast with a quarter of the egg salad, some of the remaining chives, 2 slices of tomato, then a few leaves of reserved arugula.

QUICKEST MINI FRITTATA

OF GARLIC GREENS AND FETA

SERVES 1 OR 2

3 large eggs

¼ cup half-and-half

½ teaspoon roughly chopped fresh thyme, or 1 teaspoon sliced fresh mint

½ teaspoon kosher salt, plus a large pinch

Freshly ground black pepper

3 tablespoons crumbled feta cheese

2 teaspoons extra-virgin olive oil or grapeseed oil

½ teaspoon minced fresh garlic

Pinch of red pepper flakes

2 cups very thinly sliced mature kale or collard greens (stemmed), or 2 cups zucchini "noodles" or julienne

Sour cream or Greek yogurt (optional)

¼ medium avocado, cut in half and sliced (optional)

2 to 3 teaspoons Quick-Pickled Corn, Jalapeños, and Onions (page 199)

If you've got an 8-inch nonstick skillet, you can make a quick and yummy little frittata simply by sautéing a few greens and pouring a mix of eggs, cream, and cheese over them. It's that easy. Not in the mood for greens? Sauté zucchini "noodles" (a fun way to use your Spiralizer or julienne peeler!) and add mint. We're not going for a thick frittata (like the big Kitchen Garden Frittata on page 185) here; this is more like an open-faced omelet or egg pancake, cooked on the stovetop and finished under the broiler instead of baked in a hot oven. Preheat your broiler before you start your sauté, because the cooking happens very fast. Slices of this little frittata are great to pack for lunch the next day.

1 Move an oven rack to the top position, a few inches from the broiler element, and preheat the oven broiler to high. In a medium bowl, whisk together the eggs, half-and-half, thyme, ½ teaspoon of salt, and several grinds of pepper. Whisk in the crumbled feta.

2 In a small (8-inch) ovenproof nonstick skillet, heat the oil over medium heat. Add the garlic and a pinch of red pepper flakes, and cook, stirring, until fragrant, about 30 seconds. Add the sliced kale and a big pinch of salt and cook, stirring, until wilted, about 45 seconds (1 to 2 minutes for zucchini, which can pick up a little nice browning, too, after some of the moisture cooks out).

3 Carefully pour the egg mixture into the pan and slide a silicone spatula around the edges of the pan and across the mixture a few times to evenly distribute the veggies and cheese, then let the mixture cook, undisturbed, until the edges look like they are beginning to set (you might also see a few bubbles in the custard), about 2 minutes.

4 Transfer the skillet to the hot oven and broil the frittata until the middle is set and the top is nicely golden brown in most places (the edges will be puffed up), about 3 minutes (it happens fast!). Remove from the oven and let cool for 5 to 10 minutes before slicing and eating. Garnish with a little sour cream, a few slices of avocado, and a few quick pickles (if using).

HERBED CHICKPEA FLOUR PANCAKES

WITH MUSHROOMS, PEAS, AND HUMMUS BUTTER

MAKES 7 OR 8 PANCAKES

1 tablespoon plus 1 teaspoon unsalted butter, plus more as needed

3 tablespoons plus 2 teaspoons extra-virgin olive oil, plus more as needed

2 cups thinly sliced cremini mushrooms

¾ teaspoon kosher salt

¼ cup thinly sliced scallions (all parts)

¾ cup chickpea flour

½ teaspoon ground cumin

½ teaspoon baking powder

3 large eggs

½ cup frozen peas, thawed, or fresh peas, blanched or microwaved for 30 seconds

3 tablespoons chopped fresh cilantro or a combination of cilantro and fresh mint

½ teaspoon fresh lime zest

continued opposite

I love the nutty flavor of chickpea flour, which is the traditional base for a Provençal pancake called *socca*. My untraditional pancake brings eggs into the mix, along with lots of fragrant herbs and some vegetables. The result is a hearty, satisfying supper pancake (or pancakes, I should say) that can be eaten alone or topped many ways. My favorite topping is warm Hummus Butter (page 183), which makes it a double hit of chickpeas in one supper. (This should be freshly made and still warm so it has a loose consistency.) These pancakes are pretty darn tasty just like that, but sometimes I embellish them further with chopped dates or toasted sesame seeds, pine nuts, or coconut flakes. You can play around with other toppings, too. A simple lemon butter would do, or even a few sautéed greens. For a vegan version of these (gluten-free) pancakes, replace the butter with coconut oil. Chickpea flour stores best in the freezer, where it will keep for several months. If possible, dial in 30 minutes (or up to a few hours) to let the pancake batter rest after mixing.

1 In a medium (10-inch) nonstick skillet, heat 2 teaspoons of the butter and 1 tablespoon of the oil over medium heat. When the butter has melted, add the mushrooms and ¼ teaspoon of the salt and cook, stirring, until shrunken and golden brown, about 8 minutes. Stir in the scallions and cook until softened, about 1 minute. Remove from the heat and set aside.

2 In a medium bowl, whisk together the chickpea flour, cumin, the remaining ½ teaspoon of salt, and the baking powder. In a separate medium bowl, whisk together the eggs, 2 tablespoons of the olive oil, and ⅓ cup of water. Whisk the egg mixture into the chickpea flour mixture. (It's OK if it's a little lumpy.) Let the batter rest for 30 minutes, if you have the time. (Or make it a few hours ahead and hold in the fridge.)

3 Add the mushroom mixture, peas, cilantro, and lime zest into the batter. Wipe the skillet clean and return it to medium heat. (Or alternatively, switch to a 12-inch nonstick skillet.) Add the remaining 2 teaspoons of butter and 2 teaspoons of oil to the skillet. When the butter has melted and is bubbling, use a ¼ cup measure to scoop some batter into the pan. There should be room for 2 or

1 recipe Hummus Butter (recipe follows), still warm, or 3 tablespoons melted butter seasoned with lemon or lime juice or zest

¼ to ½ cup optional garnishes (choose from chopped pitted Medjool dates, toasted unsweetened coconut flakes, toasted pine nuts, or toasted sesame seeds)

3 pancakes at a time. Cook until bubbles begin to form around the edges and a bit on the top, about 2 minutes. Check to be sure the bottom is golden brown, then flip over. Cook until golden on the bottom, about 2 minutes more.

4 Transfer the pancakes to a warm plate (or a plate in a warm oven) and cover loosely. Repeat the cooking process with the remaining batter, adding more butter or oil to the pan as needed. Serve the pancakes warm, topped with warm Hummus Butter and garnishes (if using).

Hummus Butter

MAKES ABOUT ⅓ CUP

3 tablespoons unsalted butter

½ teaspoon freshly grated lime or lemon zest

¼ cup prepared chickpea hummus or Lemony Chickpea Hummus (page 139)

Yes, you read that correctly. Hummus Butter. It is a warm, delicious thing, I promise. It is simply melted butter with a little hummus and lime or lemon zest stirred in to make a drizzly topping for chickpea flour pancakes or for greens, grains, toast—many things! I got the notion to make Hummus Butter when I saw that Middle Eastern restaurants were serving warm hummus with butter drizzled over the top. It makes perfect flavor sense, because both butter and chickpeas have nutty qualities. So I simply inverted the proportions and stirred some hummus into melted butter—yum! If using store-bought hummus, add a little lime or lemon zest. If using the Lemony Chickpea Hummus from page 139, omit the zest. Either way, make this at the last minute—it's not a sauce that holds together, so it is best served warm, straight from the saucepan. Scale up the recipe as needed.

1 In a small saucepan, melt the butter over medium-low heat until bubbly and starting to smell nutty and fragrant. Reduce the heat to low and whisk in the zest (if using store-bought hummus) and the hummus until as well incorporated as possible, keeping in mind it will be a slightly "broken"-looking sauce.

2 Immediately spoon the sauce over warm pancakes or cooked veggies or grains.

SILKY EGG RICE

WITH ASPARAGUS, SCALLIONS, PARMESAN, AND BLACK PEPPER

SERVES 3

1 tablespoon plus 1 teaspoon unsalted butter

1 tablespoon extra-virgin olive oil

1 cup white long-grain rice

1¼ teaspoons kosher salt

2 cups thinly sliced asparagus (about 1 bunch, trimmed and cut at a sharp angle)

½ cup thinly sliced scallions (any parts)

2 large eggs

½ cup coarsely grated Parmesan cheese

½ teaspoon freshly ground black pepper, plus more to taste

1 to 2 tablespoons chopped fresh tender spring herbs, such as mint, parsley, and tarragon

I first learned this method of enriching cooked rice with beaten egg from cookbook author Deborah Madison when we did a story with her at *Fine Cooking* magazine. I couldn't believe how simple and satisfying a dish like this is. The egg gets "cooked" by the hot rice (sort of like hot pasta cooks the egg in a carbonara sauce) but still stays saucy. Since then, I've adapted the technique to showcase seasonal veggies, and here a generous amount of sautéed asparagus lends a lot of flavor to the rice. Black pepper, fresh herbs, and Parmesan cheese round out this comforting and uplifting supper. Be sure to transfer the rice from the pot to a wide bowl before mixing in the egg.

1 In a medium saucepan, heat 2 teaspoons of the butter and 1 teaspoon of oil over medium heat. When the butter has melted, add the rice and ½ teaspoon of the salt. Cook, stirring, until the grains begin to lose their opacity and smell a bit toasty, 1 to 2 minutes. Add 1¾ cups of water and bring to a boil, then reduce to very low, cover, and simmer for 20 minutes. Remove the pan from the heat.

2 While the rice is cooking, heat the remaining 2 teaspoons of butter and 2 teaspoons of oil in a large (12-inch) nonstick skillet. Add the asparagus and ½ teaspoon of the salt and cook, stirring frequently, until the asparagus turns bright green and then takes on some nice browning, 5 to 7 minutes. Add the scallions and cook until just slightly softened, about 1 minute. Remove from the heat.

3 Warm a shallow mixing bowl by rinsing it under hot water and then drying. In a small bowl, whisk the eggs with the remaining ¼ teaspoon of salt until well combined. Transfer the hot rice to the prewarmed bowl, leaving behind any excess water in the bottom of the saucepan. Immediately add the beaten eggs to the hot rice, stirring with a silicone spatula to gently but thoroughly coat the rice. Stir again a few times so that the egg reaches the hottest parts of the rice. Immediately stir in the hot asparagus and scallions, as well as the Parmesan, black pepper, and 1 tablespoon of the herbs. Taste, and add more black pepper and/or the remaining 1 tablespoon of herbs if desired. Spoon into three deep bowls and serve right away.

KITCHEN GARDEN FRITTATA

WITH FINGERLING POTATOES, LEEKS, FRESH HERBS, AND GOAT CHEESE

SERVES 4

12 ounces unpeeled fingerling potatoes, cut crosswise into ⅜-inch slices

1¾ teaspoons kosher salt

Freshly ground black pepper

2 tablespoons unsalted butter

1 tablespoon plus 1 teaspoon extra-virgin olive oil

2 cups thinly sliced leeks, well rinsed but not dried

2 teaspoons minced fresh garlic

2 handfuls baby spinach, baby Swiss chard leaves, arugula, or other greens (about 1 cup packed)

8 large eggs, ideally at room temperature

⅔ cup half-and-half

½ teaspoon freshly grated lemon zest

⅓ cup coarsely grated Parmesan cheese

4 ounces cold fresh goat cheese, well crumbled while still chilled

continues on page 187

While we're on the subject of all-in-one veggie suppers, we surely can't overlook the nearly perfect qualifications of a fully loaded frittata like this one: satisfying potatoes, golden sweet leeks, tangy goat cheese, a handful of greens, and whatever lovely herbs (and even flowers) you can gather, all in one pan. (Plus eggs, of course.) And, although frittatas with potatoes aren't necessarily the quickest to prepare, they are the most hearty, and they tend to make the best leftovers, too. (This frittata tastes better after sitting out of the oven for a bit, and even better the next day.) Be generous with the herbs, and don't forget the salt and pepper, because egg custards need exuberant seasoning before cooking. For a pretty look, use whole herb leaves or edible flowers such as chive blossoms or nasturtiums to garnish the top of the frittata.

1 Place an oven rack in the middle of the oven. Preheat the oven to 375°F.

2 Put the potatoes and 1 teaspoon of the salt into a medium saucepan and cover with water by 1 inch. Put over high heat and bring to a boil, then reduce the heat and simmer until tender, 10 to 12 minutes. Drain the potatoes well in a colander and let cool for several minutes. Transfer the potatoes to a large bowl and season with a sprinkling of salt and a few grinds of black pepper.

3 In a medium (10-inch) heavy nonstick skillet that is ovenproof, heat 1 tablespoon of the butter and 1 tablespoon of the oil over medium-low heat. Add the leeks (with any residual water clinging to them) and ¼ teaspoon of the salt, cover, and cook, uncovering occasionally to stir, until softened and translucent, 6 to 8 minutes. Uncover the skillet, raise the heat to medium, and continue to cook, stirring frequently, until the leeks are shrunken and browned in places, another 6 to 8 minutes. Add the minced garlic and cook, stirring, until softened and fragrant, about 30 seconds. Add the spinach and cook, stirring, until completely wilted, about 1 minute. Transfer the leek mixture to the bowl of potatoes and toss well; reserve the skillet. Let the veggie mixture cool for 10 minutes.

continued →

KITCHEN GARDEN FRITTATA,

continued →

1 tablespoon chopped fresh thyme, or 1 to 2 tablespoons any combination of chopped fresh herbs, such as dill, parsley, mint, thyme, lemon thyme, oregano, chives, and sage

10 to 15 whole herb leaves or edible flowers, such as nasturtium petals, chive blossoms, or dill or basil flowers

4 In a large bowl, whisk together the eggs, half-and-half, lemon zest, the remaining ½ teaspoon of salt, and several grinds of black pepper. Stir in the Parmesan, goat cheese, and thyme. Add the veggie mixture and stir well.

5 Return the skillet to medium-high heat and add the remaining 1 tablespoon of butter and 1 teaspoon of oil. When the butter has melted and begun to sizzle, pour and scrape all the veggie-custard mixture into the skillet. Using a silicone spatula, gently stir and move the contents of the pan around to evenly distribute, then let the mixture cook, undisturbed, until the edges are just beginning to set, 1 to 2 minutes. Transfer the pan to the hot oven and broil until the frittata is puffed, golden, and set in the middle, 26 to 28 minutes.

6 Let the frittata cool in the pan for 15 to 20 minutes, then transfer to a cutting board and cut into squares or wedges. Serve warm. Alternatively, let it sit for 30 minutes to heighten the flavors, and serve at room temperature.

YUKON GOLD POTATO AND BRUSSELS SPROUTS HASH

WITH PARMESAN-FRIED EGGS

SERVES 2

2 teaspoons maple syrup

1 teaspoon lemon juice

½ teaspoon freshly grated lemon zest

3 tablespoons extra-virgin olive oil

2 medium Yukon Gold potatoes (about 12 ounces), cut into small dice (about 2½ cups)

1¼ teaspoons kosher salt, plus more to taste

2 cups thinly sliced brussels sprouts (6 to 7 ounces)

½ cup diced red onion

1 teaspoon minced fresh garlic

2 teaspoons loosely packed fresh thyme leaves

1 tablespoon unsalted butter

2 large eggs

Freshly ground black pepper

3 tablespoons finely grated Parmesan cheese

Comfort in a skillet here. Diced Yukon Gold potatoes slowly sauté to a crispy brown, while sliced brussels sprouts and red onions jump in the mix halfway through cooking to lend their earthy and sweet flavors. A bit of garlic and thyme and a finish of just a tiny bit of lemon and maple make this "hash" super delicious on its own—and even better when you scootch it to the side of the skillet and add a couple of eggs. Dust the eggs with Parmesan and thyme—and plenty of black pepper, of course—and fry to your liking. Supper in a skillet is served. For the most even cooking, cut the brussels sprouts lengthwise into thin slices (no need to core them).

1 In a small bowl, stir together the maple syrup, lemon juice, and lemon zest. Set aside.

2 In a large (12-inch) nonstick skillet that has a lid, heat the oil over medium heat. Add the potatoes and 1 teaspoon of the salt. Stir and cover loosely. Cook, uncovering occasionally to stir, until the potatoes have shrunken a bit and are browning, about 12 minutes. (Listen for a gentle sizzle; if there is a lot of loud popping, reduce the heat just a bit so that the potatoes will cook and brown more slowly.) Uncover and add the brussels sprouts, onion, and the remaining (scant) ¼ teaspoon of salt. Cook, stirring more frequently, uncovered, until the potatoes are tender and everything is deeply browned, 10 to 12 minutes more. (Toward the end of

cooking you will have to stir—or flip with a spatula—even more frequently to get nice browning without burning. Don't undercook, though!) Add the garlic and 1 teaspoon of the thyme. Cook, stirring, until fragrant, about 30 seconds.

3 Push the vegetables to one side of the pan. (It's OK to bunch them up.) Add the butter to the empty side of the pan. When the butter has melted and is bubbly, crack the eggs into the pan (try to keep them a bit separate). Sprinkle with salt and black pepper. When the whites are firm, sprinkle the tops of the eggs with about ½ teaspoon of thyme and 1½ tablespoons of the Parmesan, then flip them over. Sprinkle the eggs with the remaining ½ teaspoon of thyme and 1½ tablespoons of Parmesan. Cook until the Parmesan on the bottom has

crusted a bit and the yolk is cooked to your liking, 1 to 2 minutes.

4 Remove the pan from the heat. Sprinkle the lemon-maple mixture over the veggies and gently stir. Divide the veggies between two plates and top each with an egg. Season with more black pepper if you like.

PUFFY OVEN PANCAKE

WITH SAVORY TOPPINGS

SERVES 2

3 large eggs, preferably at room temperature

⅔ cup whole milk

⅔ cup flour

½ teaspoon table salt

3 tablespoons grated Parmesan or other hard cheese

1 teaspoon vegetable oil

2 teaspoons unsalted butter

1 recipe Kale and Cremini Sauté with Gruyère; Sweet Corn and Cherry Tomato Sauté with Parmesan; or Spiced Cauliflower Sauté (recipes follows)

I grew up on popovers—my Dad's breakfast specialty—and have since made them in all kinds of muffin pans, popover pans, and ramekins. But I only recently migrated to a skillet—and one big popover—when my supply of fresh eggs began to overwhelm me. Happily, I found this oven pancake to be one of the best quick suppers ever. It's like an eggy pizza: it can take a variety of toppings (choose from those below or create your own), and you can eat it with your hands! Room-temperature eggs, mixing by hand, and a hot pan produce the puffiest pancakes. And don't be alarmed—they will deflate quickly after coming out of the oven. They can also sit a bit if your topping isn't ready.

1 Preheat the oven to 425°F.

2 In a medium bowl, whisk the eggs and milk well. In a separate medium bowl, stir the flour and salt to combine. Make a well in the center of the flour. Slowly pour the egg-milk mixture directly into the well, whisking as you pour and gradually widening your circle of whisking to incorporate more flour a little at a time. When well combined, stop whisking. (Don't worry if there are a few lumps of flour.) Stir in the Parmesan.

3 Heat the oil and butter in a medium (10-inch) heavy, ovenproof nonstick skillet over medium-high heat. When hot, swirl to coat the bottom and sides of the skillet. Pour the batter into the hot skillet and let it cook, undisturbed, for 30 seconds to begin to set the edges. Transfer the skillet into the hot oven and bake for 18 to 20 minutes, until the pancake is nicely puffed up, brown, and set. Remove from the oven and let rest for a few minutes (it will deflate).

4 Transfer the pancake to a serving plate and cover with topping. Cut or tear into wedges, and eat with forks or roll up and eat with your hands.

Kale and Cremini Sauté with Gruyère

MAKES 1½ TO 2 CUPS, OR ENOUGH TO TOP 1 PUFFY OVEN PANCAKE

1 tablespoon vegetable or grapeseed oil, plus more if needed

2 cups thickly sliced cremini mushrooms (cut in half before slicing)

2 cups stemmed and very thinly sliced Tuscan kale (about ½ bunch or 4 ounces before stemming)

Kosher salt

½ teaspoon minced fresh garlic

⅓ cup grated Gruyère cheese

I'm a fan of crispy, or "dry," kale—cooked quickly over fairly high heat so that it doesn't just wilt but takes on a nutty, dark flavor. Combined with earthy sautéed mushrooms, the flavors and textures make a nice foil for the eggy custard of a Puffy Oven Pancake (page 190), but you could use this topping on toast, over grains, or with beans in tacos, too.

In a medium nonstick skillet, heat 2 teaspoons of the oil over medium heat. Add the mushrooms and a pinch of salt and cook, stirring, until browned and somewhat shrunken, about 4 to 6 minutes. Add the remaining 1 teaspoon of oil, the kale, and a pinch of salt and cook, stirring, until wilted, about 1 minute. Using the back of a spatula, stir the kale and press against the hot pan so that it cooks further and crisps up, getting slightly brittle around the edges, about 2 minutes. Add the garlic and cook, stirring, for 30 seconds. Remove from the heat and spoon onto a warm pancake or over another dish and garnish with the cheese.

Sweet Corn and Cherry Tomato Sauté with Parmesan

MAKES 1½ TO 2 CUPS, OR ENOUGH TO TOP 1 PUFFY OVEN PANCAKE

1 tablespoon cold unsalted butter

1 teaspoon vegetable or olive oil

1 cup fresh corn kernels (from about 2 medium ears)

¼ teaspoon kosher salt

½ teaspoon minced fresh garlic

1 cup halved cherry tomatoes

1 teaspoon fresh lemon juice

1 tablespoon finely sliced fresh chives

3 to 4 tablespoons grated Parmesan cheese

½ avocado, diced (optional)

A quick sauté of sweet corn, cherry tomatoes, and a little garlic makes a savory summertime topping for a Puffy Oven Pancake (page 190) or a filling for omelets or frittatas. Add fresh chives, a touch of lemon, and optional diced avocado to brighten the mix, and top with a bit of grated Parmesan.

In a medium skillet, heat 2 teaspoons of the butter and the oil over medium heat. Add the corn and salt and stir. Reduce the heat to medium-low and cook, stirring, until the corn kernels are glistening and slightly shrunken, 5 to 6 minutes. Stir in the garlic and tomatoes and cook, gently stirring, until the tomatoes are heated through and starting to soften and lose their shape, about 2 minutes. Remove from the heat and stir in the lemon juice, the remaining 1 teaspoon of cold butter, and the chives. Spoon onto a warm pancake or over another dish and garnish with the Parmesan. Toss on the avocados (if using).

Spiced Cauliflower Sauté

MAKES ABOUT 1½ CUPS, OR ENOUGH TO TOP 1 PUFFY OVEN PANCAKE

½ teaspoon ground cumin

½ teaspoon ground coriander

¼ teaspoon paprika

¼ teaspoon red pepper flakes, or to taste

2 teaspoons grapeseed or vegetable oil

2 cups small (1-inch) cauliflower florets

½ teaspoon kosher salt

2 teaspoons unsalted butter

1 teaspoon minced fresh garlic

Lemon wedge

1 to 2 tablespoons chopped fresh parsley, to taste (optional)

My friend Eliza created this quick cauliflower sauté to top one of our Puffy Oven Pancakes (page 190) one night. But in addition to being delicious with eggs, we've gone on to use it in burritos (Spiced Cauliflower, Chickpea, and Brown Rice Burrito with Arugula, page 173) and with grains and beans, too. The warm spices pair well with anything creamy, whether you're going Indian (yogurt) or Mexican (say Lime-Chipotle Sauce, page 164). This recipe yields enough to top a puffy pancake. To use it for four burritos, you'll want to double the recipe. In that case, use a large (12-inch) nonstick pan and expect a slightly longer cooking time.

1 In a small bowl, stir together the cumin, coriander, paprika, and red pepper flakes. Set aside.

2 In a medium skillet, heat the oil over medium-low heat. Add the cauliflower and salt and stir, then cover and cook, uncovering occasionally to stir, until the cauliflower has lost its opacity and is browning in spots, 7 to 9 minutes. Push the cauliflower to one side, and add the butter. When the butter has melted, add the garlic and the spice mixture, and cook until softened and fragrant, about 30 seconds. Stir together the sautéed spices and cauliflower. Remove from the heat and season with a squeeze of lemon. Toss in the parsley (if using). Spoon onto the warm pancake or add to another dish.

BAKED EGG PIZZIOLA

SERVES 1

2 teaspoons butter, plus more for ramekin

4 to 5 frozen artichoke-heart quarters

A small handful of baby spinach

Kosher salt

3 tablespoons coarsely grated Parmesan cheese

1 ounce fresh mozzarella, cut into thin slices

Scant ½ cup Quick-Roasted Plum Tomato Sauce (page 12) or best-quality store-bought marinara, reheated until simmering hot

½ teaspoon black olive tapenade, or 1 teaspoon prepared basil pesto

1 large egg

1 tablespoon heavy cream

Pinch of crushed Aleppo pepper, black pepper, or red pepper flakes

1 or 2 slices warm crusty bread (I like focaccia), cut or torn into pieces for dipping

Break an egg into a ramekin filled with creamy tomato sauce, two cheeses, and some sautéed veggies, and you're less than 15 minutes away from a hot saucy supper, ready for bread dipping. Whenever I make a batch of my Quick-Roasted Plum Tomato Sauce (page 12), I always save a little for making one of these gooey, comforting egg dishes later in the week. (Store-bought tomato sauce works fine, too; it will just give off a bit more liquid.) I like to tuck a few veggies into the bottom of the ramekin—a combination of spinach and sautéed quartered artichoke hearts (I keep a box of these in the freezer) is nice, but mushrooms and/or onions would be great, too. This recipe makes one serving; multiply it to make as many servings as you like. You'll need a large ramekin (about 1¼ cups) for this. Be sure your tomato sauce is hot before assembling.

1 Preheat the oven to 425°F. Rub the entire inside of a 1¼-cup ramekin with butter.

2 In a small skillet, melt 2 teaspoons of butter over medium heat. Add the artichoke hearts (they can still be partially frozen) and cook, pressing down with a spatula, until browned on one side, 4 to 6 minutes. Flip over and brown the other side, 3 to 4 minutes. Transfer the artichokes to a plate. Add the spinach to the pan, season with a pinch of salt, and cook, stirring, until wilted, about 30 seconds. Transfer the spinach to a cutting board and chop coarsely. Put the artichokes and spinach in the bottom of the ramekin.

3 Add 2 tablespoons of the Parmesan and half of the mozzarella slices into the ramekin. Pour in the hot tomato sauce. Swirl in the tapenade a bit with a spoon. Crack the egg into a small bowl and then carefully transfer to the ramekin. Spoon the heavy cream over the egg and top with the remaining 1 tablespoon of Parmesan and the rest of the mozzarella slices. Season with crushed pepper and a big pinch of salt. Bake for 14 to 16 minutes, until the sauce is quite bubbly and the top is browning in spots. (Store-bought marinara will give off much more liquid than homemade roasted tomato sauce, so it will bubble more. With home-made, you can also jiggle the ramekin to see if the egg has mostly set.) Serve warm with bread.

ENGLISH MUFFIN EGG SANDWICH

WITH SPINACH, AVOCADO, CHEDDAR, CRISPY SHIITAKES, AND PICKLED JALAPEÑOS

MAKES 2 SANDWICHES

2 tablespoons plus
2½ teaspoons unsalted butter

2 whole English muffins

Kosher salt

1½ cups packed baby spinach

2 large eggs

2 tablespoons half-and-half

1 tablespoon sliced chives
(optional)

Freshly ground black pepper

2 ounces aged cheddar or
Gruyère cheese, cut into
thin slices

½ small avocado, cut in
half and sliced

8 to 10 slices of quick-pickled
jalapeños (see Quick-Pickled
Corn, Jalapeños, and Onions
recipe that follows)

⅓ cup Quick-Roasted Crispy
Shiitakes (page 87)

½ cup pea shoots (optional)

2 tablespoons Lime-Chipotle
Sauce (page 164), sour cream,
or Greek yogurt (optional)

Some people may think of an egg sandwich as a treat, but I think of it as one of the most perfectly satisfying all-in-one meals. Egg sandwiches are also eminently customizable, which makes supper prep easier right off the bat. I like to start with an English muffin (usually broiled), then my unscrambled "scrambled" egg—sort of a pancake that I fold into quarters, which is perfect for melting cheese on top of. From there I add flavor and texture with avocados, crispy roasted shiitakes (vegetarian bacon alert!), some of my quick-pickled jalapeños, and maybe a few wispy green things like pea shoots. And, I almost forgot: I like a little bit of sautéed spinach under the egg. That way I actually have four or five different vegetables in one egg sandwich. You'll customize your own sandwich I'm sure, but this is a great template for you to tweak.

1 Preheat the oven broiler to high. Split the English muffins in half and place the halves, split-side up, on a rimmed baking sheet. Dot or spread about 1 teaspoon of butter on each half and sprinkle with a pinch of salt. Broil until golden brown on top, about 3 to 5 minutes. Remove from the oven. Keep the bottom halves on the baking sheet, and set the top halves aside. Keep the broiler on.

2 In a small (8-inch) nonstick skillet, heat about ½ teaspoon butter over medium-low heat. Add the spinach and cook, tossing, until wilted, about 30 seconds. Transfer the spinach to paper towels and pat or squeeze dry, then arrange half of the spinach on each English muffin bottom (still on the baking sheet). Reserve the skillet.

3 In a small bowl, whisk together 1 egg, 1 tablespoon of the half-and-half, ½ tablespoon of the chives, a pinch of salt, and a few grinds of pepper. In the small skillet, heat 2 teaspoons of butter over medium-low heat until bubbly. Pour in the egg mixture and let cook, undisturbed, until just set around the edges and underneath, 30 seconds to 1 minute. Lift the edge of the egg pancake up gently with a spatula and let any uncooked egg run to the sides, then set it down again. Let it cook, undisturbed, until the top of the pancake looks mostly set, about 1 minute. Gently flip the pancake over and cook

continued →

ENGLISH MUFFIN EGG SANDWICH,

continued →

the bottom lightly, for about 30 seconds. Transfer the pancake to a cutting board and fold in half and then again into quarters, then arrange on top of the spinach on one muffin half. Repeat with the remaining 1 egg, 1 tablespoon of half-and-half, and ½ tablespoon of chives, a pinch of salt, and a few grinds of black pepper.

4 Arrange half of the cheese slices over each folded egg, then put the baking sheet back under the broiler. Broil until the cheese is just melted, rotating the pan as necessary, about 1 to 2 minutes.

5 Arrange as many avocado slices as you like over the melted cheese on each sandwich. Top each with several slices of pickled jalapeños and a nice little pile of crispy shiitakes. Garnish with pea shoots (if using). If you like, spread 1 tablespoon of Lime-Chipotle Sauce on the top half of each English muffin. Put the top halves on the sandwiches and squish them down. Eat them standing up (!), or cut in half and serve on a plate.

Quick-Pickled Corn, Jalapeños, and Onions

MAKES 2 PINTS

1 pound fresh corn kernels, sliced jalapeños, or sliced red onions (or any onion, including scallions), or a combination of all three

1 teaspoon fresh or dried coriander seeds

2 garlic cloves, cut in half and lightly smashed

2 or 4 strips of lemon or lime zest (optional)

2 or 4 sprigs of fresh thyme (optional)

1½ cups white pickling vinegar

1½ cups water

¼ cup cane sugar

2 teaspoons kosher salt

While writing a magazine article on pickles, I discovered that brined refrigerator pickles are incredibly easy and tasty (and there's no canning required!). I also discovered that my favorite pickled vegetable is corn, and ever since then, I've had a jar of it in my fridge. I also keep pickled jalapeños and onions on hand, and all three go on my egg sandwiches, in tacos, over grain dishes, and more. I recommend making a jar of each vegetable separately, but you could certainly pickle a mixture of all three if you like—just know that the heat in the jalapeños will rule. Coriander seeds are my favorite pickling spice; I use fresh seeds from the cilantro that has finished flowering in my garden or dried seeds from my spice rack. Amounts of veggies are approximate—you may need a little more or less to fill a jar. You also might have a little extra brine after filling your jars. If you have an extra half-pint jar around, wash it so that you can pickle any extra as well.

1 Wash four half-pint jars or two glass pint jars with lids in warm, soapy water and rinse well. Drop 1 garlic half into each half-pint jar, or 2 halves into each pint. Fill each jar with a quarter or a half of the veggies, a quarter or a half of the coriander, a strip of lemon zest (if using), and a sprig of thyme (if using).

2 In a small saucepan, combine the vinegar, water, sugar, and salt. Bring just to a boil over medium-high heat, stirring to dissolve the sugar and salt, and immediately remove from the heat. Let the brine sit for 5 minutes, then pour it over the vegetables in the jars. Let the filled jars cool down at room temperature for 20 to 30 minutes, then cover and refrigerate overnight. You can begin tasting and using the pickled veggies the next day, but their flavor will improve over several days. They will keep for 3 to 4 weeks in the fridge.

JAPANESE VEGETABLE PANCAKES

WITH CABBAGE, COLLARDS, KIMCHI, AND SESAME

MAKES ABOUT 8 PANCAKES

3 tablespoons mayonnaise

1 tablespoon low-sodium tamari

1 teaspoon sriracha sauce

¼ cup plus 2 teaspoons chopped fresh parsley

1 cup very thinly sliced green cabbage

1 cup very thinly sliced red cabbage

1 cup stemmed and very thinly sliced collard greens

½ cup drained and chopped prepared kimchi, plus 1 tablespoon liquid from the jar

⅓ cup sliced scallions (white and light green parts), plus 2 to 3 tablespoons for garnish

3 eggs

⅓ cup all-purpose flour

1 tablespoon toasted sesame oil

½ teaspoon kosher salt

2 to 4 tablespoons grapeseed or olive oil

2 tablespoons toasted sesame seeds

When my friend Amy Miller and I decided to tackle a version of the popular Japanese pancake known as *okonomiyaki* for this chapter, I was a little skeptical about how raw vegetables would cook up in an egg pancake. But I wanted to go for it, knowing what a great vehicle for greens they can be. And then Amy hit the nail on the head: the first test was delicious (as were the second and the third and, well, you know . . . it's always the tastiest things we find an excuse for testing again!). With a tasty drizzling sauce and plenty of toasted sesame seeds for garnish, these pancakes are a fun and flavorful change of pace for supper. (Oh, and they're full of good-for-you greens, like collards and cabbage, too.) One of the ingredients is kimchi, but don't worry—you don't need to make it. A store-bought kimchi (well drained) will work fine.

1 In a small bowl, whisk together the mayonnaise, tamari, sriracha, and 2 teaspoons of the parsley. Set aside.

2 In a large bowl, combine the green cabbage, red cabbage, collard greens, chopped kimchi, ⅓ cup of the scallions, and the remaining ¼ cup of parsley and toss well.

3 In a medium bowl, vigorously whisk together the eggs, flour, sesame oil, kimchi liquid, and salt until well combined.

4 Add the egg mixture to the cabbage mixture and stir well to combine.

5 In a large (12-inch) nonstick skillet over medium-high heat, heat 2 tablespoons of the grapeseed oil. Use a ¼ cup measure to scoop the batter into the hot pan and flatten it slightly. (You can fit 3 to 4 pancakes in the pan at a time.) Cook until golden brown on the bottom, 2 to 3 minutes. (Lower the heat if pancakes are browning too fast.) Flip them over, reduce the heat to medium, and cook until nicely browned on the bottom, about 2 minutes more. Hold the cooked pancakes on a warm plate, loosely covered with foil. Repeat with the remaining batter, adding more oil as necessary.

6 Serve the pancakes right away, garnished with a generous amount of sesame seeds and some sliced scallions. Serve the sriracha mayonnaise sauce on the side.

MINI SAVORY BREAD PUDDINGS

WITH BRUSSELS SPROUTS, CHEDDAR, DIJON, AND SHALLOTS

MAKES 6

2 tablespoons plus 1 teaspoon unsalted butter, plus more for the ramekins

2 whole English muffins

Kosher salt

1 tablespoon extra-virgin olive oil

2 large shallots, cut into thin slices (about 1 cup)

2 cups brussels sprouts leaves, or very thinly sliced greens or baby greens, such as spinach, chard, kale, collards, etc.

6 eggs

1¾ cups half-and-half

1 teaspoon Dijon mustard

1½ teaspoons coarsely chopped fresh thyme

Freshly ground black pepper

1½ cups coarsely grated very sharp cheddar cheese

I love little savory bread puddings—so comforting on a chilly fall or winter evening, and really not difficult to make. I start with toasted English muffins and a good cheese and add sautéed veggies. (My favorite is the simple sauté of brussels sprouts leaves and shallots I've included here.) I season my custard well, pour it over the layered bread and veggies, and then my mini puddings bake up in no time. The flavor develops as they sit, so let them rest out of the oven for a little bit. They taste even better the next day, and because they reheat beautifully, they're a perfect make-ahead. You can cover them with plastic wrap and store them in their ramekins in the fridge for up to 4 days. Then just reheat one in the oven, or pop it out and microwave it for 2 minutes. You'll need 1-cup ramekins for this recipe—ceramic is nice, but Pyrex will do.

1 Preheat the oven to 375°F. Rub six 1-cup ramekins or custard cups all over with a little butter.

2 Split the English muffins in half and place the halves split-side up on a rimmed baking sheet. Spread about 1 teaspoon of the butter on each half and sprinkle with salt. Broil until golden brown on top, about 2 to 4 minutes. (Or toast them in the toaster and then add the butter and salt.) Cut the halves into ¾-inch cubes and put into a large bowl.

3 In a medium (10-inch) nonstick skillet, heat the remaining 1 tablespoon of butter with the oil over medium heat. Once the butter has melted, add the shallots and ¼ teaspoon of salt and cook, stirring frequently, until browned and softened, 5 to 7 minutes. Add the brussels sprouts leaves, season with a pinch of salt, and cook, stirring, until the leaves are glossy and mostly wilted, about 2 minutes. (If using other greens, wilting may take only 1 minute.) Transfer the brussels sprouts mixture into the bowl with the bread cubes.

4 In another large bowl, whisk together the eggs, half-and-half, mustard, thyme, several grinds of black pepper, and ¾ teaspoon of salt.

5 Arrange the 6 ramekins on a rimmed baking sheet. Divide half of the bread-veggie mixture evenly among the ramekins. Scatter ¾ cup of the cheese over the bread-veggie mixture, dividing it evenly among the ramekins. Add the remaining

bread-veggie mixture and then the remaining ¾ cup of cheese.

6 Pour the egg mixture over the contents of the ramekins, dividing it evenly. Using your fingers, gently press down on the bread and veggies to force the custard to surround everything. Let sit for 10 to 15 minutes.

7 Bake for about 30 minutes, until the puddings have risen and set and are golden. Let cool for 10 to 15 minutes before eating (they will deflate). Their flavor will improve the longer they sit. Leftover puddings will keep, covered, for 3 to 4 days in the fridge.

VEGGIES + BROTH

SOMEWHERE along the way, I fell under the spell of the Soup Boss, who drilled it into my head that the best soups could only be made with roasted bones, nubbins of cured meaty things, or a briny assortment of shellfish. Plus, Soup (with a capital "S") had to be simmered for a long time. Uh—no. I woke up one day in vegetarian world and realized this simply wasn't true. Not only is it possible to make a delicious, full-flavored, soul-warming broth that doesn't have any of this stuff in it, but it is also possible to do this in less time than you think.

So about that flavor thing. Here is a little fact to consider: Mushrooms, tomatoes, eggplants, onions, beans, and other power vegetables contain some (or many) of the same amino acids that meats do. Now, when you brown those ingredients, a chemical reaction occurs between sugars and those amino acids—called the Maillard reaction—and the result is rich, caramelized flavors that add serious depth to whatever they're combined with. (Our Caramelized Onion Soup with Cider, Thyme, and Ciabatta Croutons on page 227 takes advantage of this process in a big way.)

Browning vegetables over relatively high, dry heat is an excellent way to extract and multiply flavor in food, especially if you then infuse a liquid with that flavor by "deglazing" the browned bits. So, as far as rich flavor goes, we can check that one off the list (though I've got a bunch more ideas to share about how to get great flavor into broths).

Next, because this is supper we're talking about, how do we get satisfying soup flavor in a (relatively) short amount of time? Well, we use our larder ingredients (and ordinary water) to make a number of "shortcut" broths—all of which are better than store-bought vegetable broth. I do not love store-bought vegetable broth; let me be clear about that up front. I've avoided calling for boxed or canned vegetable broth in these recipes so that you don't inadvertently wind up completely overwhelming a dish with flavor that's disappointing at best, recipe-ruining at worst.

So let's go ahead and look at our strategy for creating flavorful veggie-supper soups with "shortcut" broths.

Tips and Strategies for Broth

IT'S THAT DARN PANTRY AGAIN.

Perhaps more than any chapter in this book, here is where our stocked pantry (or larder, meaning including a fridge) (see page x) makes all the difference. If we are to incorporate quick (or quick-ish) soups into our veggie-supper repertoire, we can't do it without many things we call "accessory" ingredients in the other chapters. Miso paste, dried mushrooms, coconut milk—these are the ingredients, along with water (yes, good old water), vegetables, and fresh herbs and spices that you'll use to make your shortcut veggie broths.

The recipes that follow include a number of different ingredients and methods you can use to flavor vegetable soup without using store-bought vegetable broth. I'm listing the important ones here so that you can get a sense of the range of items that can be used to create "shortcut" veggie broths whenever you want.

1. Miso paste (read more on page 223); especially good in combination with tamari and ginger

2. Dried porcini and/or shiitake mushrooms

3. Canned full-fat coconut milk

4. Cooking liquid from grains such as barley and wheat berries that have been cooked by the pasta method

5. Tomato paste (plus chili powder and sautéed onions to make chili broth)

6. Simmered fresh corn cobs (especially with bay leaves and garlic)

7. Red lentils (cooked with water, they pretty much turn into soup)

8. Roasted or sautéed vegetables (to start a vegetable broth)

9. Sofrito-style sautéed tomato, onion, and garlic base

10. Fruit "juices" (apple cider, orange juice)

Some of these ingredients may seem a little odd to you now, but you will see in the recipes that follow how they are used to impart flavor to a broth. In many cases, making a broth out of these ingredients happens naturally as part of making the soup. But there are a few broths (such as Dried Mushroom Broth, page 222, and grain-cooking liquid, see page 230) that you will have to (or want to) make separately before using them in the recipe.

After considering these great shortcut broths for flavoring soups, we're still left with an elephant in the room: homemade vegetable broth. We are making flavorful vegetarian broths out of many ingredients, but we can also make a relatively quick homemade vegetable broth as a substitute for store-bought. I've included a recipe here for a delicious one: Rich Vegetable Broth (page 213). I use it in several recipes. (The secret to deliciousness, you

won't be surprised to learn, is browning the vegetables first.)

The only silly concern I had about including this homemade broth recipe was that I felt bad "requiring" you to make something for your veggie supper (and only a component, at that) that takes more than an hour to make. (Of course, you could substitute store-bought vegetable broth and not tell me about it, but you might live to regret that.) Considering that the total preparation time is less than an hour and a half (most of it hands-off), and that the broth can be made any time and refrigerated for a few days or frozen for a few weeks, in the end I decided it was worth it. And I've given you some great ideas for using it, too, including the quick Tortellini in Rich Vegetable Broth with Parmesan, Peas, and Carrots on page 212 and the Ramen-esque Noodles in Rich Vegetable Broth with Late-Season Veggies on page 224.

DON'T FORGET YOUR FINISHING FLOURISHES.

A good soup begins with a flavorful base and gains interest as ingredients are added to it along the way. But a great soup is one where close attention is paid at the end. Always, always, always taste a soup before serving it. (Heaven forbid you have oversalted it, but in that case you can water it down or use a creamy or starchy ingredient to cut some of the saltiness.) What you're really tasting for is brightness. You want to see if the flavors are popping. If not—if the soup tastes flat—then it might need a bit more salt, but it most definitely needs a hit of acid (vinegar, citrus juice, or hot sauce) to bring all the flavors to the

foreground. I learned this trick of seasoning a soup or sauce with acid in French culinary school (she says sheepishly).

Soup garnishes are important too, because they can add a contrasting texture for interest (from crunchy nuts, croutons, or a raw salsa) or that elusive brightness via fresh herbs, citrus zest, yogurt, or a swirl of zingy pesto like the Garlic Scape Chimichurri on page 216. Plus, frilly pea shoots and fennel fronds are great eye and palate pleasers.

For the Pantry

As we talked about, there is no single, complete "broth" to buy for the pantry. (If you have time, though, you can make a batch, or a double batch, of Rich Vegetable Broth and freeze it.) We're going to use those "accessory" ingredients to build our own veggie-supper broths, so this is the time to freshen up the spice rack (the volatile oils in spices dissipate over time, so replace old spices and mark new ones with the date of purchase) and to stock up on canned tomato products, in addition to flavor boosters like miso and dried mushrooms.

And surprise! (Or maybe not.) This is the chapter (how appropriate, being the last one) where the stars of the first seven chapters come back for a reprise because, of course, grains, beans, lentils, leaves, toast, noodles, and even eggs are all great partners for broth. So if you've stocked up on those things already, you're halfway to broth heaven.

The Broths

IN THE FRIDGE OR FREEZER

Rich Vegetable Broth
(page 213)

Grain-cooking liquid
(see page 230)

Accessory Ingredients

Apple cider

Bay leaves

Black peppercorns

Canned beans

Canned diced tomatoes

Canned full-fat coconut milk
(preferably organic)

Canned tomato paste

Canned tomato sauce

Carrots

Celery

Chili powder

Citrus juice and zest

Dried porcini and shiitake
mushrooms

Fresh garlic

Fresh ginger

Leeks

Low-sodium tamari

Miso paste: white (shiro) miso
plus one other

Onions

Orange juice

Orzo and other small
pasta shapes

Parmesan cheese

Red lentils

Roasted or sun-dried tomato
paste in a tube

Shallots

Thyme

Tortellini

Variety of spices

Vinegars

Whole grains (wheat berries,
barley, farro, brown rice)

SPRING MISO BROTH

WITH STIR-FRIED ASPARAGUS, ROMAINE, SCALLIONS, TOFU, AND MINT

SERVES 3

2 tablespoons plus 2 teaspoons white (shiro) miso

1 tablespoon plus 2 teaspoons low-sodium tamari

1 tablespoon mirin (rice wine)

½ teaspoon toasted sesame oil

2 tablespoons grapeseed or vegetable oil

6 ounces extra-firm tofu, cut into ¼-inch-thick slices, then into ¾-inch squares

¾ teaspoon kosher salt

6 ounces inner romaine hearts, cut lengthwise into 1-inch-wide wedges, then crosswise into 3-inch lengths (3 to 4 cups)

1¾ cups sliced asparagus (about 6 ounces, cut at a sharp angle)

¾ cup sliced scallions (cut at a sharp angle)

½ cup frozen peas, thawed, or fresh peas, blanched or microwaved for 30 seconds

1 tablespoon chopped fresh ginger

1 teaspoon chopped fresh garlic

3 tablespoons thinly sliced fresh mint leaves

½ cup pea shoots or microgreens (optional)

A beautiful bowlful of green for supper—so pleasing. I always feel good eating this soup. Thanks to the stir-fry pan, a great spring selection of veggies—asparagus, romaine hearts, scallions, and peas—takes on some delicious caramelization. (You'll love the flavor and texture that sautéed romaine adds to a soup!) With garlic, ginger, mint, and a savory miso broth enhanced by tamari and mirin, it's got plenty of satisfying flavor but nothing to weigh you down too much. I do include some stir-fried tofu in this broth-meets-stir-fry, but you could just as easily replace the tofu with a poached egg, some rice, or noodles. This recipe makes enough for three main dish servings, but another night, you could certainly stretch it to four by keeping the tofu and adding the grains, noodles, or eggs. Serve this in shallow bowls to show off its good looks. Have fun garnishing with pea shoots or microgreens if you can get a hold of some.

1 In a glass 1-cup measure, stir or whisk together the miso, tamari, mirin, and sesame oil (it does not have to be completely combined). Set aside.

2 Put 2½ cups of water in a medium saucepan over medium-high heat. Bring to a near simmer and adjust the heat as necessary to hold the water just below a simmer.

3 In a large (12-inch) nonstick stir-fry pan, heat 1 tablespoon of the oil over medium heat. Add the tofu and ¼ teaspoon of the salt and increase the heat to medium-high. Cook, stirring gently, until lightly browned on all sides, 5 to 6 minutes. Transfer to a plate.

4 Return the pan to medium-high heat and add the remaining 1 tablespoon of oil. Add the romaine hearts first, followed by the asparagus, scallions, peas, and ½ teaspoon of salt. The pan will be crowded, so turn the heat up to a notch above medium-high. Cook, stirring frequently, until the romaine takes on some browning and the asparagus and scallions just begin browning (most of the excess moisture will be cooked off at this point), 5 to 6 minutes. Add the ginger and garlic and cook, stirring, until fragrant, about 30 seconds. Add the tofu back into the pan and toss to combine. Remove the pan from the

continued →

SPRING MISO BROTH,

continued →

heat and transfer the veggie-tofu mixture to three large, shallow soup bowls.

5 Ladle ½ cup or a bit more of the simmering water into the glass measuring cup with the miso mixture and whisk well to combine, then pour all of the miso-water mixture into the saucepan with the rest of the hot water and whisk very well to combine. Pour the miso broth into the bowls, over the veggies and tofu. Garnish each with 1 tablespoon of mint and plenty of the pea shoots (if using). Serve right away.

TORTELLINI IN RICH VEGETABLE BROTH

WITH PARMESAN, PEAS, AND CARROTS

SERVES 2

3 ounces dried tortellini (I like Barilla spinach-and-cheese)

Kosher salt

1½ cups Rich Vegetable Broth (recipe follows)

½ teaspoon balsamic vinegar, plus more to taste

¾ cup (more or less) quick-roasted carrots (see page 83)

¼ cup frozen peas, thawed, or fresh peas, blanched or microwaved for 30 seconds

1 teaspoon sliced or chopped fresh mint, basil, parsley, or chives (optional)

Freshly ground black pepper

Parmesan cheese

If you've got a batch of Rich Vegetable Broth (page 213) in your fridge or freezer, you can turn it into a quick supper with tortellini. A vegetarian riff on the classic Italian soup, *tortellini in brodo*, this simple combination is easy to put together, but it does depend on a deeply flavored broth and good-quality tortellini. I keep a bag of Barilla dried spinach-and-cheese tortellini in my pantry, but there are good varieties you can keep in your freezer, too. I add peas and quick-roasted carrots for a little color and heft, and a generous finish of grated Parmesan cheese is essential. (Instead, you could cook the carrots any way you like, or quick-roast a combination of carrots and other root veggies for variety.) Serve in a shallow soup bowl. This recipe doubles easily.

1 Cook the tortellini in salted boiling water according to the package directions. Drain.

2 In a small saucepan, gently reheat the broth over medium heat until just steaming. Season with a big pinch of salt and ½ teaspoon of balsamic vinegar. Taste, and add a bit more vinegar and/or salt as needed.

3 Divide the cooked tortellini between two warm shallow soup bowls, and pour the broth over them. Scatter the carrots and peas around the tortellini. Garnish with herbs (if using) and a few grinds of black pepper. Using a hand-held grater, generously grate Parmesan cheese over both bowls of soup. Serve right away.

Rich Vegetable Broth

MAKES ABOUT 3½ CUPS

1 tablespoon extra-virgin olive oil, plus more if needed

2 large carrots, unpeeled, cut into 2-inch pieces (5 to 6 ounces total)

2 long ribs of celery, bottoms trimmed but leaves left on, cut into 2-inch pieces

1 medium-large onion, unpeeled, cut lengthwise into thick wedges

1 large shallot, unpeeled, cut lengthwise into quarters

4 to 5 ounces cremini mushrooms, cut into quarters

2 large garlic cloves, smashed but not peeled

½ teaspoon kosher salt

5 to 6 sprigs of fresh thyme

4 to 5 large sprigs of parsley

2 bay leaves

6 to 8 black peppercorns

8 to 10 whole coriander seeds

1 tablespoon tomato paste

This homemade vegetable broth gets a deep caramel color from browning the veggies first, and also from including mushrooms and tomato paste along with plenty of onion, celery, carrot, and herbs. (The broth has a distinctive caramelized-onion flavor, too, and the whole house will smell like Thanksgiving while you're simmering it.) As I already mentioned, the total time it takes to make this broth is no more than 1½ hours, and most of that time is hands-off. I usually simmer the broth for about 1 hour and 15 minutes, but if you're in a hurry, the broth will be tasty enough to use, though light, after 30 or 40 minutes. You can double the quantities if you like (because broth freezes so well), but you'll need to simmer the broth a bit longer to reduce it. Store cooled broth in the fridge for 3 days or in the freezer for 6 weeks.

In a medium (5- to 6-quart), heavy-bottomed Dutch oven (nonstick is great if you have it), heat the oil over medium heat. Add the carrots, celery, onion, shallot, mushrooms, garlic, and salt. Cook, stirring frequently, until the mushrooms are browned, the other vegetables are lightly browned, and the bottom of the pan is brown (but not too dark), 8 to 10 minutes. (If the pan looks very dry after a few minutes, add a bit more olive oil.) Add the thyme, parsley, bay leaves, peppercorns, coriander seeds, and tomato paste and stir. Add 3 quarts of water and stir again. Raise the heat to high and bring to a boil, then reduce the heat to low and simmer for 1 hour. Check the volume and flavor by looking and tasting; if you are in a rush, you can stop cooking now. Otherwise, cook for another 15 to 20 minutes. Remove the pot from the heat and let the broth cool for about 15 minutes before straining. Refrigerate, uncovered, until completely cool, then cover and keep in the fridge for 3 days or in the freezer for 6 weeks.

FAST, FRESH SUMMER MINESTRONE

SERVES 3 OR 4

1 medium onion, peeled and cut in half

1 medium-large tomato, cut in half

1 garlic clove, peeled

2 tablespoons extra-virgin olive oil

¾ teaspoon kosher salt, plus 2 pinches

4 to 6 sprigs of fresh thyme or oregano, tied together

1 cup stemmed and chopped or thinly sliced greens or cabbage (any kind)

2 cups small-diced summer vegetables (any combination of green or yellow beans, peeled butternut squash, carrots, corn, okra, potatoes, snap or snow peas, sweet potatoes, summer squash, or zucchini)

1 cup cooked or canned pink beans or pinto beans, drained and rinsed

½ cup diced fresh plum tomato, including seeds and any juice (about 1 large tomato)

1 to 2 teaspoons balsamic vinegar

continues on page 216

Vegetable minestrones may be my favorite soups of all time. They're fun and easy to make, beautiful to look at, and filling in the best way. I've cooked many versions over the years, always when my garden is giving generously and I'm looking to use up extra bits of veg that wander into my fridge. Some years, when I grow cranberry beans (so lovely and creamy), I add them, too. But I find that canned pink beans have a similar texture, and pinto beans also work fine. This particular recipe is a lighter one I developed for quicker cooking, so there's no long simmering time. I use a trick I learned from making paella to give the broth some backbone: onions and tomatoes grated on a box grater and cooked down to a flavorful *sofrito*. Then I finish with a bold top note: fresh basil, a swirl of pesto, or a dollop of Garlic Scape Chimichurri (page 216).

1 Using the large holes of a box grater, grate both onion halves onto a rimmed plate. (Discard remaining ungrated pieces.) Grate the tomato halves onto a separate rimmed plate. (If you grate the tomato halves on their cut side, you will be left with only skin to discard.) Using a rasp-style grater, grate the garlic clove into a small dish.

2 In a medium Dutch oven or other soup pot, heat the oil over medium-low heat. Add the grated onion (including all its liquid) and a pinch of salt and cook, stirring, until softened, 2 to 4 minutes. Add the grated tomato (and its liquid) and a pinch of salt and continue to cook, stirring, until the mixture has reduced and thickened and is a nice brick-red in color, about

10 minutes. Add the garlic and cook, stirring, until well combined and fragrant, about 30 seconds.

3 Add the thyme sprigs, the greens, ¾ teaspoon of salt, and 5 cups of water. Increase the heat to high and bring to a boil, partially cover, and reduce to low. Simmer for 10 minutes.

4 Add the 2 cups of summer vegetables and bring back to a simmer. Cook until the veggies are just tender, 6 to 8 minutes, depending on which veggies you choose. Stir in the beans and the plum tomato and cook until just heated through. Remove the pot from the heat, add 1 teaspoon of the balsamic vinegar, and taste for seasoning. Add more

continued →

FAST, FRESH SUMMER MINESTRONE,

continued →

1 to 2 tablespoons Garlic Scape Chimichurri (recipe follows), basil pesto, or chopped fresh basil

¼ cup grated Parmesan cheese (optional)

salt or vinegar if desired. (The herb finish will deepen the soup's flavor, too.)

5 To serve, spoon the minestrone into soup bowls and top each with a swirl or dollop of chimichurri and some grated Parmesan (if using).

Garlic Scape Chimichurri

MAKES 1¼ CUPS

1 cup coarsely chopped garlic scapes

⅔ cup packed fresh Italian parsley leaves

⅓ cup packed fresh mint leaves

⅔ cup extra-virgin olive oil

1 tablespoon plus 1 teaspoon red wine vinegar

2 tablespoons orange juice

2 teaspoons black olive tapenade

1 teaspoon honey

½ teaspoon kosher salt

Freshly ground black pepper

If you're prowling the farmers' markets in June and July, you'll probably come across garlic scapes, the stalks of hardneck garlic. Farmers harvest them this time of year to conserve energy in the bulb below so that it can fatten up. The scapes are beautiful and aromatic (like garlic, only greener!), if a bit unwieldy. You can sauté or grill them, but they really shine in pestos and sauces. I make this version of a *chimichurri* (the Argentine herb and garlic sauce) out of them. It has a lovely bright flavor and color, and it freezes really well.

1 Put the garlic scapes into the bowl of a food processor and process until finely chopped. Add the parsley and mint and process again until chopped and well combined. Add the oil, vinegar, orange juice, tapenade, honey, salt, and several grinds of black pepper. Pulse until everything is well chopped and combined.

2 Transfer to a bowl, cover well with plastic wrap, and store in the fridge for several days or in a food container in the freezer for up to 2 months. Bring to room temperature before serving, and add more olive oil if you want a slightly looser sauce.

SWEET CORN, FINGERLING, JALAPEÑO, LEEK, AND CHIVE CHOWDER

SERVES 4

4 medium ears of sweet corn, shucked

2 tablespoons unsalted butter

2 tablespoons olive oil

2 cups thinly sliced leeks, well washed

1¾ teaspoons kosher salt

1 tablespoon minced fresh garlic

1 tablespoon seeded and minced fresh jalapeño

1 teaspoon smoked paprika

2 bay leaves

½ pound fingerling potatoes, cut into half-moons about ¼ inch thick

⅔ cup half-and-half

¼ cup sliced chives

Freshly ground black pepper

4 lime wedges

2 teaspoons sriracha sauce, plus more to serve

I love corn chowder, but sometimes it can be a bit of a production to make a truly flavorful version of it. So I set out to develop a recipe that would deliver plenty of flavor without hours at the stove. By starting with really good, fresh sweet corn, leeks, and fingerling potatoes (all fall favorites at the farm stand), I was on my way. I also used the cobs, and corn "milk" scraped from the cobs, to boost the corn flavor in this recipe. Then the broth gets spiked with garlic, jalapeño, smoked paprika, and sriracha hot sauce. Finish with a shower of chives, and the result is a fresh, flavorful chowder in about an hour.

1 Snap each ear of corn in half. Cut the kernels off the cobs, and reserve the cobs. You should have about 2½ cups of kernels. Use a knife to scrape the remaining corn "pulp" and milk off the cobs and into a large bowl. Leave the scraped cobs in the bowl with the pulp.

2 In a medium (5- to 6-quart) Dutch oven, heat the butter and oil over medium heat. Add the leeks and ½ teaspoon of salt, stir, and cover loosely. Cook, uncovering occasionally to stir, until the leeks have softened, about 5 minutes. Uncover the pot and continue cooking the leeks until they begin to brown and stick to the bottom of the pan, about 5 minutes more.

Add the garlic, jalapeño, paprika, 1¼ teaspoons of salt, and the bay leaves and stir well. Add the reserved corn cobs and pulp, the potatoes, and 5 cups of water. Bring to a boil, reduce the heat to low, and simmer until the potatoes are just tender, about 12 minutes. Add the corn kernels and simmer for 2 minutes.

3 Remove the pot from the heat, remove the corn cobs, and add the half-and-half, chives, several generous grinds of black pepper, and 2 teaspoons of sriracha. Stir well.

4 Spoon into soup bowls. Serve with the lime wedges, and pass the sriracha.

217

QUICK-ROASTED TOMATO AND BELL PEPPER SOUP

WITH FENNEL AND ORANGE

SERVES 3 OR 4

FOR THE SOUP

1½ pounds plum tomatoes (about 5 large)

2 small or 1 large red bell pepper (about 10 to 12 ounces total), seeded and cut into 1-inch pieces

¼ cup plus 2 tablespoons extra-virgin olive oil

3 large garlic cloves, cut in half

1½ teaspoons kosher salt, plus more to taste

Large pinch of red pepper flakes

2 cups thinly sliced fennel bulb (cored), plus a few short fennel fronds for garnish

1½ teaspoons fennel seeds

1½ teaspoons ground coriander

⅓ cup fresh orange juice

1 to 2 teaspoons balsamic vinegar

Plain full-fat Greek yogurt, drained (optional)

continues on page 220

This beautiful and satisfying soup takes advantage of the same method I use in my recipe for Quick-Roasted Plum Tomato Sauce (page 12) to give tomatoes and peppers deep flavor relatively quickly. Thirty minutes in a 450°F oven, and the veggies are caramelized and ready to simmer for just a few minutes in the soup pot with fennel and a bit of orange. The topping of raw fennel, oranges, and olives isn't entirely necessary, but it is pretty. (A dollop of yogurt would be fine, too.) An immersion blender makes quick work of the puréeing (the soup will still have a slightly chunky texture), but a stand-up blender works fine, too. You could easily make this ahead and eat it over the course of a few nights.

1 *Make the soup:* Preheat the oven to 450°F. Cut the plum tomatoes in half and poke or scoop out most of the seeds. (Don't worry if you don't get all the seeds. You can also notch out the stem end if you like, but don't cut the inner ribs out.) Cut each half into quarters (or into sixths if very large) and divide them between two 9 x 13-inch glass or ceramic baking dishes. (I like Pyrex.) Add the bell peppers, ¼ cup of the oil, the garlic, ¾ teaspoon salt, and the red pepper flakes, dividing the ingredients evenly between the baking dishes. Toss well.

2 Transfer both baking dishes into the oven and bake, stirring from time to time with a silicone spatula, until the tomatoes are collapsed, softened, and browned a bit, 30 to 35 minutes. (The sides of

the pans will be browned, as some of the tomato and pepper juices will have caramelized.) Remove from the oven and let cool for just a few minutes, then add 2 tablespoons of warm water to each dish to deglaze, scraping and "washing" the caramelized bits off the sides of the pan. Set aside.

3 In a medium Dutch oven or other soup pot, heat the remaining 2 tablespoons of oil over medium-low heat. Add the sliced fennel and ½ teaspoon of salt, cover, and cook, uncovering occasionally to stir, until limp and beginning to turn golden, about 5 minutes. Uncover the pot and continue cooking until much of the fennel has some browning, another 6 to 8 minutes. Add the fennel seeds and coriander and

continued →

QUICK-ROASTED TOMATO AND BELL PEPPER SOUP,

continued →

FOR THE TOPPING

¼ cup small-diced fennel bulb (cored), plus a few short fennel fronds

¼ cup small-diced navel orange (with peel on)

1 tablespoon chopped pitted black or green olives

½ teaspoon extra-virgin olive oil

Honey or agave nectar

Pinch of salt

cook, stirring, until fragrant, about 30 seconds. Add the orange juice and stir, scraping any browned bits off the bottom of the pot. Take the pot off the heat.

4 Add the roasted tomato-pepper mixture to the fennel mixture and add 4 cups of water and ¼ teaspoon of salt. Place the Dutch oven over high heat and bring the soup to a boil, stirring occasionally, then reduce the heat to low and simmer, partially covered, for about 20 minutes. Take the pot off the heat and let sit for a few minutes. Stir in 1 teaspoon of the vinegar.

5 Puree the soup using an immersion blender. (Alternatively, puree in batches in a stand-up blender. Do not fill the blender more than two-thirds full, and partially cover the lid with a dish towel while blending to prevent hot splatters.) The soup might still have a chunky texture—don't worry if it is not perfectly smooth. Taste, and season with salt and the remaining 1 teaspoon of vinegar if necessary.

6 *Make the topping:* In a small bowl, combine the diced fennel, orange, olives, olive oil, a drizzle of honey or agave, and a pinch of salt. Stir together. Stir in a few fennel fronds.

7 To serve, spoon the warm soup into soup bowls, then top each with a dollop of yogurt (if using) and garnish with the orange-fennel topping and fennel fronds.

SPICY "HOT AND SOUR" MUSHROOM, BARLEY, AND KALE SOUP

SERVES 4

2 tablespoons grapeseed or vegetable oil

4 cups thickly sliced mushrooms, preferably a combination of cremini and shiitake (7 to 8 ounces)

¾ teaspoon kosher salt

1 tablespoon chopped fresh garlic

1 tablespoon chopped fresh ginger

1 tablespoon Asian chili-garlic paste

3 cups stemmed and sliced Tuscan kale

1 cup tiny-diced sweet potatoes or peeled butternut squash

2½ cups Dried Mushroom Broth (recipe follows), plus any reconstituted mushrooms, chopped

2½ cups grain-cooking liquid from barley (see page 235)

2 to 3 teaspoons low-sodium tamari

2 to 3 teaspoons fresh lemon or lime juice

2 cups cooked barley (see page 235), rewarmed if necessary

This fresh spin on mushroom-barley soup takes advantage of two quick broths—grain-cooking liquid and Dried Mushroom Broth—that add depth of flavor to vegetarian soups without a need for store-bought vegetable stock. This nourishing soup features a hefty portion of grains and veggies piled into a bowl with a relatively small amount of broth, but you can use the recipe as a template to alter as you please. Farro or brown rice will work just as well as barley here. The mushrooms are essential for their meatiness, but spinach, chard, mustard greens, cabbage, or bok choy could stand in for the kale. If you want to eat this on a weeknight, plan ahead and cook the grains over the weekend, being sure to save the broth. The chili-garlic paste, tamari, and lemon juice provide the "hot and sour" notes; start with the amounts the recipe calls for, and you can always increase them if you like.

1 In a small Dutch oven, heat the oil over medium heat. Add the mushrooms and ¼ teaspoon of the salt and increase the heat to medium-high. Cook, stirring, until the mushrooms are browned and shrunken, about 8 minutes. Add the ginger and garlic and cook, stirring, until softened and fragrant, about 30 seconds. Add the chili-garlic paste, kale, and the remaining ½ teaspoon of salt and cook, stirring, until well combined. Add the sweet potatoes, mushroom broth, and barley cooking liquid. Bring to a boil, reduce the heat to low, and gently simmer until the kale is softened and the sweet potatoes are just tender, 6 to 8 minutes. Turn off the heat. Add 2 teaspoons of tamari and 2 teaspoons of lemon juice. Taste, and add another 1 teaspoon of tamari and/or lemon juice if you like.

2 Spoon or scoop ½ cup of warm barley into the center of each of four shallow soup bowls, and spoon broth and vegetables around the grain, distributing them evenly among the bowls. Serve right away.

Dried Mushroom Broth

MAKES ABOUT 3 CUPS
BROTH AND ABOUT ⅓ CUP
CHOPPED RECONSTITUTED
MUSHROOMS

⅓ cup dried porcini or
shiitake mushrooms

4 cups water

Dried mushrooms are certainly one of the stars of the vegetarian pantry, and it always amazes me how much flavor they deliver with so little trouble. To reconstitute them, I used to simply pour boiling water over them, but now I simmer them for a brief time to get a more flavorful liquid. I still get the reconstituted mushrooms, but more important, now I also get a tasty broth that's a perfect start to a vegetarian soup. The yield of your broth may vary, depending on how much it reduces while simmering, but you can always stretch it with a little water if your recipe calls for a bit more than you have.

1 Put the mushrooms and water into a medium saucepan and bring to a boil. Reduce the heat to low and gently simmer for about 12 minutes. Remove the pan from the heat. Line a mesh sieve with a piece of cheesecloth or a coffee filter and set over a bowl. Remove the mushrooms from the pan with a slotted spoon, and strain the broth to remove any grit. Reserve both the mushrooms and the broth.

2 Chop the mushrooms fine if desired, and use the mushrooms and/or the liquid in your recipe. You can also refrigerate the mushrooms and the broth for up to 2 days if not using right away.

MISO-GINGER BROTH

WITH CAULIFLOWER AND BABY KALE

SERVES 2

2 cups packed baby kale or baby spinach

3 tablespoons miso paste of choice, or a combination of two kinds of miso

1 tablespoon plus 1 teaspoon vegetable oil

Generous 2 cups small cauliflower florets

½ teaspoon kosher salt

1 teaspoon minced fresh garlic

1 teaspoon minced fresh ginger

1 teaspoon Asian chili-garlic paste

2 tablespoons thinly sliced scallions (white and green parts)

⅓ cup small-diced extra-firm tofu (optional)

A quick sauté of cauliflower, ginger, and garlic adds dimension to a light miso broth that also gets a green boost from baby kale. Instead of a traditional Japanese miso soup, this is a happy East-meets-West marriage that takes advantage of miso paste as a great foundation for a warming but super-quick weeknight soup. I like to use a combination of two different misos for an interesting flavor, but simply using sweet white (shiro) miso is fine, too. Remember not to boil your broth after the miso has been added. Feel free to add a bit of tofu (cut into very small dice) and to make veggie substitutions if you like.

1 Choose two wide, shallow soup bowls. Divide most of the baby kale or spinach between the two bowls (reserving a little bit for garnish).

2 Put the miso in a small heatproof bowl. (I use a glass measuring cup, because it's easy to stir.) (Have a strainer handy if using artisan miso.)

3 In a small Dutch oven or a medium nonstick skillet that has a cover, heat 1 tablespoon of the oil over medium heat. Add the cauliflower and salt and stir. Cover the pot or skillet and reduce the heat to medium-low. Cook, uncovering frequently to stir, until the florets are browned in spots all over and the cauliflower is beginning to lose its stiffness, 5 to 7 minutes. Uncover, reduce the heat to low, and push the florets to one side. Add the remaining

1 teaspoon of oil to the other side of the pot or skillet and add the garlic, ginger, and chili-garlic paste and stir. Cook just until the garlic and ginger are softened, a few seconds, then stir them into the cauliflower.

4 Add 2½ cups of water and stir, scraping the bottom of the pan. Increase the heat to high and bring the cauliflower mixture just to a boil. Remove the pot or skillet from the heat, and ladle about ⅓ cup of its hot liquid into the bowl with the miso. Stir or whisk until the miso is dissolved. Pour or strain your miso mixture back into the cauliflower mixture.

5 Ladle or spoon the cauliflower and the broth over the greens in the soup bowls. Sprinkle with the scallions, diced tofu (if using), and the remaining greens. Serve right away.

RAMEN-ESQUE NOODLES IN RICH VEGETABLE BROTH

WITH LATE-SEASON VEGGIES

SERVES 2

4 to 5 ounces dried Chinese curly wheat noodles or baked ramen noodles

½ teaspoon kosher salt, plus 2 pinches

1 tablespoon white (shiro) miso

1 tablespoon low-sodium tamari

½ teaspoon toasted sesame oil

1 tablespoon grapeseed oil

3 cups late-season vegetables, sliced or chopped into similar-size pieces (a combination of four or five of the following: bell peppers, onions or shallots, mushrooms, eggplant, cauliflower or broccoli, bok choy, napa cabbage, and/or red or green cabbage)

1 tablespoon minced fresh ginger

3 cups Rich Vegetable Broth (page 213)

continues on page 226

It's happy news for vegetarians that a hearty bowl of ramen noodles and veggies doesn't need pork or chicken broth to be delicious. In fact, our Rich Vegetable Broth, enhanced by miso, tamari, and ginger, makes a lovely destination for a tangle of noodles and a variety of sautéed vegetables. A poached or soft-boiled egg slipped into the mix is a bonus, and a topping of toasted sesame seeds, scallions, and cilantro ties it all up nicely. I mentioned in the Veggies + Noodles chapter (page 5) that I like to buy Chinese curly wheat noodles (Kame brand) rather than ramen. They are quite similar to ramen, only baked instead of fried. But you can sometimes find organic baked ramen, too, and either will do. Ideally, serve this soup in extra-wide, deep soup bowls, but if you don't have such a thing, no worries: just use a smaller bowl, and help yourself to seconds.

1 Bring a medium pot of salted water to a boil and cook the noodles until done, about 2 minutes. Drain them well in a colander and rinse briefly under cold water. Let dry a bit in the colander, then transfer to a medium bowl and season with a big pinch of the salt.

2 In a glass measuring cup, whisk together the miso, tamari, sesame oil, and 2 tablespoons of water. Set aside.

3 In a medium Dutch oven or large saucepan, heat the grapeseed oil over medium heat. When the oil is hot, add the vegetables and ½ teaspoon of the salt and increase the heat to medium-high. Cook, stirring, until the vegetables are browned in places and starting to shrink but still a little bit firm, 5 to 7 minutes. (Alternatively, you can stir-fry each type of vegetable individually and set aside separately, for arranging in the bowls at serving time; add a little oil to the empty stir-fry pan before continuing with the recipe.) Add the ginger and cook, stirring, until just softened and fragrant, about 30 seconds. Add the Rich Vegetable Broth and bring to a boil, then turn off the heat. Whisk the miso mixture into the hot broth and remove the pot from the stove.

4 Divide the cooked noodles between two wide, deep soup bowls

continued →

RAMEN-ESQUE NOODLES IN RICH VEGETABLE BROTH,
continued →

2 soft-cooked eggs
(see page 238) or poached eggs
(see Note), optional

Freshly ground black pepper

1 to 2 tablespoons chopped
fresh cilantro

1 to 2 teaspoons toasted
sesame seeds

¼ to ⅓ cup sliced scallions
(any parts)

and ladle the broth and vegetables over all. (Or arrange the separately cooked vegetables "around the clock" over the noodles, then pour in the hot broth.) Add 1 egg to each bowl and season the eggs with a pinch of salt and a couple of grinds of black pepper. Garnish with generous amounts of chopped cilantro, sesame seeds, and scallions. Serve right away with a fork, spoon, and napkin.

Note: *To poach 2 eggs:* Fill a wide, deep skillet with water. Add ½ teaspoon of white vinegar and ½ teaspoon of salt, and bring to a very gentle simmer (about 180°F). Crack 1 egg into a small bowl and slip it gently into the simmering water. Repeat with the other egg. Lower the heat to just below a simmer and leave the eggs to cook for 4 minutes. Use a slotted spoon to lift the eggs from the water and serve immediately, or if cooking ahead, transfer to a plate to hold.

CARAMELIZED ONION SOUP

WITH CIDER, THYME, AND CIABATTA CROUTONS

SERVES 4

½ cup apple cider

1 tablespoon low-sodium tamari

1 teaspoon apple cider vinegar

4 tablespoons unsalted butter

2 tablespoons extra-virgin olive oil

5 cups sliced yellow onions (about 1 pound)

1 teaspoon kosher salt

Freshly ground black pepper

1½ teaspoons chopped fresh thyme

4 cups Rich Vegetable Broth (page 213)

4 slices of ciabatta (about 1 inch thick)

½ to ⅔ cup Gruyere, Swiss, or cheddar cheese

Onion soup is traditionally made with beef broth, but I think you'll be amazed at how delicious and satisfying this vegetarian version is. It takes advantage of a batch of our Rich Vegetable Broth, which already gains some of its character from onions. The broth gets spiked with a little apple cider and tamari, and the caramelized onions add their deeply sweet and earthy flavor. (If your batch of Rich Vegetable Broth does not amount to quite as much as this recipe calls for, just add enough water to make up the difference.)

1 In a small bowl, stir together the apple cider, tamari, and cider vinegar. Set aside.

2 In a large straight-sided stainless-steel skillet, heat 2 tablespoons of the butter and the oil over medium-low heat. Add the onions and salt and stir. Cover and cook, uncovering frequently to stir, until the onions are wilted, have lost their opacity, and have begun to brown a bit, 8 to 10 minutes. Uncover and continue cooking, stirring frequently to distribute brown bits, until all the onions are very well softened and greatly reduced in volume, and most of them are a lovely golden brown, 15 to 20 minutes more.

3 Add the thyme and the cider mixture to the onions and cook for 1 minute, stirring and scraping up any browned bits on the bottom of the pan. Add the vegetable broth and bring to a gentle simmer. Cook, stirring occasionally, for 5 minutes.

Take the pan off the heat, cover, and set aside.

4 Place an oven rack in the top position in the oven. Preheat the oven broiler to high. Arrange the ciabatta slices on a baking sheet and spread the top of each slice with ½ tablespoon of the remaining butter. Broil until the tops are golden brown, about 2 minutes. Flip the slices over and broil the other side until golden, about 2 minutes. Remove from the oven. Flip the ciabatta slices back over. Top with equal amounts of the grated cheese and return to the oven. Broil for about 2 minutes, just until the cheese has melted. Remove from the oven and transfer the toast to a cutting board. Cut each piece into 12 to 14 large croutons.

5 Ladle the caramelized onions and the broth into four deep soup bowls. Top with the cheese croutons, divided evenly among the four bowls, and serve.

SPICED RED LENTIL AND SWEET POTATO SOUP

WITH TURMERIC, COCONUT MILK, AND CILANTRO

MAKES 6 TO 7 CUPS, SERVES 4

2 tablespoons grapeseed or vegetable oil

1 cup diced onion

1½ teaspoons kosher salt, plus more to taste

1 tablespoon chopped fresh garlic

2 teaspoons chili powder

1 teaspoon ground ginger

1 teaspoon ground turmeric

2 tablespoons tomato paste

1 large sweet potato, peeled and cut into small dice (about 12 ounces)

¾ cup red lentils

½ cup canned full-fat coconut milk (preferably organic), well stirred

¼ cup chopped fresh cilantro

½ lime

2 to 3 tablespoons chopped toasted almonds, toasted coconut, pita croutons, or other garnish (optional)

You've got to love red lentils—they cook so quickly, and they add instant body and flavor to anything they're hanging out with. In this recipe, while they simmer (in water) with sweet potatoes and a combination of ginger, turmeric, and chili powder, they pretty much make themselves into their own soup—with a little help from coconut milk and the immersion blender. No vegetable stock required. The turmeric gives an especially warm feeling to this soup.

1 In a medium Dutch oven or soup pot, heat the oil over medium heat. Add the onion and ½ teaspoon of salt, stir, and cover the pot loosely. Cook, uncovering occasionally to stir, until the onions are translucent and starting to brown, 5 to 6 minutes. Add the garlic and cook, stirring, until softened, about 30 seconds. Add the chili powder, ginger, and turmeric and stir to combine. Add the tomato paste and stir, breaking it apart as much as possible. Add the sweet potato, lentils, 1 teaspoon of salt, and 6 cups of water and stir well. Bring the mixture to a boil, then reduce the heat to medium-low, cover the pot loosely, and simmer until the sweet potatoes are quite tender, about 25 minutes. (You may have to adjust the heat down as the time goes on to maintain a moderately gentle, not rapid, simmer.) Remove the pot from the heat and let sit for 10 minutes.

2 Use an immersion blender to puree the soup. (Keep the blender blades submerged while operating it to avoid splashing the hot soup. Alternatively, puree the soup in batches in a stand-up blender. Do not fill the blender more than two-thirds full, and partially cover the lid with a towel to prevent hot splashes.) When the soup is smooth, well combined, and a lighter orange color, add the coconut milk and puree again. Taste for salt and season with a bit more if necessary. Add the cilantro and a good squeeze of lime and puree again until well combined. Taste again, and add salt if needed.

3 Return the pot to the stove and gently rewarm the soup if necessary. Serve the soup in deep bowls, alone or with any garnishes you like.

SOOTHING WHEAT BERRY BROTH

WITH LEMON, SPINACH, SQUASH, AND SHALLOTS

SERVES 1

1 tablespoon vegetable oil

1 large shallot, sliced

½ cup small-diced peeled butternut squash or carrots or sweet potatoes

Large pinch of kosher salt

⅛ teaspoon ground coriander

2 cups grain-cooking liquid from wheat berries (see page 235)

½ cup cooked wheat berries (substitute any cooked grain)

Large handful of baby spinach (about ¾ cup)

2 teaspoons fresh lemon juice

1 to 2 teaspoons low-sodium tamari

The first time I made a soup with a base of grain-cooking liquid, it was a total revelation—I couldn't believe what a nourishing (and easy) broth grains provide. I guess I had completely forgotten about traditional barley and rice soups: they have a velvety viscosity thanks to grains, not meat or anything else in the soup! So the next time you cook wheat berries, don't throw out the cooking liquid. (And save a few wheat berries for later, too.) Then you can make this almost-instant supper on another night by adding just a few flavorful ingredients. The bright combination of lemon and spinach works well in the earthy broth, and a quick sauté of shallots and squash or carrots adds sweetness and color. Make this once, then make a version with your own favorite veggies another time. Double the recipe to serve two people.

1 In a medium saucepan, heat the oil over medium heat. Add the shallot, squash, and a big pinch of salt. Cook, stirring, until the veggies are very lightly browned and beginning to soften, about 5 minutes. Add the coriander and stir. Add the wheat berry cooking liquid and bring to a boil, then reduce the heat to low and simmer, stirring occasionally, until the veggies are tender, 7 to 9 minutes. Spoon off any foam that gathers on the top of the broth. (Pay close attention: if the broth is boiling too rapidly and reducing too much, cover the pan loosely with a lid and lower the heat a bit.)

2 Add the cooked wheat berries, spinach, lemon juice, and tamari. Stir well to wilt the spinach. Ladle into a bowl and enjoy.

ACKNOWLEDGMENTS

Simple Green Suppers is my fourth cookbook, and never have I had such a great collaboration of so many talented people. The secret? This magical little island I live on. Martha's Vineyard seems to spawn and attract creative folks, all of whom happen to be pretty cool to work with, too. In fact, this time around, not only are author (*moi*) and photographer (Randi Baird) both year-round Vineyarders but our fabulous editor (Jennifer Urban-Brown) grew up here, too! The photo shoots were all done here on Martha's Vineyard, the props were provided by Vineyard artisans, the food was styled by Vineyard cooks, and so on. Of course, there were some hugely valuable contributions by off-Islanders (people who live in America!), from my can't-do-it-without long-time recipe cross-tester and best friend, Eliza Peter, in York, Maine (whom we also lured to a photo shoot on Martha's Vineyard), to seriously talented book designer Toni Tajima in San Francisco to all of the amazing folks at Roost Books and Shambhala Publications in Boulder, Colorado.

Honestly, I guess the point is this: A great team makes a great cookbook. And on that note, if I don't quit extolling and start listing, I will (as usual) run out of space for these acknowledgments:

All of my books begin under the eagle eye of my beloved agent, Sarah Jane Freymann, to whom I am ever grateful.

Huge appreciation and thanks to Roost editor Jennifer Urban-Brown for snagging my proposal, signing me on, and kindly, gently, and confidently steering the manuscript—and design—to its sweet spot. To everyone else at Roost and Shambhala—publisher Sara Bercholz, art director Daniel Urban-Brown, assistant editor Julia Gaviria, sales and marketing manager K. J. Grow, publicist Jess Townsend, and marketing manager Claire Kelly—my hat (each and every one!) is off to you. I am a true admirer of all you do to produce the most beautiful, useful, and inspiring books. Thank you for making *Simple Green Suppers* so incredible.

To photographer Randi Baird, so much love and appreciation for a totally inspiring, fun, and productive collaboration, and for your boundless energy, enthusiasm, and searing talent. You went the extra mile on this, and I can't thank you enough. We were so lucky to have cook (now food stylist) extraordinaire Amy Miller with us through the long hours and many days of shooting. There's no way to express how grateful I am to Amy, not only for her fine kitchen skills, her organization, and her thoughtful suggestions but also for her friendship and support. And our photo-shoot quartet was completed in style by the wonderful Mary Shea, who assisted Randi on each shot and also offered excellent propping suggestions and kept our enormous prop collection organized.

We were so fortunate to have a beautiful house and gorgeous kitchen with lovely light to photograph our recipes, and for that we thank homeowners Bob and Helen Bernstein and Bill and Lori Bernstein.

We are over-the-top grateful to artist Leslie Freeman (check out Lesliefreemandesigns on Etsy) for her generous loan of so many beautiful ceramic bowls, plates, and platters. Every dish she leant us made the food look even more beautiful, and we turned to them again and again. Enormous thanks to Suzanne Wesley of Halfacre Vintage Rentals, who gathered an eclectic and stunning collection of platters, baskets, silverware, and glasses for us to use. Really special thanks to Anne-Marie Eddy, owner of Refabulous Décor in Vineyard Haven, and to painter Bill Croke for providing us with supercool custom-painted wooden surfaces to use in our photos.

Our friends at three Vineyard Haven retail shops—Robert Cropper at Juliska, Heather Kochin at Rainy Day, and Scott Mullin at Brickyard—were also incredibly generous in lending us beautiful props from their stores. Many thanks.

Developing the recipes and writing the text for a book is an arduous and consuming project and it simply can't be done without the support of friends and family. For me, there are many to thank: Judy Fraser-Pearse, Laura Watt, Alasdair Watt, Mary Wirtz, Jim Costello, Laura Roosevelt, Liz Durkee, Renee Balter, Ann Dewitt, Fae Kontje-Gibbs, Heidi Feldman, Kay Goldstein, Katie Hutchison, Chris Hufstader, Mary Margaret Chappell, Trip Barnes, Andra Spurr, Dawn Braasch, Molly Coogan, and all of my coworkers at Bunch of Grapes Bookstore; Paul Schneider and Alley Moore at *Martha's Vineyard Magazine*; and all of my friends at *Fine Cooking* magazine. And to my very special girl Libby Riley and her amazing mom, Kelly Crocker, undying thanks. As always, I'm grateful for the wonderful support of my mom and dad and my sister Eleanor Evans, and most of all, for my best fried Eliza Peter (and the whole Peter family), who not only cross-tested every recipe in *Simple Green Suppers* but also offered her love and support at every turn. Thanks always, Lou.

ESSENTIAL TECHNIQUES

From both culinary school and my time at *Fine Cooking* magazine, I learned the importance of mastering a few good cooking techniques. When you can turn a little knowledge into hundreds of different dishes, what's not to love? Here I've gathered a few techniques that are especially useful for making vegetarian suppers every night. These methods will get you consistent (and delicious) results every time.

How to Cook Grains Using the Pasta Method

This method of cooking hearty grains as if they were pasta (in a lot of boiling water) is so easy! Just throw a big pot of boiling water on, toss in some grains, and set the timer. You don't have to worry about measuring the exact amount of water—or about whether the texture will be right when the water is absorbed. Simply begin tasting a grain or two after the timer goes off, and if they are still a little too al dente, leave them to boil a little longer.

As a bonus, cooking times for many grains cooked this way are shorter than they would be if the grain were cooked pilaf style (that is, simmered in an exact measure of water). Quinoa, for instance, cooks in only 10 to 12 minutes by the pasta method, as opposed to 20 to 25 minutes. Some grains, like wheat berries, will benefit from an overnight soak first, which will further speed up their cooking time. All grains should be rinsed well before cooking.

After cooking and cooling, these grains store well in the refrigerator for up to 5 or 6 days or in the freezer for a few weeks. Because they're unseasoned, you can use them in endless ways—in salads, soups, tacos, or egg dishes—throughout the week. You can (and should) save the cooking water and use it as broth for a quick soup (such as Soothing Wheat Berry Broth with Lemon, Spinach, Squash, and Shallots, page 230).

I love this method for brown rice (especially short grain—my favorite), red rice, black rice, wheat berries, barley, and farro. I do prefer the pilaf method for starchy grains like white rice and for when I want to infuse flavor into grains like quinoa during the cooking process.

1 To make 5 to 6 cups of cooked grains, fill a small (5- to 6-quart) stockpot three-quarters full of water. Add ½ teaspoon of kosher salt and bring it to a boil. Rinse 2 cups of grains in a fine-mesh colander or strainer and add them to the boiling water. Set a timer for the short end of the grain's suggested cooking time and begin tasting for texture when the timer goes off. Continue timing and tasting until you like the texture of the grains. (When you are cooking long-cooking grains, a bit too much water may boil off. If the water level comes down to within a half inch of your grains, add a saucepan of boiling water to bring it back up.)

Barley: 35 minutes

Black or red rice: 20 to 25 minutes

Brown rice: 28 to 32 minutes

Farro: 30 to 35 minutes

Quinoa: 10 to 12 minutes

Wheat berries (soaked overnight): 50 to 70 minutes

Wheat berries (not soaked): 60 to 90 minutes

2 Put a colander inside a heat-proof bowl (to capture cooking liquid) and pour the cooked grains and liquid into the colander (keep the pot nearby). Lift the colander out of the bowl and allow the grains to drain well. Shake the colander a little to get out any excess liquid, then return the drained grains to the warm pot (off the heat). Cover the pot with a lid and let sit for 10 to 15 minutes; the grain will absorb the remaining moisture, be slightly drier, and fluff up a bit.

3 If serving right away, season with tamari or salt and add a bit of butter or olive oil if you like. Or season as directed by your recipe. If cooking the grains ahead, let them cool completely, then portion the grains into airtight containers (I like to divide them into 1- or 2-cup batches) and refrigerate or freeze.

Note: If you have time, soak wheat berries overnight in filtered or unchlorinated water. Cover the grains with three times as much water and cover the bowl. Soak for up to 24 hours. Drain and cook.

How to Cook Chickpeas

The day before you plan to cook chickpeas, pick through them and discard any discolored or broken beans, then put them in a bowl, cover with three times their volume of filtered or unchlorinated water, and pop them in the fridge to soak overnight. (They can also soak at room temperature for 6 hours or so.) If you run out of time to cook them the next day, change the water, return them to the fridge, and cook them the following day.

The best way to tell when chickpeas are done cooking is to simply start tasting them after about 1 hour of cooking (this is a good time to add a little salt, too). Continue tasting one or two chickpeas every 5 to 10 minutes until you like the texture. Chickpeas should have a firm but pleasantly creamy texture—you don't want to undercook them. (It's a misconception that beans should be cooked "al dente"; chickpeas and all beans are definitely more easily digested when cooked until tender.) Some of the skins will pop off when cooking, and you can discard these. Some cooks go crazy getting rid of all the skins, but I am not one of them.

You can use this method to cook any kind of dried bean (don't forget to soak them first). When cooking other dried beans, you will just need to taste them sooner and more frequently, because dried beans vary a lot in cooking times depending on their variety and how old they are. Beans that cook for a long time may need to be topped off with more hot water before they are done.

1 Soak 2 cups of chickpeas overnight in cold filtered or unchlorinated water. Drain the chickpeas, then put them in a large pot and cover with at least 3 inches of water. Add 1 bay leaf, 2 sprigs of thyme, and 2 garlic cloves to the pot and bring it to a boil. Reduce the heat to low and gently simmer for 1 hour. (If the water level gets too close to the chickpeas, add more hot water.)

2 After 1 hour, season the chickpeas with 1 teaspoon kosher salt. Also, taste a chickpea for tenderness. If needed, continue to simmer for 10 to 25 minutes, tasting a chickpea every 10 minutes or so, until the texture is nicely creamy. Drain well, reserving the cooking liquid if you'd like to use it in hummus. Remove the bay leaf and discard.

3 Store the drained chickpeas and the liquid (if desired) separately in the fridge for up to 5 or 6 days, or in the freezer for up to 1 month.

How to Cook Lentils

Cooking lentils is quick and easy. First, of course, you need to choose which type of lentils to cook (see page 60). Use this method for all types of lentils—regular brown or green lentils, French or du Puy lentils, or black beluga lentils—*except* red lentils, which break down when cooked. (Red lentils are usually cooked with flavorings, so instructions will vary by recipe. See individual recipes, such as Red Lentils and Roasted Root Veggies with Spicy Lime-Chili Oil on page 82, for appropriate cooking instructions.)

1 Pick through 1 cup of lentils and discard any pebbles.

2 Bring 6 cups of water to a boil in a large saucepan. Add the lentils, return the water to a boil, and reduce the heat to very low. Gently simmer for 15 minutes, then taste a few lentils for tenderness. Continue to simmer, tasting every couple of minutes, until done to your likeness, usually no more than 25 minutes total. Smaller lentils, such as black belugas and French lentils, can be tender in as little as 16 to 18 minutes. Larger brown or green lentils can take the full 25 minutes. (Be aware that the larger varieties cook less consistently from lentil to lentil—some will already be breaking up when the rest are just getting tender.)

3 Drain the lentils very well and spread on a baking sheet to cool down and dry a bit.

How to Toast Nuts

You can toast nuts in a skillet on the stovetop, but I prefer the oven method because the nuts toast more evenly in the indirect heat, and you do not need to stand at the stove actively stirring them. However, you do still have to pay attention. Set a timer and begin checking the nuts after 5 minutes. (Most will take somewhere between 6 and 10 minutes.) But use your sniffer, too—smell is one of the best ways to follow the progression of toasting nuts to avoid overtoasting. You want to get the nuts to a deep golden (often somewhat reddish) brown for the best flavor. If it looks like they have darkened too much, cut one in half to see if it is still only a light brown and taste it to see if it hasn't yet become bitter—some may be salvageable. Take note that many toasted nuts do not crisp up until they have cooled completely, so color is a good indicator of doneness.

Place an oven rack in the center of the oven. Preheat the oven to 375°F or 400°F. Arrange whole or sliced nuts in a single layer on a baking sheet. Bake until the nuts are an appealing deep golden brown and smell roasty-toasty. Let cool on the countertop for 10 to 15 minutes to crisp up. Once they are completely cool, store in an airtight container at room temperature, in the fridge, or in the freezer.

How to Hard-Cook Eggs

To avoid overcooking eggs (and getting that dreaded green, sulfurous ring around the yolk), don't boil them. Instead, steep them. Bring the water and eggs just to a boil and remove the pan from the heat. Cover the pan with a lid and let the eggs sit to finish cooking. Then follow a few tips for easier peeling. But remember: very fresh eggs will be the most difficult to peel, no matter what you do. (As eggs age, the air pocket between the shell and the membrane increases slightly, which ultimately makes peeling easier.)

Start with 4 to 6 fresh large eggs. Put the eggs into a medium-large saucepan and cover with cold water to about 1 inch above the eggs. Slowly bring the water to a boil over medium-high heat. When the water boils, immediately remove the pan from the heat, cover, and set the timer for 12 minutes. (If you want a soft-cooked egg, reduce the steeping time to 4 minutes.)

When the timer goes off, carefully drain off the hot water and run cold water over the eggs until they are cool to the touch. Transfer them to the refrigerator to chill completely for the easiest peeling. Alternatively, you can plunge the eggs into ice water to cool them down quickly.

To peel, first warm the egg a bit by rubbing it with your hands. Tap the narrow tip of the egg (where the air pocket is) against a hard surface and also rap the rest of the egg against the surface to gently crack the shell all over. Peel the egg over the sink (under running water if necessary).

To slice, use a handy-dandy old-fashioned egg slicer or a hollow-edged Santoku-style knife. Run the knife under hot water between slices.

How to Grill or Broil Bread for Toast

Surely toasting is a simple task, you say. But trust me: there are nuances to getting the best results. The most important thing to remember is that you need a fairly hot, direct heat source, like a grill or a broiler, so that your bread really does toast instead of bake. A baked slice of bread is tough. Toast should be crisp on the outside with some tenderness still remaining in the interior. As I mentioned before (see page 121), because I like to brush bread with oil or butter before toasting, I rarely use a conventional toaster.

To grill: Dial a gas grill to medium heat (medium-high if your grill runs cool) and scrape the grill grates clean with a metal brush. Cover the grill. (Always lower the lid on a gas grill when cooking, as it encourages convection, moving the heat around.) Let the grates heat up for

10 minutes or so. Brush both sides of your bread generously with olive oil and season with a little salt. Put the slices directly on the grill, cover again, and set a timer for 1½ minutes. Check the bottoms for browning and grill marks; if needed, continue cooking on that side for 30 seconds and check again. Flip the slices over with tongs when nicely marked. (The edges may get slightly dark.) Grill for 1 to 2 minutes on the second side, then immediately transfer to a plate. Do not walk away from the grill when bread is on!

To broil: Move an oven rack to the highest position, 4 to 5 inches from the broiler element, and preheat the oven broiler to high. Arrange your bread slices on a small baking sheet and brush both sides (or just one) with either olive oil or melted butter. (Know that melted butter will brown more quickly, leaving you with some delicious but more tender moist spots on your toast.) Broil until the top side of all the slices is nicely golden, about 2 minutes. (Move the baking sheet around for even cooking, or use tongs to move the bread slices if necessary.) Flip the slices over and broil again until golden, 2 minutes more. Remove from the oven.

How to Grill Veggies

Grilling vegetables is all about getting to know your own grill—how hot it gets, where the cool spots are, and so on. As a result, recipe times and directions can really only be guidelines. There are "doneness" clues you can look for: the obvious one being exterior color but also, in many vegetables, the texture and appearance of the flesh. If you consider vegetables like eggplant and zucchini (onions, too), you'll notice that not only do they become slightly

floppy when tender, but their flesh also turns from opaque to almost translucent as they cook. The trick is to keep the exterior of the vegetables from burning while the interior fully cooks. (If all else fails, you can take seared veggies off the grill and wrap them in foil to let the steam finish cooking them.)

Over the years I've grilled vegetables a number of different ways: directly on the grill grates, on a grill topper or in a grill basket, in a foil pouch, and on skewers. Skewers are my least favorite because vegetables cook very inconsistently on them. Foil pouches are for relatively long, slow cooking. For our veggie suppers, grilling directly on the grates, on a grill topper, or in a grill basket are the best methods.

Grilling directly on well-scraped, oiled grates works well for large, flat slices of veggies that aren't too thin. Brush or toss them with plenty of oil, use medium or medium-high heat, and don't move the pieces for the first few minutes of cooking to prevent tearing.

Using a grill topper, or enameled grill tray, is great for smaller slices of vegetables or long, thin veggies like asparagus that might fall through the grill's grates. Cooking may be a bit slower than directly on the grates.

Using a grill basket (my favorite method) is like stir-frying on the grill. As you move the veggies around in the basket, they release moisture, which helps them steam while they're browning up, with less chance of burning—perfectly cooked and delicious veggies. Any veggies, most any size, can go into a grill basket.

How to Warm Tortillas

There are several great ways to heat tortillas, and after you've tried them, you will settle on your own favorite. Whichever method you use, be sure not to overheat the tortillas or they will become stiff and tough.

If you've already got a covered gas grill going or your oven is hot, wrap the tortillas in foil packets (3 or 4 tortillas per packet—roll the tortillas up first if you like). Put the packets on the grill grate and cover the grill, or place in the hot oven, and heat for 5 to 10 minutes, until steamy hot. (Corn tortillas may need less time.) That's the best way to get a bunch of tortillas heated and ready to go, and they will also stay warm in the foil for 10 to 15 minutes.

(Alternatively, you can stack several on a plate, cover with damp paper towels, and microwave for 30 seconds.)

To heat one tortilla at a time—and to toast it a bit, too—drop a tortilla into a hot cast iron pan or directly onto a hot grill grate, let sit for several seconds, then flip it over and heat for a few seconds more. You can also use tongs to hold the tortilla over a gas flame. With these methods, you'll want to fill or top the tortilla right away, as it won't stay hot for long.

INDEX OF BONUS RECIPES

It's the little things—the tips, the tricks, the flavor boosts—that wind up making the difference between a good dish and a great one. And I'm not talking about complicated food. Even the simplest recipes benefit from the addition of a little something special (Lemon-Miso Butter, Balsamic Glaze, Spicy Lime-Chili Oil). I want you to have absolute confidence that you've got the tools you need to make delicious one-dish veggie suppers, so I've compiled this index for you. It contains all the little "bonus" recipes in the book that will get you to "great."

Think of this list as a treasure chest—there's gold here, I promise. Open it up, pull a little something out (Creamy Blender Caesar Dressing, Grilled Maple-Tamari Mushooms, Pita Crisps) and use it. Certainly you will use these recipes when making the main recipes they accompany in this book, but I do hope you'll go on to improvise with them to create some dishes of your own.

Salsas and Slaws

Infused or Flavored Oils and Pestos

Butters

Dips and Spreads

Roasted, Grilled, and Sautéed Veggies

Crunchies

Broths

Legumes and Grains

INDEX

ABOUT THE AUTHOR

Cook/writer/farmer SUSIE MIDDLETON is the author of *Fast, Fresh & Green*; *The Fresh & Green Table*; and *Fresh from the Farm*, an NPR top cookbook of 2014. She is the former chief editor and current editor-at-large for *Fine Cooking* magazine. Susie operates a small farmette and farm stand on the island of Martha's Vineyard, where she lives year-round. She blogs about cooking and growing vegetables on her website Sixburnersue.com. You can also follow Susie on Instagram @sixburnersue. Susie is a columnist for *Martha's Vineyard Magazine* and a frequent contributor to *Vegetarian Times*. She is a blue-ribbon graduate of the Institute of Culinary Education (ICE) in New York, and was chosen as an inaugural member of the ICE Alumni Hall of Achievement.

ABOUT THE PHOTOGRAPHER

RANDI BAIRD is a Martha's Vineyard–based editorial and commercial photographer specializing in food, lifestyle, and portrait work. For more than thirty years, she has used her photographs as a means for communication, education, and social change. Her images, which have been distributed worldwide by the Associated Press and United Press International, can be found in *Food & Wine*, *Edible Manhattan*, and *Cape Cod Magazine*. She is a regular contributor to *Martha's Vineyard Magazine* and is a founding member and board president of Island Grown Initiative, a nonprofit that supports the small family farms and food growers of Martha's Vineyard. Randi is a backyard grower of fruits, vegetables, and poultry and tends bees with her family in West Tisbury, Massachusetts. Visit her website at randibaird.com.